THE

EMPTY

GRAVE

A TRUE STORY OF MURDER, SMALL TOWN SECRETS,
& A FAMILY'S FIGHT FOR JUSTICE

JOY BRUNNER

CONTENTS

~

CHAPTER 1

The ending of this tragic case is that Corey Wood will be brought out periodically throughout time for educational purposes at the Texas State University Forensic Department until the end of time.

Corey Wood
God's Justice.
Your choice.

American Forensics

P.O. Box 550846 • Dallas • Texas • 75355
(214) 221-2700 • FAX (972) 692-6676 • csaforensics.com

Case number: AF-0512-12   **Name:** COREY A. WOOD

Age: 22 years   **Gender:** Male   **Race:** White

Authorization: Sharon Joy Brunner, mother of the deceased.

Date and Time of Death: 09/28/1999 at unknown time.

Date and Time of Examination: 05/16/2012 at 10 a.m.

Forensic Pathologist: Amy C. Gruszecki, MSFS, DO

Final Autopsy Report

I.   Burial coffin received filled with water.
II. Body markedly decomposed to skeletal remains.
III. Gunshot wound to the head.
   A. Entrance: 3/8 inch defect left side of skull.
   B. Path: Bullet would cause injury to brain.
   C. Bullet: None recovered.
   D. Exit: A defect on right side of skull.
   E. Course: Left-to-right.
   F. Range: Soot deposit around the bone of the entrance wound.
IV. Deceased was reportedly right handed.
V.   Questionable circumstances regarding death of the deceased (see Conclusion).

CAUSE OF DEATH: Gunshot wound to the head.

MANNER OF DEATH: Undetermined.

2nd Autopsy

2

AUTHORIZATION

This examination is performed at the request of Sharon Joy Brunner, mother of the deceased. No restrictions are requested for this examination.

EXTERNAL EXAMINATION

The body is received in a burial coffin. When the coffin is pried open, murky, malodorous water is found to be filling the casket. All of the items that were buried with the deceased along the remains of the deceased are soaked with water. The deceased's body has markedly decomposed and consists only of skeletal remains covered with paste remains of skin and a plastic bag likely containing viscera.

The coffin contains funeral blanket and pillows. The lining is unattached in many places. Identified within the coffin are black boots, which are generally intact; remnants of blue jeans, a black belt, white socks, and a plaid white and blue T-shirt. The white-blue plaid shirt is destroyed per the request of the family. The remaining items are returned with the remains. Received separately from the family is a plaid blue shirt on a hanger, a gun and a black cloth bag. The gun and the shirt are returned to the family. See description below regarding black cloth bag.

Photographs are taken. A radiograph of the head is taken.

General: The skeleton is consistent with that of an adult white male. Black hair mass is on the head. The skeleton as found is disarticulated and has pasty remains of soft tissue on the head and covering some bones. No ligaments are noted. The growth plates and suture lines of the calvaruim are closed.

The cranium has saw marks, which are consistent with previous autopsy examination. The maxilla and mandible are in one piece. Teeth are present. The hyoid bone is not found. All ribs appear to be present. The body of the sternum was not recovered. The xipoid and manubruim are present. The cervical, thoracic, lumbar and sacral vertebrae are present. The right and left pelvic bones are present. The subpubic angle is acute. The sciatic notch is narrow. The pelvis when reconstructed has a small pelvic outlet. The bony surfaces of the pubic symphysis are smooth. The left humerus, left ulna, and both radii, femurs, tibiae, fibulae are present and are largely intact. The feet bones are all generally intact and were found within the socks. The bones of both the right and left hands are mostly present. All torso and extremity bones are free of discernible injury.

Notably absent are the right humerus and the right ulna.

The approximate length of the left arm is approximately 2 feet.

A plastic bag is recovered which contains the apparent remains of the viscera. The viscera are markedly decomposed with few anatomical landmarks. No evidence of injury or natural disease is able to be identified.

2nd Autopsy

3

GUNSHOT DEFECT TO THE HEAD

The skull and calvarium are cleaned, re-approximated, examined and photographed.

Entrance: On the left side of the head is a 3/8-inch round gunshot defect, which is just above the lateral portion of the left zygomatic arch on the side of the head. it is centered 4 inches from the left of the midline anteriorly and 4.5 inches from the top of the head. The defect has inward beveling and is surrounded by black soot deposit.

Path: The projectile would have passed through the brain.

Exit: An apparent exit wound was on the right side of the head as the skull bones were reconstructed. The actual characteristics of the boney defect were unable to be re-approximated due to the absence of fragmented bones.

EXAMINATION OF THE GUN

The gun was provided which was allegedly the gun used in the injury to the deceased. Photographs of the gun were taken. A muzzle to trigger length is measured at 23.5 inches.

ADDITIONAL INFORMATION RECEIVED FOR CASE EVALUATION

Inside the black cloth bag received from the family, are the following items:
1. A death certificate for the deceased.
2. Thirty eight photos of alleged blood spatter from the decedent's home.
3. A photo card index.
4. A red folder which contains numerous sheets of bank account information from Huntington State Bank.
5. A white envelope, which is written an address of "Mitch Wood."
6. A yellow note sheet and fragments of a yellow note sheet with addresses and phone numbers written on it.
7. A packet of "Herbal Life Total Control" which contains one pill. The package states that it originally contained three pills.
8. DVD packaging and three blank DVDs.
9. A green hanging file folder, which contains a CD labeled "Affidavit Form" which is labeled "Luminol; Affidavit for Mom; Lillian Armstrong; Tammy Womack." The folder is empty.
10. Another green hanging file folder, labeled "Sherriff's Department" which contains numerous newspaper clipping regarding local news articles regarding the Sherriff's Office, and 2 papers which are labeled, "General Fund" and appear to be accounting information.
11. A schematic of the scene of death.
12. A DVD labeled, "Luminol".
13. A DVD of a family event and news coverage in video case.

2nd Autopsy

4

14. A DVD with videos of the scene and Luminol preparation.
15. A green hanging file folder, which contains numerous letters, court documents, affidavits regarding the attempted investigation by the family of this case.

Received separately through the US Mail is a microcassette tape which contains recorded phone messages from the family to various authorities regarding trying to receive information on this case.

All of these above items are reviewed for the purpose of rendering an opinion in this case and are returned to the family at the conclusion of this investigation.

CONCLUSION:

Based on my examination of the skeletal remains, my findings are consistent with the primary autopsy report in that the deceased received a gunshot wound to the left side of the head along with a (probable) right exit wound. Soot is present around the entrance wound, so it is consistent with a contact gunshot wound.

A gunshot wound of the head in and of itself is not usually diagnostic medically or scientifically of a suicide or a homicide. The manner of death is based largely upon the case investigation that is completed around the time of the death. The measurements of the skeletal remains make it possible, in my opinion that the deceased would be able to pull the trigger on his own with the gun at the left side of the head.

Other factors to be considered in evaluating this case include that the deceased Mr. Corey Wood was a generally happy, well-established man looking forward to his career. He had just purchased a house. The deceased was right handed and the gunshot wound to the head was on the left side of the head. The deceased had 3 other people in the house at the time of the injury. The deceased also allegedly had large sums of money stolen from his bank account by these friends or acquaintances of these friends. These factors should at least shed doubts upon the ruling of suicide.

The family performed their own investigation and found what is suspicious for blood to be elsewhere in the house and on a baseball bat. They have even attempted luminal evaluation. I will defer an opinion on blood spatter analysis, but it does again raise questions as to what the original evaluation of the death scene was.

2nd Autopsy

Considering all of these investigative findings and the additional lack of other investigative findings regarding this case, it is my opinion that the manner of death is best classified as undetermined.

The above represents my opinion regarding the information I have reviewed in this case. I reserve the right to modify my opinion if additional information becomes available for my review. Thank you for the opportunity to participate in this case. Please do not hesitate to contact me if you have any further questions.

Signature: _____   Date: June 14, 2012

Amy C. Gruszecki, MSFS, DO
Forensic Pathologist

2nd Autopsy

1st Exhumation

TEXAS STATE
UNIVERSITY
SAN MARCOS
The rising STAR of Texas

Anthropological Report

September 8, 2015

Ms. Darci Holloway
Darciholloway@yahoo.com
(254) 541-8908

Re: F04-2015: Anthropological Analysis of Corey Wood's Skeletal Remains

Prepared by: Dr. Daniel J. Wescott, Devora Gleiber, Chloe McDaneld, Lauren Meckel, and Courtney C. Siegert

Summary

The remains of Corey Woods were examined at the request of his sister Darci Holloway on behalf of his family. The nearly complete skeleton reveals evidence of a close contact gunshot wound to the head. The bullet entered the temple region on the left side of the skull and exited the right side above the ear. The manner of death cannot be determined from the injury pattern alone.

Background

The remains of Corey Adam Wood were delivered to the Forensic Anthropology Center at Texas State (FACTS) in a burial coffin on 11 August 2015 by Darci Holloway and transferred to the custody of Sophia Mavroudas (FACTS Coordinator) for anthropological analysis. The remains were locked in a secure area of the Osteological Research and Processing Laboratory on Freeman Ranch in San Marcos, Texas during processing. After processing the skeletal remains were brought to the Grady Early Forensic Anthropology Laboratory for analysis and photography.

The postmortem examination was conducted by Dr. Daniel Wescott with the assistance of Texas State University graduate students (forensic team) at the request of Darci Holloway, sister of Corey Wood. Ms. Holloway requested that Dr. Wescott complete an inventory of the skeletal remains, examine the skeletal remains for fractures and other signs of trauma, and provide an opinion on the possible manner of death. Darci Holloway also provided FACTS with two previous postmortem examination reports conducted on the remains of Corey Wood. No documentation about the death scene or law enforcement investigation was provided.

The first postmortem examination of Corey Wood was conducted by Dr. James R. Bruce on 28 September 1999 at the Lufkin Pathology Laboratory in Lufkin, Texas. He concluded in his report (A-99-226) that there was a "penetrating gunshot wound to the left side of the head consistent with suicide." The second examination was performed by Dr. Amy C. Gruszecki at the request of Sharon Joy Brunner, mother of Corey Wood, at American Forensics in Dallas, Texas on 16 May 2012. Dr. Gruszecki concluded in her report (AF-0512-12) that the cause of death was due to a

3rd Autopsy

gunshot wound to the head and the manner of death was undetermined. She states that other factors "at least shed doubts upon the ruling of suicide."

Initial Examination and Processing

Condition of the Remains:

On 12 August 2015 the FACTS forensic team opened the coffin, which was partially filled with black water and contained a black body bag and a bag with coffin lining materials. The remains of Corey Wood were discovered in the black body bag, in rough anatomical position. Also in the body bag were remnants of clothing, a pair of boots, and a bag with abdominal organs. The skeletal remains were removed and inventoried. The remains of Corey Woods were mostly skeletonized with some adipocere (wax-like organic matter). The bones were black, brown, and blue in color. The skull, ribs, and clavicles were previously cut during the first autopsy. The skull was fragmentary. Sixteen fragments were recovered. Some cortical bone loss was observed on the bones.

Maceration and Reconstruction:

The FACTS forensic team cleaned the skeleton in water with a mild detergent and allowed it to completely dry. Adipocere was removed to the extent possible without causing damage to the skeleton. After drying the skull was reconstructed to the extent possible using a cement glue to aid the analysis of trauma.

Analysis of Skeletal Remains

Inventory: The skeleton is mostly complete (Figure 1). Missing was the hyoid, xiphoid process of the sternum, part of the sternal body, and several phalanges of the hands and feet. All teeth are present.

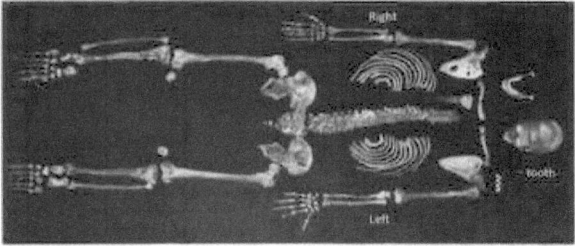

Figure 1. Skeletal remains of Corey Woods.

Biological Profile: Skeletal indicators of age, sex, and ancestry observed are consistent with a 22 year old, white, male.

3rd Autopsy

9

Nonmetric Traits and Healed Trauma:

Unique traits observed on the skeletal remains include bridging of the 7th and 8th left ribs at the neck (Figure 2), bilateral (biconcave) depressions on the inferior endplate of the lumbar vertebrae (Figure 3), and antemortem fractures of the left ankle (Figure 4). The bridging of the ribs is likely due to a developmental anomaly but could have resulted from earlier trauma. The biconcave depressions of the endplates of the lumbar vertebrae appear to exhibit reactive bone formation. The etiology of the depressions is unknown but they are commonly present in the inferior endplate of the lumbar vertebrae. The fractures of the ankle include a curved oblique fracture of the distal end of the fibula. The fracture edges exhibit evidence of osteoclastic rounding and smoothing but the two ends have not rejoined resulting in a healed nonunion fracture. There is also evidence of healed fractures of the left navicular and left talus. Most likely the ankle fractures resulted from a single injury during life caused by a combination of bending and compressive forces or bending and torsion (twisting).

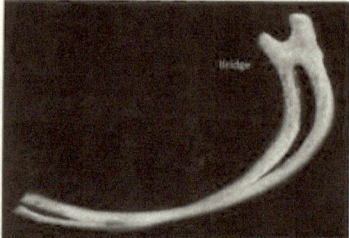

Figure 2. Bridging of the 7th and 8th left ribs.

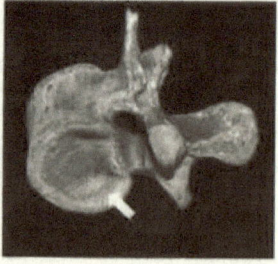

Figure 3. Lumbar vertebra showing bilateral depressions of the inferior endplate.

3rd Autopsy

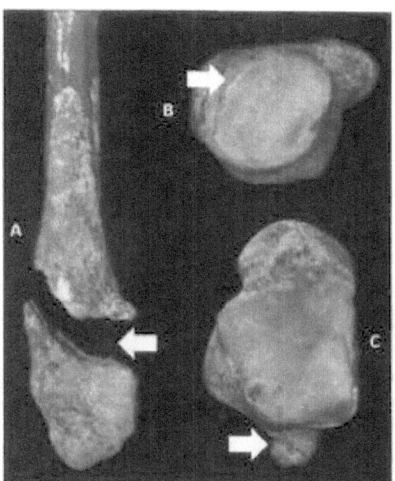

Figure 4. Fibula (A), Navicular (B) and talus (C) with antemortem fractures indicated by arrows.

Projectile Wound:

Two defects associated with a single close contact gunshot to the skull were observed. The bullet entered the skull at the temple region (near the junction of the temporal, sphenoid, and frontal) on the left side (Figure 5A). The bullet exited the skull on the right side above the ear (Figure 5B). The path of the bullet from left to right was posterior and slightly inferior (Figure 6). That is, the exit wound was slightly towards the back of the skull and at a lower position than the entrance wound when the skull is in anatomical position. However, the position of the head at contact is unknown. Figure 6 shows the path of the bullet from a front (A) and top (B) views. The bullet would have passed through the brain and resulted in death.

The entrance wound is round defect 9.5 mm (3/8 inch) in diameter with a faint soot ring on the outside and inward beveling on the inside. There are four radiating fractures associated with the entrance defect. While the soot ring is only faint during our examination this is most likely due to years of burial. The black ring deposit around the entrance wound is consistent with a close contact gunshot wound.

3rd Autopsy

11

The exit wound is a round defect approximately 9.5 mm (3/8 inches) in diameter. However, due to fragmentation of the bone on the top margin of the exit wound the size and shape of the defect can only be approximated. There are a few radiating fractures and fragmentation of the temporal bone associated with the exit wound.

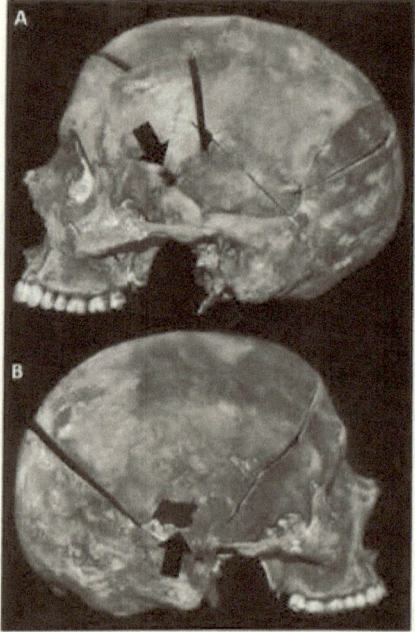

Figure 5. Cranium showing entrance wound on left side (A) and exit wound on the right side (B).

3rd Autopsy

Comparison of Postmortem Examination Reports

Two previous postmortem examinations were conducted (see background). Below is a comparison of the postmortem examinations.

Inventory and Morphology

There are some differences between our findings and those of Dr. Gruszecki regarding the bones present and absent. Dr. Gruszecki wrote "Notably absent are the right humerus and the right ulna." However, both bones were recovered from the coffin. Why she did not observe them is unknown. She also stated that the xiphoid process of the sternum was present but the sternal body was absent. We recovered a portion of the sternal body but no xiphoid process. It is possible that Dr. Gruszecki confused the two parts of the sternum. Also contrary to the report by Dr. Gruszecki, most of the bones of the right and left hands are present and most of the fragments of the right skull (associated with the exit defect) are also present.

With regard to the pubic bones, Dr. Gruszecki wrote "The bony surfaces of the pubic symphysis are smooth." However, there are still remnants of ridges and furrows on the surfaces of the pubic symphyses, which is consistent with the morphology of a young adult. The "smoothing" of the pubic symphyseal faces is due to postmortem degradation and not age-related changes.

Gunshot Wound

The findings of our postmortem examination of the gunshot wound are consistent with those of Drs. Bruce and Gruszecki. Dr. Bruce noted that the entrance wound had a 2 mm rim of soot. In our examination the soot ring was faded but still observable. The fading is due to 15 years of postmortem change. We also agree with Dr. Gruszecki that based on the evidence available the manner of death should be classified as undetermined. There is nothing characteristic about the gunshot wound defects that point conclusively to homicide or suicide. What is troubling is that Dr. Bruce notes that the wound is "consistent with suicide" but does not provide any evidence about the investigation that would lead him to conclude the manner of death was suicide.

3rd Autopsy

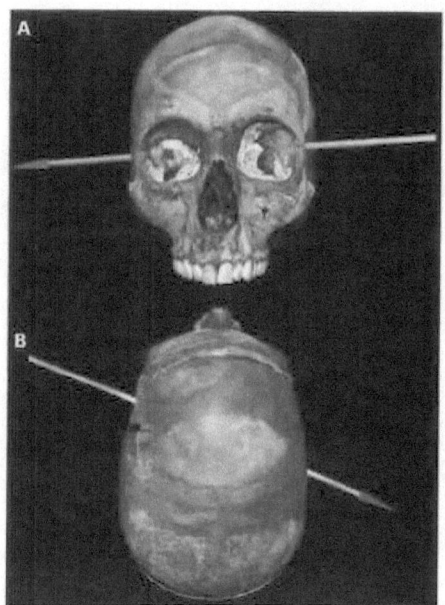

Figure 6. Front (A) and top (B) views of the cranium illustrating the path of the bullet. Arrow indicates direction.

Taphonomy/Postmortem Damage:

Postmortem damage to the skeleton is due to saw cuts associated with autopsy, mortuary fastener placement, and normal decomposition. The cranium was cut in a wedge shape during autopsy (Figure 5), and the saw cuts to the clavicle (Figure 7) and several ribs are consistent with the Y-incision performed by Dr. Bruce during the original postmortem examination. Mortuary fasteners were observed on the mandible and maxilla that are used to connect the upper and lower jaws and keep the mouth closed during funerary events. Postmortem damage was also observed on the left maxilla body and both scapulae (Figure 7). This damage is due to decomposition of the thin bone. There is also some cortical bone loss on several bones due to decomposition. Several small bones are missing, but this is to be expected for a body that has

3rd Autopsy

undergone two previous postmortem examinations and burial for fifteen years. Finally, postmortem processes have caused the coloration changes of the bones. The black color is associated with years of water in the coffin. The blue color is probably due to staining by clothing in the coffin or blue gloves present in the coffin.

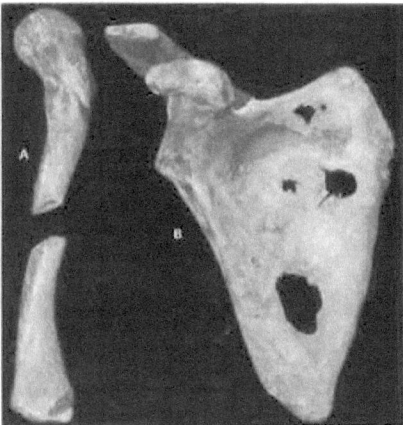

Figure 7. Right clavicle (A) and right scapula (B) showing postmortem damage. The clavicles were cut during autopsy. The missing parts of the scapula result from decomposition and fragmentation of the thin bone. Bones not to scale.

Time-Since-Death: On or before 28 September 1999 based on previous postmortem examination records.

Conclusions

Based on the examination of the skeletal remains of Corey Wood, our finding is that he experienced a single gunshot wound to the head that entered the left side near the temple region and exited above the right ear. The dark soot ring around the entrance defect is consistent with a close contact gunshot wound. The radiating fractures are consistent with a high velocity weapon. These findings are in agreement with the other two postmortem examinations performed by Drs. Bruce and Gruszecki. There are no specific characteristics of the gunshot wound that allow for a determination of the manner of death. The defects observed could have resulted from either homicide or suicide. Other damaged areas of the skeleton noted by the family are due to postmortem processes. The cranium, clavicles, and ribs were cut during the autopsy performed by Dr. Bruce.

3rd Autopsy

JOY BRUNNER

Signatures

Daniel J. Wescott, PhD
Director, Forensic Anthropology Center at Texas State
Department of Anthropology, Texas State University

Devora Gleiber, MA candidate
Department of Anthropology, Texas State University

Chloe McDaneld, MA candidate
Department of Anthropology, Texas State University

Lauren Meckel, MA candidate
Department of Anthropology, Texas State University

Courtney Siegert, MA candidate
Department of Anthropology, Texas State University

3rd Autopsy

16

TEXAS STATE
UNIVERSITY
SAN MARCOS
The rising STAR of Texas

September 21, 2015

Dear Mrs. Brunner,

I would like to take this opportunity to thank you and your family for facilitating the generous donation of your son, Corey A. Wood to the Forensic Anthropology Center at Texas State University. This type of donation is the most invaluable contribution one could make to our program. Your donation will help further education and research within the fields of forensic anthropology and forensic science. The type of research we conduct at Texas State's Forensic Anthropology Research Facility will address a number of real-world questions that are important for forensic anthropology, law enforcement, and medical examiner investigations. This research can be grouped into two categories.

The first category is the investigation into the postmortem interval, or time since death. This kind of research looks at the timing and sequence of events that happen after someone dies. This will help us as forensic anthropologists with interpreting the time since death interval specifically in Texas and other regions with similar environments and climates. Currently, no research has been conducted on these questions in Texas, so it is vital that we establish a baseline as quickly as possible to aid law enforcement with medico-legal investigations.

The second category is a long-term goal of the Forensic Anthropology Research Facility and will yield an incredible amount of information that will help with establishing the identity of unknown individuals, and assessing skeletal trauma. This will be the creation of a permanent documented skeletal collection made up of donated individuals, with known ages, sexes, heights, and ancestries. This collection will be invaluable. Currently, there are only two large documented skeletal collections of modern individuals in the U.S., and Texas State is beginning to assemble the third. Donated bodies and the documented human skeletal collection which will result from these donations will provide opportunities for research in developing new methods and techniques of identification for unidentified skeletal remains and missing persons. Our skeletal collection will be maintained in perpetuity to allow for the education of future generations of forensic anthropologists and forensic scientists. Further, research from this skeletal collection will result in faculty publications, national and international visiting scientist projects, and law enforcement-sponsored investigations.

We simply cannot express how deeply we appreciate the generous donation you and your family have made to our program, and we want to assure you that your loved one's permanent legacy will be one of education, instruction, and assistance to other families in need.

Sincerely,

Sophia R. Mavroudas, MA
Coordinator – Forensic Anthropology Center
Texas State University
REF:D52-2015

DEPARTMENT OF ANTHROPOLOGY
601 UNIVERSITY DRIVE | SAN MARCOS, TEXAS 78666-4616 | *phone* 512.245.8272 | *fax* 512.245.8076 | WWW.TXSTATE.EDU

Texas State University-San Marcos, founded in 1899, is a member of The Texas State University System.

2nd Exhumation

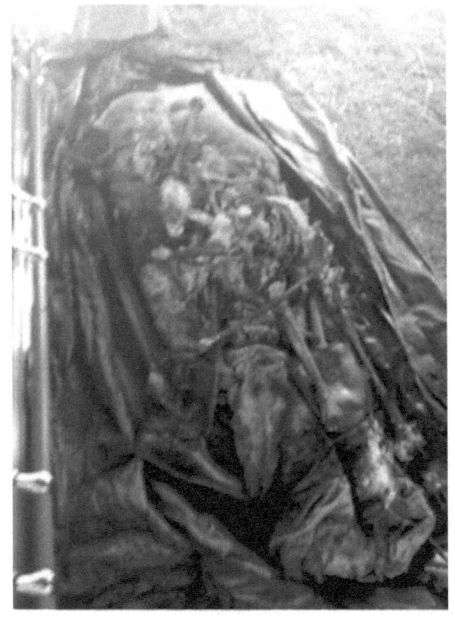

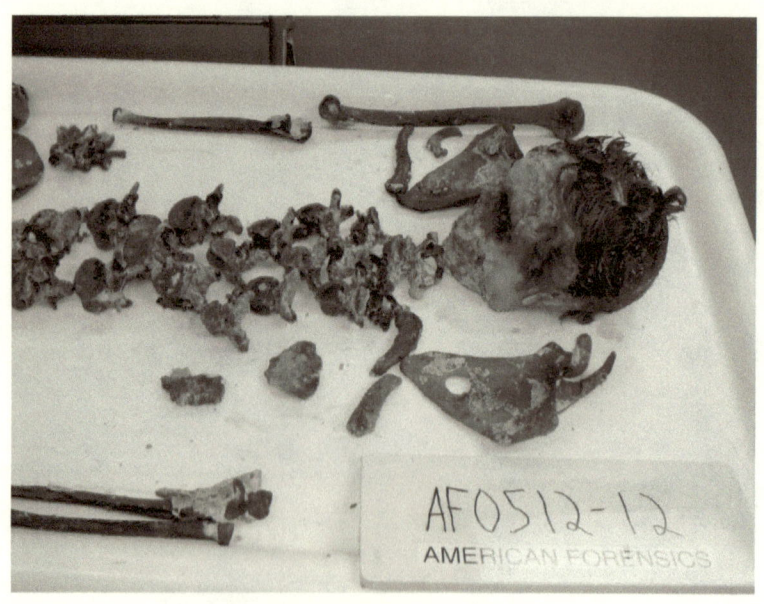

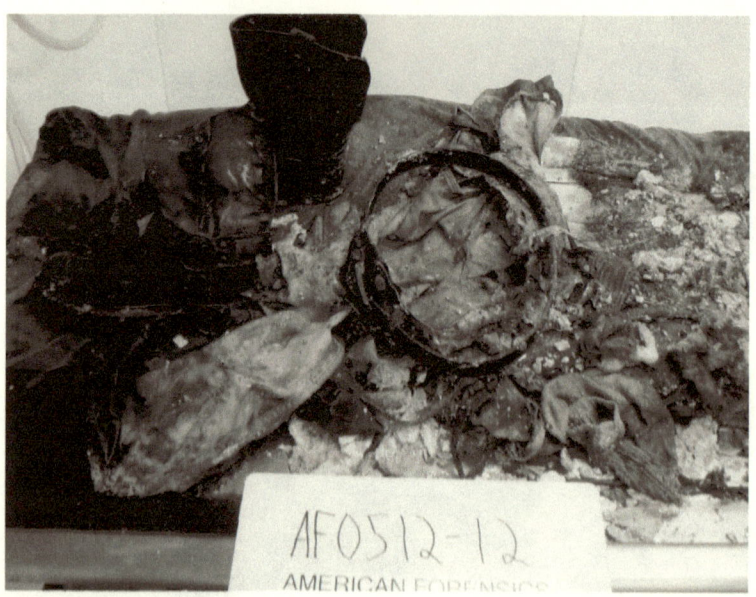

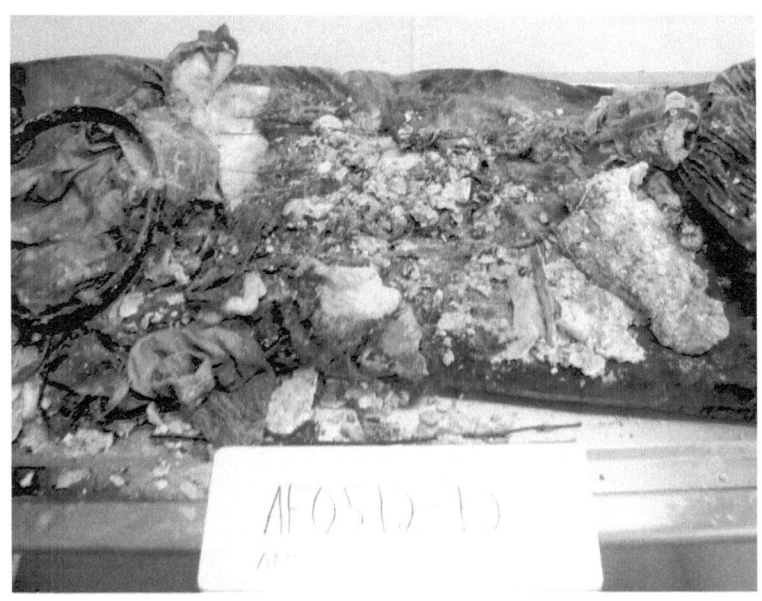

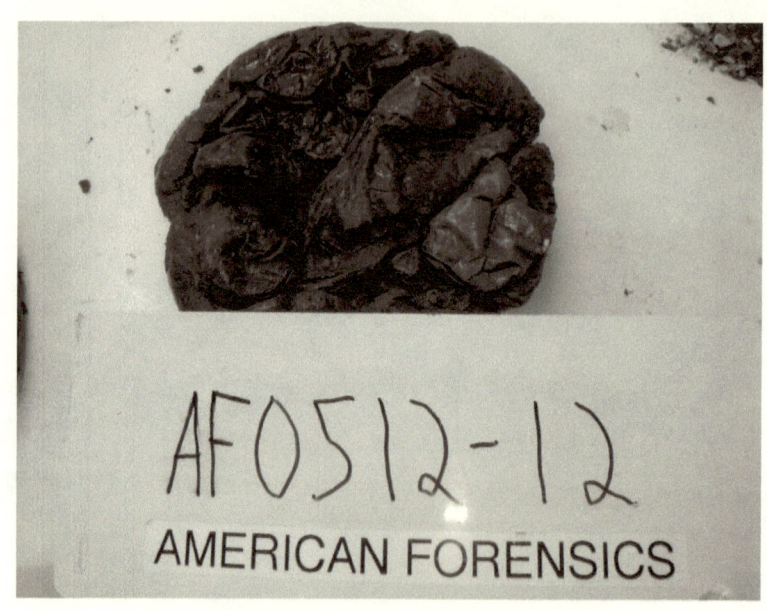

AF0512-12

AMERICAN FORENSICS

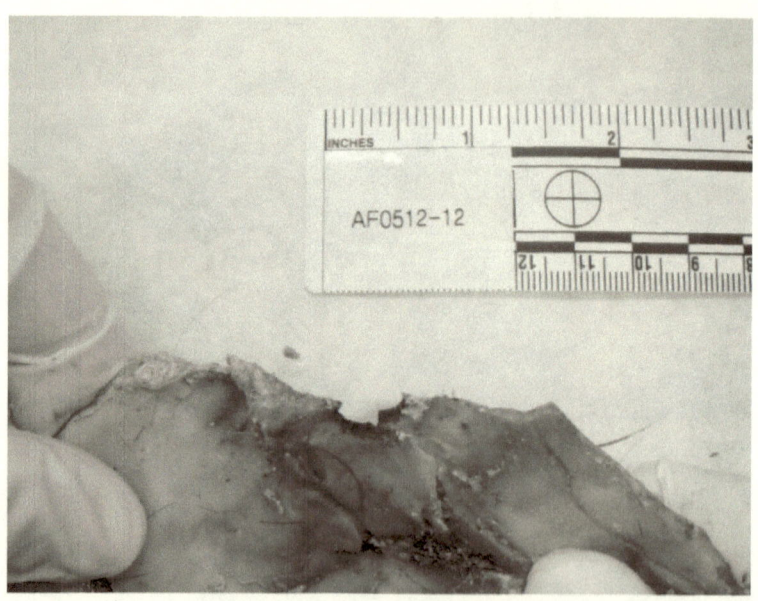

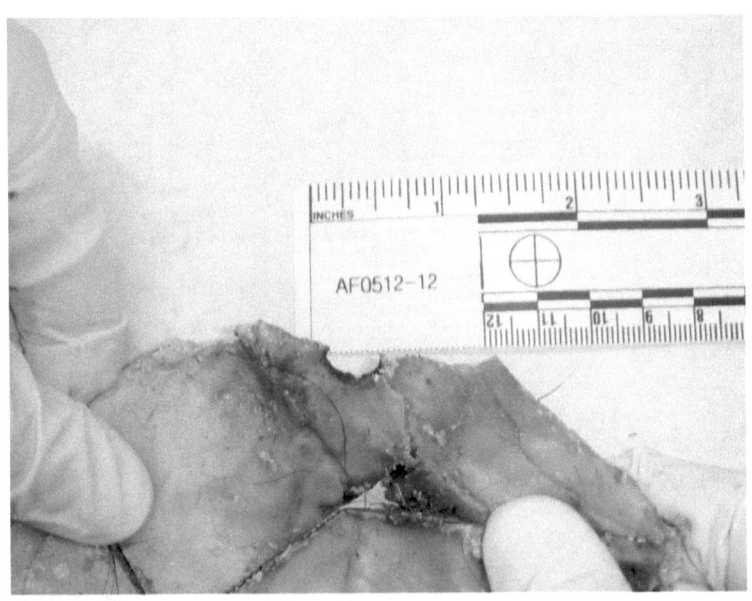

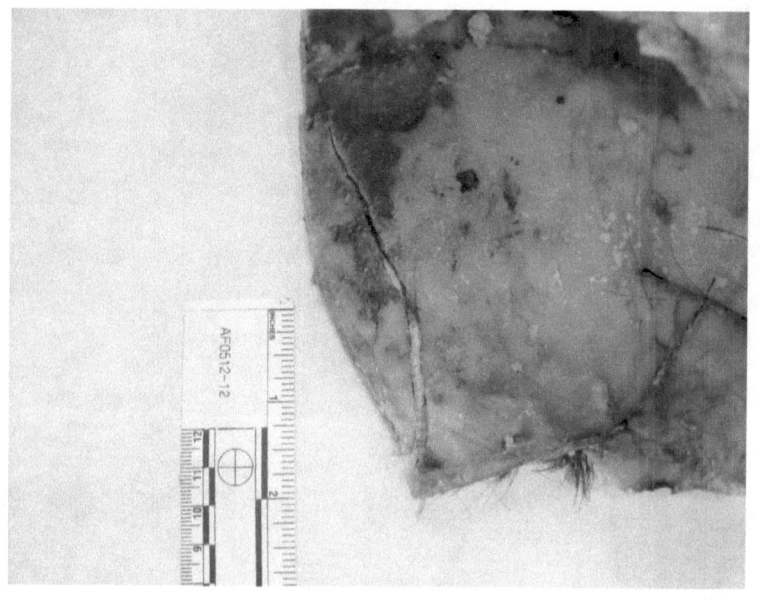

LUFKIN PATHOLOGY LABORATORY

James R. Bruce, M.D., F.C.A.P.
P.O. Box 150110, Lufkin, Texas 75915
409-632-5992 or 409-634-8311
Fax 409-632-5470

Diplomate American Board of Pathology
Certified Forensic Pathology, American Board of Pathology

AUTOPSY REPORT
A-99-226

Patient:	WOOD, Corey Adam	Expired:	9-28-99
Race:	White	Postmortem:	9-28-99
Sex:	Male	Limitation:	None.
Service:	Claude Marshall	Prosector:	James R. Bruce, M.D.

PRINCIPAL DIAGNOSES

Contact penetrating gunshot wound to head with:
a) Brain lacerations and parenchymal hemorrhage.
b) Traumatic subarachnoid hemorrhage.
c) Gunshot defects to skull.

Dr. Burtenje
no Microscopic
usually for
police

DIAGNOSIS BY ANATOMIC SYSTEM

General:	Tattoos; bilateral periorbital contusions.
Cardiovascular:	No pathologic diagnosis.
Respiratory:	Pulmonary edema; aspirated blood.
Gastrointestinal:	No pathologic diagnosis.
Genitourinary:	No pathologic diagnosis.
Endocrine:	No pathologic diagnosis.
Hemic/Lymphatic:	No pathologic diagnosis.
Integumentary:	See general.
Musculoskeletal:	See principal diagnoses.
Central Nervous System:	See principal diagnoses.
Cause of Death:	Contact gunshot wound to head.
Manner of Death:	Suicide.
Date Reported:	10-19-99

Suspition
Some doubt
Keep investigating
some one may
have done it!

Dr. Bruce Autopsy Report
(page 1)

27

A-99-226

GROSS DESCRIPTION

General Information: Postmortem examination of this 22-year-old white male identified as Corey Adam Wood is performed on September 28, 1999 and commences at 9:30 a.m. at the Lufkin Pathology Laboratory, Lufkin, Texas. The body is transported to the Lufkin Pathology Laboratory from Gipson Metcalf Funeral Home, Lufkin, Texas and, following postmortem examination, is transported to said funeral home by representatives of said funeral home.

The decedent arrived clothed as follows:

1. Two boots.
2. Gold colored chain necklace with round pendant.
3. Two gray socks.
4. Check book.
5. Belt.
6. Jeans.
7. Cigarette lighter.
8. Pocket knife.
9. Two white socks.
10. Underwear.
11. Twenty-five dollars and seventy-eight cents ($25.78).

External Examination: The deceased is a normally-developed white male of average build appearing the recorded age of 22 years. He measures 70 inches in total length and is of average nutritional status weighing approximately 170 pounds. Preservation is good in the absence of embalming. Normal lividity is fully-developed. Rigidity is slightly-developed. The temperature is cool to touch, the body having been refrigerated prior to postmortem examination. The hairline is normal. The head hair is full, straight, brown, and measures 3 cm in maximum length. Neither beard nor moustache are present. Body hair is of the male distribution and is of slight amount. Neither the right ear nor the left ear is pierced. The eyes are slightly open; the cornea are clear and the irides brown. No arcus senilis, lens opacities or conjunctival petechiae are noted. The pupils measure 4 mm and are equal. The teeth are natural.

Scars are present as follows:

1. Linear skin indentations with drying, left anterior and lateral chest, dorsal left wrist, left lateral arm and left lateral buttock.

Tattoos are present as follows:

1. Numerous uninterpretable tattoo designs of right and left shoulders.
2. Lion, left chest.
3. Skull with flames, right lower lateral leg.
4. Cross, mid back.
5. Face surrounded by flames, right scapula.
6. "Wood", across abdomen.

tattoo [illegible]

Evidence of injury is as follows:

1. 4 mm in diameter round gunshot entrance wound of left lateral head, 4.5 cm lateral to and 1 cm above the lateral corner of the left eye. A 2 mm in width rim of soot surrounds the entrance wound. No powder tattooing is present.

Soot - A black substance formed from burning matter
to cover or foul with soot.

Page 2

Dr. Bruce Autopsy Report

(page 2)

A-99-226

2. Bilateral periorbital contusions, left greater than right.

Internal Examination: The body is opened with the usual Y-shaped incision to reveal no significant fluid or fibrinous adhesions within any of the body cavities. Examination of the neck musculature reveals no traumatic injuries.

Cardiovascular: The heart weighs 300 grams and has a normal configuration on external examination. Examination of the left main coronary artery reveals no arteriosclerosis. Following bifurcation of the left main coronary artery, the left anterior descending coronary artery shows no significant arteriosclerosis. The circumflex artery is patent without significant arteriosclerosis. The right coronary artery shows no significant arteriosclerosis. No fibrinous or fibrous adhesions are noted on the pericardial sac. Opening the heart along the course of blood reveals the right atrium to be of normal volume. No significant distention of the superior or inferior vena cava is noted. The tricuspid valve shows three delicate leaflets. The chordae tendineae show no significant thickening. Papillary muscles show no significant fibrosis or any present or past ischemic changes. The right ventricle contains the normal coarse trabeculations. No endocardial thickening is noted and no significant dilatation or hypertrophy is present. The left atrium again shows no significant dilatation. The mitral valve contains two delicate leaflets and the chordae tendineae and papillary muscles show no significant changes. The left ventricle shows no evidence of dilatation and hypertrophy and measures 8 mm in thickness along its lateral free wall. No present or past ischemic changes are noted. The aortic valve and pulmonic valve each consist of three pocket leaflets. The coronary artery ostia are patent. The aortic root shows no dilatation. The major branches of the aorta are present in their normal positions. Examination of the descending thoracic and abdominal aorta reveals no evidence of aneurysm or significant arteriosclerotic change.

Respiratory: The tongue shows no gross abnormality. The lips show no contusions or lacerations. The trachea and major bronchi are patent. Examination of the vocal cords reveals them to show no significant pathologic change. Laryngeal petechiae are absent. The hyoid bone and thyroid and cricoid cartilages show no fractures or hemorrhage. The trachea shows no significant congestion or mucous accumulation. No pulmonary emboli are noted. The right lung weighs 670 grams and the left lung 600 grams. Bilateral pulmonary edema is present. No foci of consolidation are present. No tumors or granulomatous inflammation is noted. Both lungs contain aspirated blood.

Gastrointestinal: The esophagus is lined by the typical white squamous epithelium. The G-E junction shows no significant pathologic change. The stomach is empty. No ulcers or tumors are noted. The small intestine shows no significant pathologic change upon palpation. No areas of obstruction are identified. The colon shows no significant dilatation. No diverticula are noted. No tumors are identified. The liver weighs 1670 grams and has a reddish-brown color on cut surface. No cirrhosis or tumors are identified. The gallbladder contains no stones. The pancreas shows no significant pathologic changes and has a coarse lobular configuration on cut surface.

Genitourinary: The left kidney weighs 180 grams and the right 180 grams. The cortical surface is smooth. Cut surface reveals a cortex measuring 7 mm in thickness. The cortical-medullary junction is distinct. No significant pathologic changes are noted in the renal papillae or renal pelvis. The ureters appear to drain freely into the bladder.

Page 3

Dr. Bruce Autopsy Report

(page 3)

A-99-226

Endocrine: The thyroid gland shows its typical beefy-red color and is of normal size and configuration. The adrenal glands are of normal size. Cut surface reveals the typical yellowish color of the cortex and gray medulla. No focal lesions are noted.

Hemic/Lymphatic: The thymus is of normal size for age. The spleen weighs 130 grams and shows no focal lesions on external or cut surface examination. It has the typical dark reddish parenchyma on cut surface with multiple pin point foci of white pulp.

Integumentary: See external examination.

Musculoskeletal: See central nervous system.

Central Nervous System: Reflection of the scalp reveals a 6 mm in diameter gunshot entrance defect of the anterior aspect of the left middle fossa. There is traumatic subarachnoid hemorrhage over each convexity. The projectile traveled from left to right, horizontally and front to back, macerating the inferior right and left temporal poles and midbrain before exiting the right lateral temporal skull leaving a 1.5 cm externally beveled defect. The projectile is found in the soft tissue of the right temporal region. The brain weighs 1340 grams and has a diminished gyral-sulcal configuration. The pituitary gland shows no enlargement. The meninges are clear and glistening. The cerebral arteries show no arteriosclerosis. Examination of the base of the brain reveals traumatic subarachnoid hemorrhage. Basilar skull fractures are present in each frontal region.

MICROSCOPIC DESCRIPTION

None.

FINAL SUMMARY

Postmortem examination of this 22-year-old white male revealed a contact penetrating gunshot wound to the left side of the head consistent with suicide. *self-murder*

fixed firm
compatible
not contradictory → *thought only consistent*

James R. Bruce, M.D.

Beveled to cut a bevel angle
defect - a blemish - fault - flaw

Dr. Bruce Autopsy Report
(page 4)

CHAPTER 2

Here is Corey Wood's story.

On September 28, 1999, Corey Wood was found in his home slumped over an end table. The smallest space in his room. He was laying on his side between his bed and an L-shaped end table that ran down the side of the wall across from his bed.

Law enforcement arrived early that morning of the 28th at almost 8:00 am. EMT's had already answered a call to his address close to 6:00 am the same morning, there is an affidavit that will verify this 1st ambulance, there is also a claim in that affidavit that states there was a blond-haired boy in that ambulance at that time, we still do not know who this boy is, and can only believe that a sworn affidavit is the truth and the boy was in that ambulance.

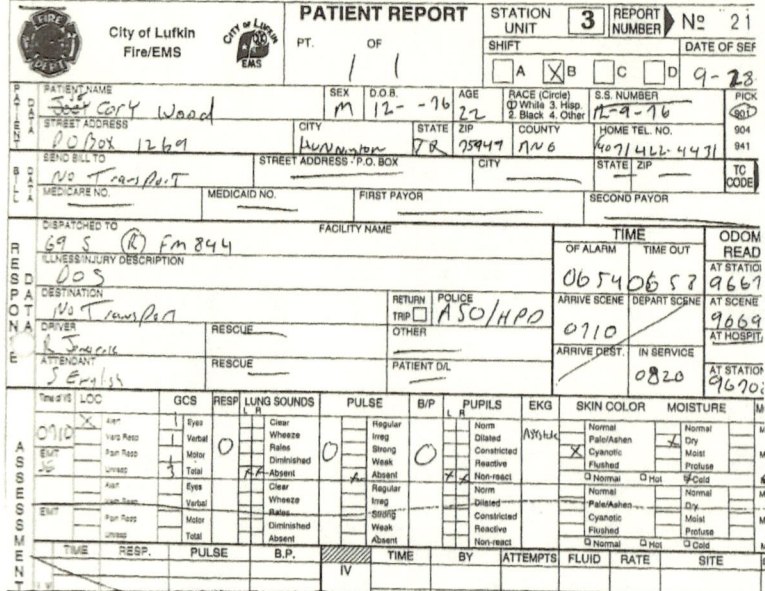

EMS Report

People that were in the home the night and into the morning of the 28th, Brian Wilson (shooter, room-mate), Jeremy Holder (another room-mate), Melinda Boles (Brian's girlfriend), and John Havard (friend and classmate of all that were there) John Havard said he was leaving, I heard him tell Corey just after 12 midnight that he was leaving, I don't have any idea when he returned, he was there when law enforcement arrived, he told the officers on-scene that Corey and I were fighting, this is one of the 1st of the many lies that have been told about the events leading up to Corey's killing.

DR YVONNE MARSHALL
936 422-5342

JANUARY 26 2008

REF: TO MR BURFINE'S LETTERS ON JANUARY 11, AND 13, 2008. ACCUSES
ANGELINA COUNTY SHERIFF KENT HENSON OF BOTCHING THE INVESTIGATION
OF CANDICE ALEXANDER'S MURDER

THANK YOU DETECTIVE DAVID CAMPBELL AND TEXAS RANGER PETE
MASKUNAS F OR YOUR HARD WORK THAT BROUGHT THIS TO JUSTICE.

I SUPPORT MR. BURFINE ON HIS BRAVERY AND COURAGE TO STAND UP AND
WRITE THESE TWO LETTERS ABOUT HOW THE INVESTIGATIONS HAVE BEEN
DONE IN OUR COUNTY. I KNOW FIRST HAND ABOUT HOW, IF ANY
INVESTIGATIONS ARE DONE IN ANGELINA COUNTY. THE CASE I KNOW VERY
WELL IS THE CASE OF COREY ADAM WOOD, MY GRANDSON, ON SEPTEMBER 28TH
1999. I RECEIVED A PHONE CALL AROUND 8AM FROM MY SISTER TELLING ME
SOMETHING HAD HAPPENED AT COREY'S TRAILER, AS I HUNG UP ANOTHER
CALL CAME IN, A FRIEND WAS GOING TO WORK AND SAID SHE SAW SEVERAL
SHERIFF'S CARS AT COREY'S. MY HUSBAND AND I HURRIED TO CHECK ON
COREY. HIS TRAILER WAS ABOUT HALF A MILE FROM OUR HOUSE ON 69 S.
WHEN WE GOT THERE KENT HENSON AND SEVERAL OTHER MEN WHERE IN THE
STREET LAUGHING AND TALKING WHILE GIPSON'S FUNERAL HOME WAS
BRINGING THE BODY OF COREY OUT IN A BODY BAG. NO ONE WANTED TO
TALK TO US. WE LEFT TO TELL COREYS MOM OF HIS DEATH. NO ONE HAD
COME TO OUR HOUSE TO TELL OF COREY'S DEATH. EVERYONE THAT HAD
BEEN AT COREY/S THE MORNING OF HIS DEATH HAD TO PASS OUR HOUSE, BUT
NOONE STOPPED TO TELL US.

THE FAMILY BURIED COREY THINKING IT WAS AN ACCIDENT. COREY DID NOT
HAVE A GUN NEVER HAD A GUN COREY LIKED TO FISH. COREY HAD TWO
ROOMMATES BRIAN WILSON AND JEREMY HOLDER THEY HAD GUNS.

SIX DAYS AFTER COREY/S DEATH THE FUNERAL IS OVER, FAMILY AND FRIENDS
ARE GONE BACK TO WORK OR OUT OF TOWN BACK TO THEIR JOBS AND HOMES.
I GET THIS PHONE CALL FROM CLAUDE MARSHALL, THE JUSTICE OF THE PEACE
IN ZAVALLA SAYING HE IS RULING COREY'S DEATH A SUICIDE. I ASK ON WHAT
GROUNDS OR PROOF HE HAS? HIS WORDS WERE SHERIFF HENSON'S
INVESTIGATION STATED SUICIDE. I TOLD JUDGE MARSHALL WE NEEDED MORE
THAN JUST SAYING SUICIDE ON A PIECE OF PAPER. THE FAMILY HAD BEEN

WITH COREY AND SPOKE TO HIM ON THE PHONE BEFORE HIS DEATH AND THE FAMILY DID NOT BELIEVE COREY COMMITTED SUICIDE. WE NEEDED AND WANTED TO TALK TO SHERIFF HENSON.

MY HUSBAND AND I WENT TO THE SHERIFF'S OFFICE. WE DID NOT TALK TO KENT HENSON AND AS OF TODAY HE WILL STILL NOT TALK TO US.

I HAVE A COPY OF COREY'S AUTOPSY. WHAT I HAVE READ IN THE AUTOPSY IS THAT COREY WAS SHOT IN THE LEFT SIDE OF HIS HEAD WITH THE GUN FIRED GOING TO THE FRONT OF HIS HEAD ON THE LEFT SIDE. COREY WAS RIGHT HANDED. IT ALSO STATES THE SIZE AND MEASURE OF ORGANS. COREY WAS OF NORMAL SIZE A BIG HEALTHY YOUNG MAN OF 22 YEARS OF AGE.

COREY ALSO HAD A BLACK EYE AND MARKS AROUND HIS WRISTS. HE ALSO HAD BRUISES ON HANDS AND UP ARMS AS FAR AS WE COULD SEE. WE WERE NEVER ALLOWED TO SEE COREY UNTIL AFTER THE AUTOPSY AND FUNERAL HOME WAS THROUGH. COREY'S FAMILY WONDERS IF THE PICTURES OF CANDICE ALEXANDER SHOWED SUCH A BEATING WHAT DID COREY LOOK LIKE. WE WERE NOT ABLE TO SEE HIM AND TO THIS DAY HAVE BEEN DENIED BY SHERIFF KENT HENSON ANY INFORMATION ON THIS CASE.

THREE YEARS AFTER COREY'S DEATH OUR GREAT GRANDDAUGHTER TWO AND HALF BAILEY HEALD WAS MURDERED BY HER BABY SITTER. AS WE WALKED INTO THE SHERIFF'S OFFICE THE FAMILY WAS TOLD BY THE OFFICER'S WORKING THE CASE THAT HE WOULD NOT TALK ABOUT COREY'S CASE TO US. THE FAMILY DID NOT KNOW AT THE TIME THAT BAILEY HAD BEEN MURDERED. WE THOUGHT OR BETTER SAID WE WERE LET TO BELIEVE BAILEY'S DEATH WAS AN ACCIDENT AT FIRST ALSO. AS WE HAD COREY'S. YOU NEVER WANT TO THINK THERE IS SOMEONE OUT THERE THAT WILL TAKE THE LIVES OF YOUR LOVED ONES. WE NEED SOMEONE THAT WILL AND CAN FIGHT TO FIND JUSTICE FOR THEIR MURDERS AND PUT THEM AWAY.

ON COREY'S CASE NO INVESTIGATION HAS BEEN DONE. IT IS AS IF THERE IS SOMETHING TO HIDE, OR JUST FORGET ABOUT IT. THIS DOES MATTER TO THE FAMILY.

PEOPLE COME UP TO ME ALL THE TIME TALKING ABOUT WOOD, THIS IS WHAT COREY'S FRIENDS CALLED HIM. THE OTHER DAY THIS YOUNG MAN CAME UP TO ME TELLING ME HE WAS WITH COREY THE DAY BEFORE HIS DEATH, COREY HAD FOUND OUT HIS ROOM MATE BRIAN WILSON WAS TAKING MONEY FROM HIS ATM, AND COREY WAS LOOKING FOR HIM. THAT COREY WAS UPSET ABOUT THIS AND HAD BEEN LOOKING FOR BRIAN ALL DAY. WHEN I SAY UPSET, FIGHTING MAD ARE BETTER WORDS.

AFTER COREY'S DEATH I FOUND IN HIS CHECKS THAT RANDY WILSON, BRIAN'S

DAD HAD WRITTEN 6500 DOLLARS IN CHECKS ON COREY'S ACCOUNT, NOT ON HIS SIGNATURE CARD. COREY'S MOM JOY BRUNNER AND MYSELF WENT TO THE BANK ON THIS MATTER- NO HELP THERE EITHER. EVEN THOUGH THE PRESIDENT OF THIS BANK KNEW COREY WANTED TO TALK TO HIM ABOUT SOMETHING THE DAY OF HIS DEATH.

YES WE DO NEED SOMEONE, SOMEONE TO STAND UP AND BRING JUSTICE FOR THE PEOPLE OF ANGELINA COUNTY AND THEIR FAMILIES.

JOY COREY'S MOM HAS WORKED ON THIS CASE FOR OVER EIGHT YEARS. AT THIS TIME SHE HAS A REWARD FOR ANYONE WITH INFORMATION LEADING TO THE CONVICTION OF COREY'S MURDER. THE FAMILY NEEDS THIS PUT TO A CLOSE AND FIND JUSTICE FOR COREY. WE PRAY THAT SOMEONE WILL COME FORWARD AND TELL WHAT, WHEN, AND HOW COREY DIED. COREY WAS A LOVING PERSON AND LOVED HIS FAMILY AS WE DID HIM.

MR. BURNFINE YOU HAVE THE SUPPORT OF MY FAMILY TO PUT THESE MURDERS AWAY AND BRING JUSTICE TO ALL OUR LOVED ONES.

DR. YVONNE MARSHALL
HUNTINGTON TEXAS
936 422-5342

William R, Campbell
P.O. Box 553
Broaddus, TX 75929

July 25, 2017

To whom it may concern:

My name is William R. Campbell and I am a retired Crime Scene Investigator with the Harris County Sheriff's Office in Houston, Texas. I was employed as a full time Crime Scene Investigator from August 2005 until I retired on October 2012. In addition, I have over 30 years experience as a Law Enforcement Officer with a Master Peace Officer's Certificate. Listed below are the following schools that I have attended and successfully completed in regards to Crime Scene Investigation:

- Courtroom Testimony Techniques – October 2004
- Collection, Documentation, and Preservation of Footwear and Tire Track Evidence – October 2004
- Basic Forensic Ridgeology – November 2004
- Fundamentals of Latent Print Examinations – December 2004
- Footwear Impression Comparison & Examination - January 2005
- Intermediate Crime Scene Investigations – February 2005
- Basic Homicide Investigation – March 2005
- DNA and Expert Witness Seminar – June 2005
- Crime Scene Search – October 2005
- Practical Homicide Investigation – October 2005
- FBI Fingerprint Classification – November 2005
- DNA Evidence – November 2005
- Medical Death Investigation – January 2006
- Bloodstain Pattern Analysis – Level One – February 2006
- Basic Photography – September 2006
- Develop, Lift, and Document Fingerprints - November 2006
- Fluorescein Training- Latent Blood Stain Detecting Agent – May 2007
- Use of Force Concepts – Police Officer Involved Shootings – July 2007
- Advanced Forensic Digital Imaging – August 2007
- Video Camcorder Techniques for Law Enforcement – January 2009
- Homicide Investigation Procedure and Tactics – December 2009

- Advanced Latent Print Comparison – January 2010
- Forensic Photography – August 2010
- Advanced Palm Print Comparison Techniques – July 2011
- Advanced Bloodstain Pattern Analysis – July 2012

During my 7 years in Crime Scene Investigations I worked the night shift with 5 other Crime Scene Investigators and we conducted almost exclusively death investigations. These included capital murders, murders, suicides, infant deaths and some industrial deaths; at least one of these occurred almost every night. In addition, I have been certified as an expert witness in the Harris County Criminal Court 186 in the fields of Blood Spatter and Fingerprints.

Around July of 2015, Darci Holloway and I met with Lieutenant Pete Maskunas of the Angelina County Sheriff's Office at which time I was able to review the case file (Case # 9910690) of the death investigation of Corey Adam Wood, white male, D.O.B. 12-15-1976.

My initial response upon reading the first responding deputies' and the investigator's reports was that of shock, due to the small amount of information that was recorded from the crime scene. All death investigations should be investigated as a homicide until proven otherwise, This investigation lacked good photographic and video evidence and did not have a crime scene sketch with measurements included. I did not see any mention of blood spatter evidence or lack thereof or any other detailed crime scene information.

Investigator Casper in supplemental report number 91367.4 in paragraph two stated he attempted to dust the rifle for fingerprints, but was unable to lift any prints that would be usable. The proper procedure would be to place the rifle into a paper bag for transportation to a facility that would have a Cyanoacrylate fuming chamber in order process the weapon for any possible latent fingerprints.

Based on my review of the case, I cannot make any determination as to suicide, murder, or any other manner of fowl play due to the lack of evidence and lack of proper case documentation from the initial crime scene investigation.

William R. Campbell
Retired Crime Scene Investigator
Harris County Sheriff's Office

Bradley Steffen
A&H Adjuster
AIG Accident & Health
Consumer Lines
913 495 2127 Telephone
866 831 5745 Facsimile
800 551 0024 Customer Service
brad.steffen@AIG.com

On Behalf Of National Union Fire Insurance Company of Pittsburgh Pa

November 29, 2017

Ms. Sharon Joy Brunner
2101 Church Street, #305
Galveston, TX 77550

RE: Insured: Corey Wood
     Policy Number: BSC 8052554
     Policyholder: Tidewater, Inc.
     Claim Number: 645-088586
     Date of Loss: 9/28/1999

Dear Ms. Brunner:

This letter is with respect to the above-captioned claim submitted in the death of your son, Corey Wood.

You previously indicated you were seeking the second report, but I could not tell if you meant the second from the beginning or from the end. Because neither of those reports contained any significant information I decided to send you a copy of every ICS report submitted to us by ICS Investigator Robert Bull.

As you are aware, this claim was originally denied by letter dated July 19, 2001. You subsequently filed an appeal which was denied by letter from the ERISA Appeals Committee dated September 25, 2002. With this your administrative remedies have been exhausted and any legal remedy must be pursued through the Courts.

Sincerely,

Bradley Steffen

Bradley Steffen
AD&D Adjuster

Encl.: ICS reports dated 1/08/2001, 1/25/2001, 2/12/2001, 3/09/2001, 3/22/2001, 4/04/2001, 11/07/2001, 5/15/2002, 6/20/2002, 7/01/2002, 7/09/2002, 7/15/2002, 7/24/2002, 8/26/2002, and 10/04/2002.

DR. YVONNE MARSHALL

November 12, 2001

ASSESSMENT & EVALUATION

STEPHANIE WILSON:

TO WHOM IT MAY CONCERN:

ASSESSING STEPHANIE WILSON AS A MOTHER OF TWO SONS. I FIND IT VERY STRANGE THAT WHEN SHE HEARD OF COREY'S DEATH THAT SHE DIDN'T TRY TO CONTACT COREY'S MOTHER OR STOP BY THE GRANDPARENTS HOUSE, THAT IS MY HUSBAND AND MYSELF. WE LIVE ABOUT TWO MILES BEFORE YOU GET TO COREY'S HOUSE. MRS. WILSON HAD TO PASS BY OUR HOUSE ON THE WAY TO COREY'S TRAILER. SHE HAD TO PASS BACK BY OUR HOUSE ON HER WAY FROM COREY'S.

WHEN MRS. WILSON, MR. WILSON, AND BRIAN CAME TO MY HOUSE A FEW HOURS AFTER COREY'S DEATH. MY HUSBAND AND MYSELF WERE STILL NOT BELIEVING COREY WAS DEAD.

THE WILSON'S WHERE VERY STRANGE ACTING, NO TEARS, THEY WERE TELLING ABOUT THE TIME THEY GOT THE CALL, THE TIME THEY ARRIVED AT COREY'S. FAMILY MEMBERS AND FRIENDS STATED THEY TOO FOUND THE WILSON'S TO BE VERY STRANGE. MRS. WILSON STATED SHE FLEW BY MY HOUSE ON HER WAY TO COREY'S HOUSE THAT MORNING. FAMILY AND FRIENDS HAVE COMMENTED ON HER ACTIONS, AND AS TO WHY SHE WOULD NOT STOP ON HER WAY TO OR FROM COREY'S TO LET HIS FAMILY KNOW HE WAS GONE. MRS. WILSON WAS DOING MOST OF THE TALKING AND TELLING WHAT HAD HAPPENED, VERY FAST AND CONTRADICTIVE. MRS. WILSON HAS BEEN VERY DEFENSIVE EVER SINCE COREY'S DEATH.

EVALUATION OF MRS. WILSON, MRS. WILSON NEEDS TO BE BROUGHT BEFORE A JUDGE AND ASKED ABOUT COREY'S DEATH, ALSO ABOUT THE CLEANING OF THE TRAILER THE MORNING OF COREY'S DEATH.

Sincerely,

DR. YVONNE MARSHALL

PRESENT IF POSSIBLE.

DOCUMENTATION AND ASSESSMENT OF AUTOPSY

*ALL INVESTIGATORS AND LAW ENFORCEMENT PERSONAL, FBI,
TEXAS RANGER, DISTRICT ATTORNEY CLYDE HARRINGTON
SHERIFF KENT HENSON, CHIEF DEPUTY JIM CASPER, TONY
GALLOWAY, AND DAVID CASPER. IF NOT PRESENT
DOCUMENTATION AS TO THEIR INVESTIGATION.*

JUDGE MARSHALL: ASSESSMENT OF INVESTIGATION: INQUEST

*EDDIE MATTHEWS: DOCUMENTATION AS 1ST OFFICER ON SCENE;
INVESTIGATION INTO THEFT AT HUNTINGTON STATE BANK;
COREY ADAM WOOD (DECEASED) MONEY FORGED OUT OF
CHECKING ACCOUNT, ALL OF INVESTIGATION: DOCUMENTATION*

Sincerely,

JOY BRUNNER

INQUEST FORM

NOTIFIED BY: *Suffin S.O.* AT 7:30 M. A.M. 9-28-1999

NAME OF DECEASED: COREY ADAM, WOOD

ADDRESS OF DECEASED: Rt. 2, Box 348 Huntington Tx (NE/Rd off 844

DATE OF BIRTH: 12-15-76 DL# 13225597 SS# 451-61-3497

TESTIMONY: *Was found in room by Roomate Brian Wilson. Jeremy Halden another roomate had already went to work. Home, Ph# 422-443 Medicine found that he was taking were Cefadroxil 500 mg prescribed by Dr. McClure the parameters said it was for a cold*

TIME FOUND: 6:30 AM. DATE: 9-28 1999 PLACE: Home

AUTOPSY ORDERED: (YES) or NO
(circle one)

CAUSE OF DEATH: *Gunshot wound to the head, the bullet went in the left temple and appeared to be lodged in the head. It appeared to be self-inflicted. Autopsy was ordered for final Judgment.*

TIME OF DEATH: 7:45 AM. DATE: 9-28 1999

FAMILY MEMBERS (or friends): *Officers present were G. Torres, Chris Ward, Larry Wright and Jim Casper Casper. officer took wallet out of pocket for identification. Sheriff Kent Henson was also on the sene. Mother Joy Brumer from Central was notified and Grand Parents Mr. & Mrs. B. D. Marshall came to sene.*

REMARKS: *Cory was in bedroom laying off left side of bed on floor, left arm hanging down right had hold of forearm of gun he was laying across th gun head on nightstand. Box of 22 shells spilled out on tols. lent up against the wall*

Claude Marshall Jr.

Claude F. Marshall Jr.
Justice Of The Peace
Precinct #4
Angelina County, Texas

RELEASED TO: *Gibson* FUNERAL HOME

SUITE 5
LUFKIN, TEXAS 75904
(409) 639-3266

NOVEMBER 3, 1999

RE: COREY WOOD

COREY WOOD WAS SEEN IN MY OFFICE ON 09-24-99
WITH PHARYNGITIS AND TRACHEOBRONCHITIS. HE
WAS GIVEN KEFZOL 500 IM AND PLACED ON
DURICEF 500 AND TUSSI-ORGANIDAN DM, WHICH ARE
NON-NARCOTIC COMPOUNDS. THERE WERE NO
SIGNS OF DEPRESSION. THERE WERE NO SIGNS
OF ANY ATTEMPT TO HURT HIMSELF OR ANYONE ELSE.

C. H. MCCLURE, M.D.

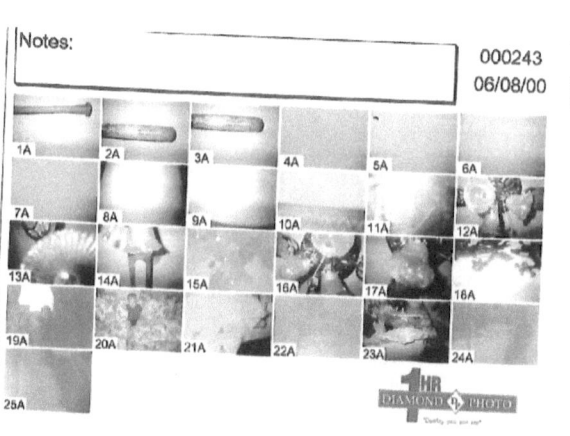

CAUSE NO. 34,564-01-09

JOYBRUNNER, AS PERSONAL   IN THE DISTICT COURT OF
REPRESENTATIVE OF THE ESTATE
OF COREY A. WOOD AND JOY
BRUNNER, INDIVIDUALLY
    PLAINTIFS

VS.   OF ANGELINA COUNTY,
TEXAS

BRIAN WILSON, RANDY WILSON
STEPHANIE WILSON, ROBERT
HEATH TALBERT, JEREMY HOLDER
AND MELINDA BOLES
    DEFENDANTS   JUDICIAL DISTRICT

COURT OF APPEALS
STATE OF TEXAS
NINTH DISTRICT

RE: CASE NUMBER: 09-02-00132-CV
    TRIAL COURT CASE NUMBER: CV-34564-01-09

NEW CASE NUMBER: 04-02-00288-CV

AFFIDAVIT

BEFORE ME, THE UNDERSIGHNED NOTARY PUBLIC, ON THIS DAY
PERSONALLY APPEARED KIMBERLY Y. HILL, WHO BEING BY ME DULY
SWORN ON HER OATH DEPOSED AND SAID:

PLAINTIFF'S EXHIBIT

I AM KIMBERLY Y. HILL, UNDER OATH AM OVER THE AGE OF 18 YEARS, HAVE NEVER BEEN CONVICTED OF A CRIME, AND AM OTHERWISE COMPETENT TO MAKE THIS AFFIDVIT. THE FACTS DATED IN THIS AFFIDAVIT ARE WITHIN MY PERSONAL KNOWLEDGE AND ARE TRUE AND CORRECT

ON THE MORNING OF SEPTEMBER 28, 1999, SOMETIME BEFORE OR AT 5:30 AM I WAS GOING TO WORK. I LIVE ON NEAL RD IN HUNTINGTON TEXAS, I STOPPED AND ASK AN AMBULANCE TO PLEASE MOVE, THE AMBULANCE WAS PARKED ACROSS THE ROAD ON NEAL RD. IN FRONT OF THE DRIVE-WAY OF COREY WOOD'S HOME.

SUBSCRIBED AND SWORN TO BEFORE ME ON THE ___14th___ DAY OF __January__, 2003. TO CERTIFY WHICH WITNESS MY HAND AND OFFICAL SEAL

Angela Harris

ANGELA HARRIS
MY COMMISSION EXPIRES
JANUARY 3, 2006

NOTARY PUBLIC IN AND FOR THE
STATE OF TEXAS
MY COMMISSION EXPIRES.
___1/3/06___

The call came in after I had hung up from Rhonda and darci.   3 way, talked about heelies and Christmas.   November 28th 2007. Around 11:30 maybe after 12:00am

Kimberly started by saying she told Roland that she had not been avoiding me and had just got back into town, that she would call me soon.   We talked about how Roland only gives half of the message

then she preceded in telling me about who she saw that day, Kent Henson in a out of the way Mexican resuarnt . I knew it, and the day I was there or night there were want to be cops there too. Sheriff reserves.

Kent Henson was sitting with a table full of Texas rangers and other deputies under cover, that when she went to the pisser, her words.   He stood up and called her name and waved real big, her and mat had sat in smoking and she had one beer and made sure that was all.

Then she told me about how crazy that was because she had showed the tape of corey, a reporter came to investigate from Austin about the case file, Kent Henson is showing his rear on this tape. So matt knew who he was. She went on about how weird that was how he acted.

I laughed and said he probably thinks you put up the money for the 10,000 dollar reward I just put up for coreys killers.

She went nuts, why didn't you tell me you were going to do that???

How could you do that, why would you do that, you and aunt sandi won't let this go, I can see why you won't, but don't understand why you won't let it go.   Just what do you want out of this?

I said what do you mean what do I want, you know what I want.   I want them dead or in jail

she said well you will go to hell if you kill them, I will go to Kent Henson and tell him if he will just change that death certificate to accident all of this will just go away.

J   it is too late for accident now it will have to me homicide
k oh they are not ever going to change I to homicide
j well maybe at this point unknown, but no way accident
k I thought that was the whole point to get the death certificate changed, not to get the killers

j you have known what we wanted from the beginning I thought you knew any way

 at some point in this conservation I ask what she knew that she was not telling me, she said she would tell me later, it was mat's last night and she was going to spend time with him.

We hung up, said bye and that we loved each other,
I went to bed, back to bed, and the phone rang about 5 to 10 minutes later. It was Kimberly
wanting me to promise to do 2 things for her the next day.

1, go to the court house and get the evidence that the judge sealed, a copy of it so she could put it
in a safety deposit box for her mother in case she was killed over this, made me promise over and
over. I did promise to find out maybe even said I would, she told me to get the girl at work to
notarize the paper work if I had to. Then the 2nd thing was for me to get on the computer and
look up what you are supposed to do if some one steels your guns, and she ask me if I
remembered jay and Jessie self stealing her guns, and she sure did not need them to come back
used in a murder.

That is when I knew she really did know more about corey's death than she has said all along and
started to put some things to gether my self about the was things have happened since corey's
died. I called the dps and told Pete on answering machine, I told her I would and she said don't
because of some dps officer named Paul. Something about his wife and the department. I called
anyway and left the message. Hope I did the right thing   Nov 30 2007 11:41 pm joy Brunner
oh they killed Logan and now they will kill me, they put a bullet in Logan head and they can just
as easily put one in mine.
I cant believe you did not tell me about this, you should have give me a heads up, I and going to
punch you right in the stomach when I see you

j you better not

k well I need to hit you somewhere,

j if you hit me any where on my body, I will beat the shit out of you, do you not remember the
first time you reached over and hit me, I will whip your ass all over this house or where ever.
Laughing

k well I can not believe you would not tell your best friend you were gong to do this
they will be able to place me down at corey's house by the security camera at my school. They
are going to kill me.

J what in the world are you so drama about they already know you were at corey's house what is
the big deal now.

K I just can't believe you would do something like that and not tell me, you are standing on the
mountain top on snow white ground and the ball is rolling down hill and going to hit me like a
rock smash me down. All of this stuff with nataasa and all these people all that has been going
on. You should tell someone before you do something like this

you just plow into something and don't ease into anything, in 3 months I can have Kent Henson
where I want him.

J if you want to fuck him why don't you just do it

k well first we can get the death certificate changed to accident and from there, well I really won't be lying we can wait for a while and then go back and ask for unknown or even homicide. What do you want me to tell him?

J I really don't care what you tell him or what you do with him, as far as I'm concerned Im though with Kent Henson,

k well we started talking while you were gone. I saw him at the lunch box he was getting a cake for some 50 retirement party, ask me if I thought I could park my big yellow truck any where I wanted and not get towed, I said in this town there is not a tow truck that will touch it.   I thought he was a Texas ranger didn't even know who he was,

I did not say anything and really have just thought about it now, that was a lie to my face, you know she know's who the sheriff is, he's been the sheriff for ever.

J you've probably already have funked him, laugh.

K well you need to tell me before you do something like this again,

j well I called you a bunch of times and did not want to leave a message like this on your phone.

K oh you can at least call me and tell me to call that you are going to do something with corey's case.   You know I'm up at the court house saying I was at corey's.

j ok I'm sorry I had know idea you would get so upset

k you know they can kill both of us a bullet in the head is an easy thing to do.

J ok then we hung up

she called back in just a very short time, I had just layed back down.

She made me promise to go to the court room and ask the judge for the she called it a depostion but

I know this is detailed but it's the whole conversation as well as I can remember. There are some things in here that sent red flags up for me.

This woman was the only one that knew I was going across the river the night I was pulled over, I was at her house when Bailey died, there is a lot of things this woman has been at in our lives that may be questionable. There when our house burnt and told the people that Roland started it. Any one that knows roland knows he saves every thing, he was beside himself.

I drank with this woman for the last eight years, and now that I am sober I believe she has keep someone informed about what we are doing. By her reaction to the reward.

Clyde my mother and family tried to tell me she was involved and not to trust her.

sharon joy brunner dec 13, 2007

FEB 2 2002

MY GRANDSON WAS MURDERED,
FAMILY DECIDES TO FIND OUT WHY,
WHO DID THIS?
BY YVONNE MARSHALL, PH.D.

The County medical doctor who performed the autopsy ruled the death a self-inflicted gunshot to the left temple. The projectile traveled from left to right, horizontally and front to back. The autopsy also states there was a subarachnoid hemorrhage in the base of the brain with basilar skull fracture in the front region.

Two roommates were living with my grandson at the time of his death. They are saying in their statements that they did not hear the gunshot. One roommate states he was running late for work and did not see my grandson in his room, but turned off the TV in the living room and the light in the kitchen. We found out later, he took the time to stop and take his dog to work with him.

The other roommate states he got up after the first one left, he turned off the light, and found my grandson slumped over the gun. No 911 call, the call went straight into the sheriff's office. We have been told it was placed from a public phone. Also, that several calls were made to the sheriff's office the morning of my grandson's death, but only one call was recorded for the record.

The trailer had been cleaned all but my grandson's room.

The people that were at my grandson's trailer have been asked by the DA to take a polygraph test. There were several people at the trailer, girlfriends of the roommates as well as parents. They all have refused a polygraph test and have hired a criminal lawyer.

Money was forged out of my grandson's checking account prior to his death. This was found out two months after his death. The bank had allowed this man, the father of one roommate, to take $6,500 from my grandson's checking account. No signature card, nor any permission to take the money. The bank would not offer any help on this; nor was there any help from law enforcement. However, a lawyer has told us that this is good information to put in court when needed. This is a good motive and will be good to bring up at another time.

The family was not contacted of my grandson's death. Our grandson had put his new trailer on our land about two miles from us. The law enforcement, as well as all of my grandson's friends, had to pass our house on the morning of his death. My sister who lives on my grandson's road called me after her neighbor saw all the cars at the trailer. This was several hours after his death. Whoever was responsible had more than enough time to execute an exquisite cover-up.

The Sheriff's Department investigated my grandson's homicide for one-hour and fifty-four minutes. The Sheriff will not talk to the family about this case. No one from the sheriff's office will talk.

My grandson was studying to be a ship captain. He had money in the bank and had just received a ten-dollar a day raise the day before his death. He had worked off shore for three years. He told me just hours before his death; he would be home for Christmas with money to have a great Christmas with his family. Christmas and East were great times for Cory, spending them with his family.

At this time, the DA and an investigator are working on the case. They tell us that some of the kids are talking about what happened to my grandson. The DA has made the statement that he has never worked on another case that has this many people involved, and gone this long with no one talking. However, we have been told that someone of the friend circle has talked. Sooner or later someone will have to talk, we pray.

I have assessed and evaluated the roommates and friends statements. Everyone has a lot of anger toward my grandson. Their statements are written as if pre-rehearsed in a group before going to the Sheriff's Office. The signature of one is so small you can barely make it out. Two friends also made statements that they had been at the trailer earlier with my grandson and that they were all watching Monday Night Football. My grandson was falling asleep on the couch when they left.

This investigation should never have happened this way, or gone this long without the truth coming out. The Sheriff's Office did not do an investigation. The trailer was not checked out, or the people that were in the trailer. The Sheriff's Department only took the word of the man who had forged $6,500 out of my grandson's checking account. He was at the trailer when the law enforcement arrived and he did all the talking.

We are also told, at this time, that the gun in my grandson's hand may not be the gun that killed him. No fingerprints were on the gun, not even my grandson". It had been cleaned.

Something has to be done to change this kind of quick investigation and putting suicide down, letting the people that murdered our loved one walk the street. Our family never wants another family going through what we are going through. Losing a loved one is by far hard enough, but finding out there was no investigation done to determine the cause of death is almost unbearable. We have found out thousands of families out there are experiencing the same grief and pain we are. We believe we have been given a life sentence of grief and pain, some of us without the tools to deal with it. The family and friends are praying that justice will be done. We truly believe it will. We won't stop until it is.

At this time, a law has been passed in the Texas State Legislature that is authorizing teams to review unexpected adult deaths. I am pleased about this new bill, Chapter 672, Adult Fatality Review and Investigation SB515, as amended, would authorize a county to establish a review team to conduct reviews of unexpected deaths that occur in the county. Review teams for counties with populations below 50,000 could join with adjacent counties to establish combined teams.

A Commissioners Court could oversee the team; Commissioners could designate a non-profit agency or political sub-division of the State involved in family violence, abuse or suicide treatment to oversee the team, if the agency or political sub-division agreed.

The purpose of the teams would include developing an understanding of the causes and incidences of unexpected deaths in the county and advise the Legislature, State agencies, and local law enforcement agencies about changes to law, policy or practice to reduce the number of unexpected deaths. To achieve their purpose, teams would have to meet to review fatality cases suspected to have resulted from suicide, family or abuse and recommend methods to improve coordination of services and investigations among agencies represented on the team.

My hope and goal for this team is to enable a family member to be present and be involved; because who knows their loved one better than a family member.

The bill was passed March 7, 2001. Late for my grandson, he died September 28, 1999. However, I believe with the letters and phone calls that have been made since my grandson's death, maybe just one family won't have to go through what we have in the past two years. We will fully support the bill, and I hope to serve on the team.

At this time, we are working on getting our loved one exhumed. We now feel this is our next step. Over the past two years of working on his case, we have met many closed doors, but with our hard work and prayer, another door has opened. We will continue to work and pray.

About the author:

Dr. Marshall is a Counselor in Huntington Texas. She is a Clinically Certified Forensic Counselor, specializing in forensic evaluation and counseling. Dr. Marshall may be contacted at 936-422-6342.

Sheriff:
KENT HENSON

Incident ID: 91267   Case # 9910690
Status   : CE (INACTIVE)

Initial Call Reported By:
    WILSON,VERNON
    P O BOX 1269
    HUNTINGTON, TX 75949
    4224631

Nature of Call : UNKDEATH-UNKNOWN DEATH

Offense/Incident Location:
    FM 844/NEAL RD
    FM 844/NEAL RD
    HUNTINGTON, TX 75949

Officer/Unit Assigned:
    GXT (TORRES, DELLIS)

Investigator Assigned:

Category:

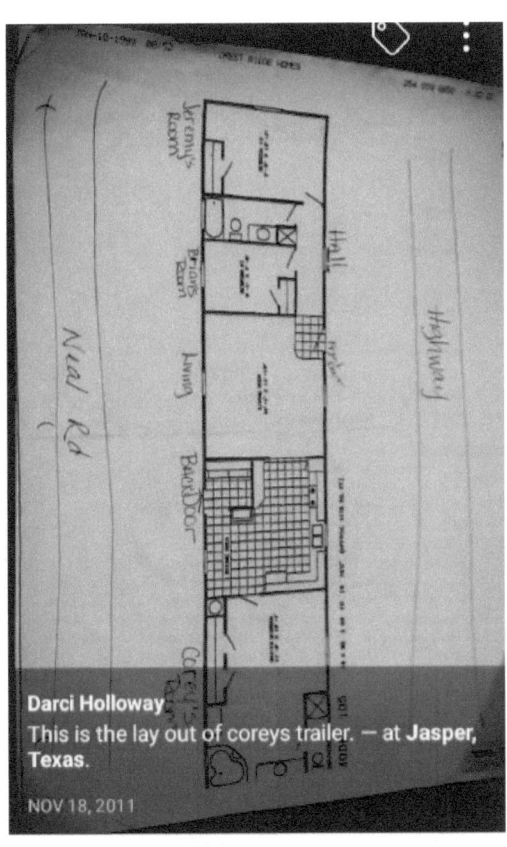

YVONNE MARSHALL, PH.D.
Route 2 Box 348 • Huntington, Texas 75949 • Phone: (409) 422-5342

November 20, 1999

RE: Reference Line I.D. No. 132377

To Whom It May Concern:

I am writing this letter after the inquest on Friday November 19,1999, because I was not allowed to make a statement with Judge Marshall.

I was under the impression the inquest would be recorded and I would be able to speak and give my statement on behalf of Corey A. Wood, my grandson, who died on September 28, 1999 from a 22 caliber rifle gunshot wound to his head at his residence in Huntington, Texas. At the inquest, Judge Marshall stated no statement or letter would be read. Therefore, I have not of this date been able to tell, or state, that I spoke with Corey on the night of September 27th around 10:30 p.m. We talked for about an hour. I knew Corey well; my husband B. D. and I helped our daughter (Joy) raise Corey. I was also Corey's Head Start teacher. I have a Master's degree in Early Childhood and Child Development, as well as a Doctorate in psychology and counseling. Corey and his sister Darci were both evaluated and assessed during my college studies. Corey had high self-esteem, very good social skills, attitude, good thoughts about himself, and enjoyed his school years. He played all sports and had a great desire to go far in life. Corey had no emotional problems during his childhood or as an adult of 22 years. He loved life and was planning for his future.

Corey called me on the night of September 27, 1999, talking about his Mom and Stepfather (Roland) having words about his Stepfather's drinking and not coming home. I told him I knew about this, because I had visited my daughter that day. Corey said he was coming the next morning to get his grandfather B.D. and go talk to Roland about going back home to his Mom and little brother Jenson, and if he had to, he would kick Roland's butt. Yes, Corey was mad about his Stepfather leaving his Mom and Jenson, but he was going to talk to Roland the next morning. Corey was a 22 year old young man—involved with his own life, making plans for his future. He had a good job, a 4-wheel drive truck, and a brand new mobile home. Corey did not want to kill anyone, least of all himself.

Reference Line ID No. 132377
Yvonne Marshall, Ph.D.
Page 2

A 22 year old with Corey's plans and future ahead of him, would not have taken his life because his Mom and Stepfather were having a disagreement over the Stepfather's drinking and staying out all night. As a matter of fact, Judge Marshall appears to be laboring under the impression that it was Corey and his Mom who were having a disagreement, which is entirely false. The disagreement was between Corey's Mom (Joy) and her husband, Corey's Stepfather. This misconception is what Judge Marshall based his final decisions of suicide on—stating it was 51%. Corey was not living in his parent's home and had been out of their home for four and a half years.

Judge Marshall would not allow me to make a statement at the inquest. I was also told by the young investigator on Corey's case, David Casper, that my statement was not necessary due to the fact that I would say the same as the others who gave statements and stated that Corey did not do it.

As I stated previously, I spoke to Corey on the telephone the night of September 27, 1999 around 10:30 p.m.; we talked for about an hour. Corey's desires for his future, as well as his family, were very high that night. His attitude and thoughts were that he would be making enough money with the raise he had just learned that morning he was getting, he could help his mom, sister and little brother if needed. He also told me that when I retired my private practice in the year 2000, he wanted me and his grandfather to go in the RV and not worry about the family; he would be making enough money to take care of the family if needed, just like his grandfather had taken care of him, Darci and his Mom.

Corey did not intend to take his own life. I feel Corey was under the assumption that the gun was unloaded and that perhaps he reached across the gun and the gun went off. "The bullets were on the table".

Our family is very much in need of information we may be able to obtain from the records of Corey's death. Please help us; all we want is to view the records and try to make sense of this tragedy—suicide simply does not fit the pattern of Corey A. Wood. Please call (409)422-5342 if you need to speak with me concerning this letter.

Sincerely yours,

Yvonne Marshall, Ph.D.

November 18, 1999

On the morning of Tuesday, September 28, 1999, I received the news that my cousin, Corey, had been found dead at his residence. The first news that I heard was that he had died from a self-inflicted gunshot, and that no suicide note had been discovered. Well, my initial response was disbelief, and my mind filled with questions. I remember thinking— "No way... not Corey! He wouldn't do something like that."

I am a psychology major, and some of my classes have dealt with the issue of suicide. In every case that I have studied, there was always some kind of "reason" linked to the suicide, and I was unable to think of any "reason" for Corey to intentionally do anything so drastic.

So... In an effort to find answers to all my questions, I called Huntington City Hall. Eddie Mathews was there, and he was able to give me the name of an officer who was on the scene at Corey's residence. I then went to the Angelina County Sheriff's Office to speak with Lieutenant Hight. The Lieutenant was very considerate, and he started answering my questions one by one. During our conversation, which lasted about 45-60 minutes, he told me about the scene, the position of Corey's body, where the gun was found and the angle of the bullet's point of entry. He also told me what type of gun it was. He gave me a very graphic account of the many details he encountered while on the scene. He then went on to say that, it was his *theory* that Corey was under the assumption that the gun was unloaded, and that Corey reached across the gun, *possibly* to get the bullets that were on the table, in order to load the gun, and the gun went off. The Lieutenant said he saw nothing at the scene that would indicate evidence of a suicide, and several times he stated that **no one** would ever be able to convince him that Corey's death was **anything** but an accident!

Lori M. Bell

YVONNE MARSHALL, Ph.D.
Route 2 Box 348 · Huntington, Texas 75949 · Phone: (409) 422-5342

December 28, 1999

Ms. Sandy Sawyer
Open Record Division Office of the Attorney General
Box 12548
Austin, Texas 78711

RE: Reference Line I.D. No. 132377

Dear Ms. Sawyer:

I knew Corey A. Wood very well. My husband B. D., Corey's grandfather, and I helped our daughter (Joy) raise Corey. Corey was a loving child, as well as a loving adult. Corey had no emotional problems. He had high self-esteem, very good social skills, and everyone loved and liked Corey. He was outgoing and loved life. He enjoyed his life and was proud of what he was doing.

Corey was a 22 year old man who worked for Tidewater Marine. He was preparing to upgrade for his mates license with the help of Captain Terry Hunter. When Corey first went on the tugboat, Mr. Hunter had taken him under his wing and treated him like a son; Mr. Hunter wanted what was best for Corey. Since Corey's death, I have talked with Mr. Hunter several times. Mr. Hunter also said there was no way Corey could or would do this, "take his own life", that he had so much to live for and he loved his family too much to do this.

Most people either talk about suicide or do something to indicate that they are going to kill themselves. There are warning signs; people see these. As many people as Corey was with, someone would have seen this if suicidal signs were there.

Many who attempt or commit suicide do not want to die, but simply want a way to escape an unbearable situation. Corey was not in an unbearable situation.

Corey had his life in order and was working on making it even better. He talked about having his own family one day. He told me this a few hours before his death. Corey did not have any suicidal signs.

As many as 80% of completed suicides occur after previous attempts. This is especially true for young people. Corey had no previous attempts.

Corey was coming to my house the next morning to make out his bills and sign his checks so I could pay his monthly bills. I paid them for him while he was out of town working. The night of September 27, 1999, I had a long talk with Corey. Yes, Corey was concerned about his Mom and little brother (Jenson). He wanted assurance they would be taken care of before he left out for work. He said he would be gone for two months working and would come back with money for Christmas. He enjoyed buying for the family at Christmas. The family knew he would be gone for Thanksgiving because he always saved his time for Christmas. We were all looking forward to this Christmas together.

I would very much like to view Corey's records at the Sheriff's office. The family needs to know more. There is not enough evidence showing accident, suicide or murder. We all know it has to be one.

Please call (409)422-5342 if there is any way you can possibly help us.

Sincerely yours,

Yvonne Marshall, Ph.D.

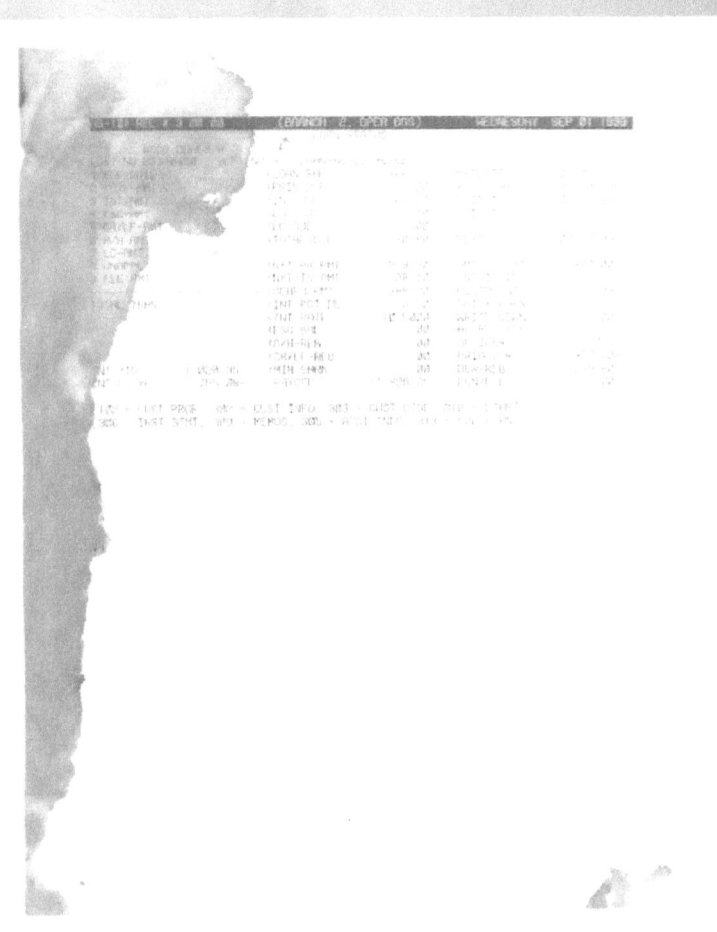

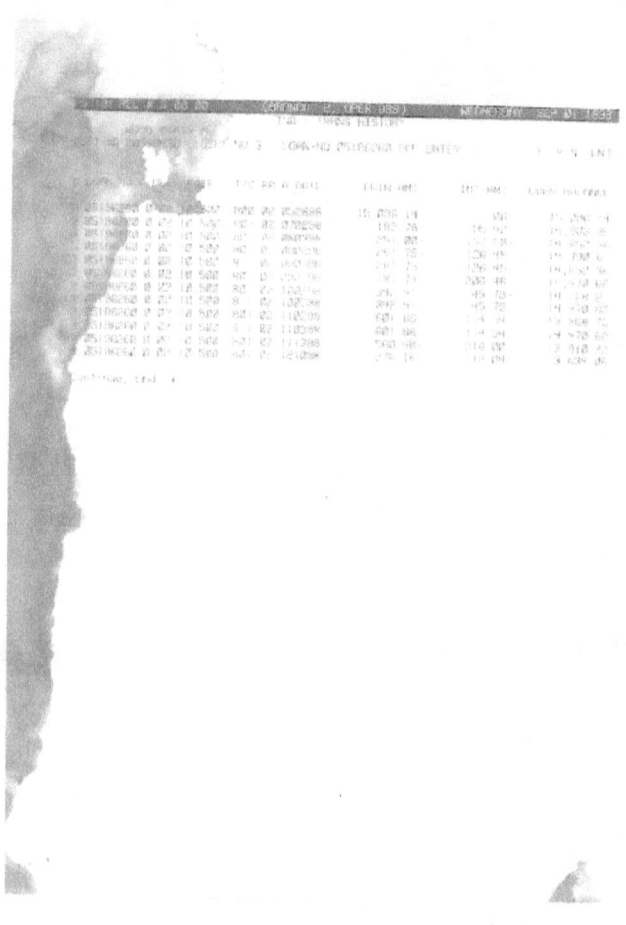

Corey Wood
3-17-99
X-Rays

Arthur W. Jordan, D.D.S.
1405 SOUTH JOHN REDDITT DRIVE
LUFKIN, TEXAS 75904
Telephone (409) 632-6609

To Whom It May Concern:
Per family's request:

Corey Wood's dental work included a temporary crown @ #8. Also, root canal and titanium post at #8. He also had multiple alloys as restorations @ #3, 14, 18, 19, 20, and 30. Resin fillings @ 2, 15, and 31. All four wisdom teeth were present and at some level impacted.

I hope this helps.

Thanks,

Art Jordan

Tidewater Marine

October 22, 1999

To Whom It May Concern:

I, Hunter J. Chasson, was the supervisor for Cory Wood at Tidewater Marine. I am writing this letter to state the future of Cory Wood's planning with Tidewater Marine. On Friday 9-24-99 Cory called me stating that he would be able to go to work the following Monday. I had Cory scheduled to report to the M/V Gulf Ace II for 0800 on Monday 9/27/99. Monday morning at 0800 Cory called me at the office and said he would not make it to the office because he needed to see a doctor for a cold. I rescheduled Cory for Wednesday 9/29/99 again for the M/V Gulf Ace II. Cory asked if 11:00 A.M. would be fine instead of 0800 due to some last minute errands he had to run, bills to pay, hair cut, etc. Cory claimed, what he could not finish he would get his Grandmother to finish for him. Cory's was preparing to upgrade for his Mates license with the help of his Captain, Terry Hunter. Captain Hunter acknowledges Cory did not have the complete time in for the license but already started training Cory at the wheel of the vessel.

In my own opinion, I feel that Cory would never take his own life. Cory was the type of person who was what I call "high on life". Cory was always cheerful and willing to learn and help with any task given to him on the vessel or in the office. For such a young man, Cory was always looking toward the future to better himself professionally and personally. I can say he loves his family dearly. Cory was always talking about how close they were. Again, in my opinion I can not see a young man taking his own life with so much to give to those around him. After talking to Cory's mother, Joy, I can tell that Cory was loved just as much by his family. I ask that if there is anything I might be able to answer or elaborate on concerning Cory's investigation that I am contacted to clarify for the sake of Cory's memory.

I am sending this letter to Judge Marshall and the others involved in Cory's case, in hopes that I may be able to help enlighten any other opinion of Cory's life and attitude towards life that anyone else may have of a young man that they do not know. If there is any need for you to contact me for further questioning. I ask that you reach me at my office phone 1 800 634 5806.

Sincerely yours,

Hunter Chasson

Dear Cory Wood,

Subject: Outstanding Performance of Duties

You are commended on your outstanding performance on board the Mac Tide 63 from 9 February through 10 March 1999. You displayed a positive attitude and very knowledgeable of your job requirements.

You were a self-starter, always alert to the job at hand. You were very much an important element in maintaining the vessel material condition, performing at an above average level in all operations.

You are a team player always pitching in to assist your fellow shipmates when needed, and never having to be directed in the routine matters of duties. When given an assignment you accomplished it with very little if any directions.

Your positive approach to safety and Company policies and procedures has been outstanding.

It has been a privilege and a pleasure to have you aboard, and we look forward to see you aboard again as a shipmate.

Again Thank You.

Captain John Fulton

Chief Engineer Lawrence LeBlanc

Mate Charles Brinson

Lawrence LeBlanc

Ti_ _ater Marine, Inc. - Towing Di_ ion

CREW
PERFORMANCE EVALUATION

Section: 1

Name of crewman: *Cory A. Wood*		Position: *A/B*
Period of tour:	From: *2-10-99*	To: *3-9-99*

Please rate the ability of each crewman as they relate to the described subjects below by checking the appropriate box in each row.

		Excellent	Above Avg	Average	Below Avg	Poor
Knowledge	How well does this person know the job requirements?	✓				
Ability	Can this person convert knowledge and instruction into performance?	✓				
Attitude	Describe this person's attitude towards the responsibilities of the job?.					
Initiative	Is this person a self-starter?					
Effort	Does this person do his or her best?					
Cooperation	Does this person work together with the others?					
Dependability	Is this person reliable or available when needed?	✓				
Ambition	Does this person show a desire to learn or upgrade?	✓				
Understanding	How well does this person take/use instructions?	✓				
Acceptance	How well do others accept this person?	✓				
Personality	How well does this person accept or treat others?	✓				
Safety	Does this person know, understand and practice safety?	✓				

Section: 2

Briefly comment where needed with regard to any of the above items:
Cory is an outstanding A/B - well versed in his Responsibilities - one of the best A/B we have worked with

CHARLES BRINSON
Name of evaluator (print)

MATE
Position of evaluator

Signature of evaluator

I have reviewed and discussed this evaluation of my performance.
My signature does not mean that I necessarily agree with it.

Employee signature

3-9-99
Date

Tidewater Marine, Inc. - Towing Division

CREW
PERFORMANCE EVALUATION

Section: 1

Name of crewman:	COREY Wood		Position:	R.B.
Period of tour:	From: JUNE 3, 1999		To: JUNE 9 1999	

Please rate the ability of each crewman as they relate to the described subjects below by checking the appropriate box in each row.

		Excellent	Above Avg	Average	Below Avg	Poor
Knowledge	How well does this person know the job requirements?			✓		
Ability	Can this person convert knowledge and instruction into performance?			✓		
Attitude	Describe this person's attitude towards the responsibilities of the job?.			✓		
Initiative	Is this person a self-starter?		✓			
Effort	Does this person do his or her best?		✓			
Cooperation	Does this person work together with the others?		✓			
Dependability	Is this person reliable or available when needed?			✓		
Ambition	Does this person show a desire to learn or upgrade?		✓			
Understanding	How well does this person take/use instructions?			✓		
Acceptance	How well do others accept this person?			✓		
Personality	How well does this person accept or treat others?		✓			
Safety	Does this person know, understand and practice safety?			✓		

Section: 2

Briefly comment where needed with regard to any of the above items:

_____

_____

_____

ALTON J. ALARIO, JR.   CAPTAIN   _[signature]_
Name of evaluator (print)   Position of evaluator   Signature of evaluator

I have reviewed and discussed this evaluation of my performance.   _[signature]_   6-9-99
My signature does not mean that I necessarily agree with it.   Employee signature   Date

Tidewater Towing

TIDEWATER MARINE TOWING, INC.
P.O. Box 802 • Harvey, LA 70059-0802
A Tidewater Company

PERSONNEL PERFORMANCE EVALUATION

NAME: _Cory Wood_ CLASSIFICATION: O/S

NO OF DAYS OBSERVED: 37 From June 26, '97 To Aug 1, 1997

	POOR	NEEDS IMPROVEMENT	GOOD	VERY GOOD	EXCELLENT
KNOWLEDGE :How well does this person know his job?	( )	☒	( )	( )	( )
ABILITY :Can this person translate knowledge and instruction into performance?	( )	( )	☒	( )	( )
INITIATIVE :Is this person a self starter?	( )	☒	( )	( )	( )
EFFORT :Does this person do his best?	( )	( )	☒	( )	( )
COOPERATION :Does this person get along with co-workers?	( )	( )	( )	☒	( )
DEPENDABILITY :Is this person "there when you need him"?	( )	( )	( )	☒	( )
AMBITION :Does this person work at learning? :Try to upgrade himself?	( )	( )	( )	☒	( )
UNDERSTANDING :How well does this person take/use instructions?	( )	( )	☒	( )	( )
ACCEPTANCE :How well do others accept this person?	( )	( )	( )	☒	( )
PERSONALITY :How well does this person accept others?	( )	( )	( )	☒	( )
SAFETY :Does this person know, understand and practice safety?	( )	( )	( )	☒	( )
ATTITUDE :Describe this person's attitude toward his employment responsibilities?	( )	( )	( )	☒	( )

COMMENTS: _Cory has THE capability of becoming a very good seaman, needs a little guidance as expected but can be molded in to a well seasoned seaman_

SIGNED: _____ DATE: Aug 1, 1997

SIGNATURE OF PERSON BEING EVALUATED: _____ DATE: Aug. 1, 1997

Tidewater Marine, Inc. - Towing Division
CREW
PERFORMANCE EVALUATION

Section: 1

Name of crewman:	Corey Wood		Position:	A.B
Period of tour:	From:	March 25, 1998	To:	April 27, 1998

Please rate the ability of each crewman as they relate to the described subjects below by checking the appropriate box in each row.

		Excellent	Above Avg	Average	Below Avg	Poor
Knowledge	How well does this person know the job requirements?		✓			
Ability	Can this person convert knowledge and instruction into performance?		✓			
Attitude	Describe this person's attitude towards the responsibilities of the job?.		✓			
Initiative	Is this person a self-starter?		✓			
Effort	Does this person do his or her best?		✓			
Cooperation	Does this person work together with the others?		✓			
Dependability	Is this person reliable or available when needed?		✓			
Ambition	Does this person show a desire to learn or upgrade?		✓			
Understanding	How well does this person take/use instructions?		✓			
Acceptance	How well do others accept this person?		✓			
Personality	How well does this person accept or treat others?		✓			
Safety	Does this person know, understand and practice safety?		✓			

Section: 2

Briefly comment where needed with regard to any of the above items:

_____

_____

_____

Terry Hunter Sr.	Captain	_signature_
Name of evaluator (print)	Position of evaluator	Signature of evaluator

I have reviewed and discussed this evaluation of my performance.
My signature does not mean that I necessarily agree with it.   Employee signature   4-27-98   Date

Were any additional pages or document copies attached?   If so, how many?

T... ...water Marine, Inc. - Towing D... ...sion

CREW
PERFORMANCE EVALUATION

*CM
9-23-98*

Section: 1

Name of crewman:	*Corey Wood*		Position:	*AB*
Period of tour:	From: *2 August 98*		To:	*18 August 98 = 16 days*

Please rate the ability of each crewman as they relate to the described subjects below by checking the appropriate box in each row.

		Excellent	Above Avg	Average	Below Avg	Poor
Knowledge	How well does this person know the job requirements?	☐	☑	☐	☐	☐
Ability	Can this person convert knowledge and instruction into performance?	☐	☑	☐	☐	☐
Attitude	Describe this person's attitude towards the responsibilities of the job?	☑	☐	☐	☐	☐
Initiative	Is this person a self-starter?	☐	☑	☐	☐	☐
Effort	Does this person do his or her best?	☐	☑	☐	☐	☐
Cooperation	Does this person work together with the others?	☐	☑	☐	☐	☐
Dependability	Is this person reliable or available when needed?	☑	☐	☐	☐	☐
Ambition	Does this person show a desire to learn or upgrade?	☐	☑	☐	☐	☐
Understanding	How well does this person take/use instructions?	☑	☐	☐	☐	☐
Acceptance	How well do others accept this person?	☑	☐	☐	☐	☐
Personality	How well does this person accept or treat others?	☑	☐	☐	☐	☐
Safety	Does this person know, understand and practice safety?	☐	☑	☐	☐	☐

Section: 2

Briefly comment where needed with regard to any of the above items:

Mr. Wood has been an asset to my crew while deckhanding, helping me break in a green seaman & has willingly & efficiently undertaken whatever tasks assigned to him.

Jim Hale	*Capt.*	*Hale.*
Name of evaluator (print)	Position of evaluator	Signature of evaluator

I have reviewed and discussed this evaluation of my performance.
My signature does not mean that I necessarily agree with it.

Employee signature

8-18-98
Date

Ti͏ vater Marine, Inc. - Towing Di͏ ion

CREW
PERFORMANCE EVALUATION

Section: 1

Name of crewman:	Corey Wood		Position:	AB
Period of tour:	From:	11/20/98	To:	12/16/98

Please rate the ability of each crewman as they relate to the described subjects below by checking the appropriate box in each row

		Excellent	Above Avg	Average	Below Avg	Poor
Knowledge	How well does this person know the job requirements?		✓			
Ability	Can this person convert knowledge and instruction into performance?		✓			
Attitude	Describe this person's attitude towards the responsibilities of the job?.	✓				
Initiative	Is this person a self-starter?	✓				
Effort	Does this person do his or her best?		✓			
Cooperation	Does this person work together with the others?	✓				
Dependability	Is this person reliable or available when needed?	✓				
Ambition	Does this person show a desire to learn or upgrade?		✓			
Understanding	How well does this person take/use instructions?	✓				
Acceptance	How well do others accept this person?	✓				
Personality	How well does this person accept or treat others?	✓				
Safety	Does this person know, understand and practice safety?		✓			

Section: 2

Briefly comment where needed with regard to any of the above items:

_____

_____

_____

Jim Hale	Captain	Signature of evaluator
Name of evaluator (print)	Position of evaluator	

I have reviewed and discussed this evaluation of my performance.
My signature does not mean that I necessarily agree with it.   Employee signature   12/16/98
                                                                        Date

Texas State Board of Medical Examiners

Mailing Address: P.O. Box 2018 • Austin, TX 78768-2018
Phone: (512) 305-7010

DECEMBER 29, 1999

SHARON BRUNNER
RT 2 BOX 159-D
HUNTINGTON TX 75949

Re: Complaint   00-5863

Dear MS BRUNNER:

This will acknowledge receipt of your information. This Board has authority to investigate allegations against its licensees. Said allegations must involve a possible violation of the Medical Practice Act or Board Rules.

The information you provided has been carefully evaluated; however, it is not reflective of a violation of the Act. Although we will not be opening an investigation at this time, your information will be retained in our file for reference.

I am very sorry for your loss of your son. The information contained in your complaint is inconclusive to open an investigation. What opinion was proffered by Dr. R.M. Gutierrez? Did you order an independent autopsy? If so, copy of autopsy by Dr. Bruce and the second autopsy would be helpful for evaluation.

Thank you for sharing this information with the Board.

Sincerely,

Kevin P. Foy
Assistant Director
Investigation Department

Hendricks Investigations
204 E. Lufkin Avenue # 204
Lufkin, Texas 75901

COPY

Please consider this letter a formal demand under the Texas Open Records Act.
[Vernon's Texas Statutes and Codes; Annotated/Government Code. Title 5 (a) 552.221 et
al] for the release of the case file concerning the death of Cory Woods.

Please include copies of any and all reports of the investigation, copies of any and all
statements taken from witnesses or other individuals related to this matter, any and all
photographs taken of the scene, and any and all evidence collected by your department.

If any fees for copies of reports, statements or photographs are required, please contact
me at the above phone number and let me know so payment can be arranged for time of
release.

Thank you for your cooperation.

Sincerely,

_____
Joe Hendricks, TX. Lic. # A-09586

_____
Joy Brunner,
Mother of Cory Wood (Deceased)

Hendricks Investigations
204 E. Lufkin Avenue # 204
Lufkin, Texas 75901
Ph: 409-634-0007
Fax: 409-634-0012
Email: jh0007@ttlcc.net

COPY

December 1, 1999

Sheriff Kent Henson
Angelina County Sheriff

Re: Cory Wood

Dear Sheriff Henson,

Please consider this letter a formal demand under the Texas Open Records Act.
[Vernon's Texas Statutes and Codes; Annotated/Government Code. Title 5 (a) 552.221 et
al] for the release of the case file concerning the death of Cory Woods.

Please include copies of any and all reports of the investigation, copies of any and all
statements taken from witnesses or other individuals related to this matter, any and all
photographs taken of the scene, and any and all evidence collected by your department.

If any fees for copies of reports, statements or photographs are required, please contact
me at the above phone number and let me know so payment can be arranged for time of
release.

Thank you for your cooperation.

Sincerely,

_____
Joe Hendricks, TX. Lic. # A-09586

_____
Joy Brunner,
Mother of Cory Wood   (Deceased)

Hendricks Investigations
202 E. Lufkin Avenue # 204
Lufkin, Texas 75901
PH: 409-634-0007
FAX: 409-634-0012

December 9, 1999

COPY

Mr. Ed Jones
Angelina County Attorney
P.O. Box 908
Lufkin, Texas 75901

Regarding: Clarification of request for case file concerning death of Corey Wood

Dear Ed,

In regard to our phone conversation of Tuesday, December 7, 1999, I am sending this letter clarifying my request for evidence in the matter.

As far as giving you a list of the physical evidence I wish to inspect, I do not know what evidence was collected. Because of not knowing what evidence was collected, how can I request to see specific items. Thus, my original request for "any and all evidence collected" by the Angelina County Sheriff's Department remains as is.

As to my request of the photographs taken of the death scene by the Sheriff's Department, I do want copies of all photographs. I will pay for the cost of copying the photographs.

Please confirm if the case file will be released by December 10, 1999, the tenth (10th) day following the presentation of the original demand to the Angelina County Sheriff's Department for release of the report.

Very Truly Yours,

Joe Hendricks, TX Lic. #A-0956
Email: jh0007@lcc.net

County Attorney

DENNIS JONES
Assistant County Attorney

JULIE CAHALANE
Assistant County Attorney

WILLIAM AGNEW JR.
Assistant County Attorney

COPY

OFFICE OF THE COUNTY ATTORNEY
ANGELINA COUNTY
Post Office Box 1845
LUFKIN, TEXAS 75902-1845

Area Code 409
Telephone 639-3929
Fax # 639-3905

Hot Check Division
Telephone 634-5905

DAVID PARISH
Investigator

December 14, 1999

VIA CERTIFIED MAIL NO. P 332 282 201
The Honorable John Cornyn
Texas Attorney General
P. O. Box 12584, Capitol Station
Austin, Texas 78711-2548

RE: PUBLIC INFORMATION OPINION REQUEST

Dear Attorney General Cornyn:

Within the last ten (10) business days, the Sheriff of
Angelina County received a written request dated December 1, 1999
from Joe Hendricks requesting the following information:

"Please consider this letter a formal demand under the Texas
Open Records Act, [Vernon's Texas Statutes and Codes;
Annotated/Government Code. Title 5(a)552.221 et al] for the
release of the case file concerning the death of Cory Woods.

Please include copies of any and all reports of the
investigation, copies of any and all statements taken from
witnesses or other individuals related to this matter, any and all
photographs taken of the scene, and any and all evidence collected
by your department."

It is the position of the Sheriff of Angelina County that the
information sought is not subject to public disclosure because of
the exception set forth in Section 552.108(a) (2) Texas Government
Code because "it is information that deals with the detection,
investigation, or prosecution of crime only in relation to an
investigation that did not result in conviction or deferred
adjudication;".

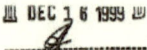 

I am submitting a copy of the request and certify that it was received on December 1, 1999.

I request that you review this special request and render an opinion in accordance with Section 552.301 through 552.306 of the Texas Government Code Annotated.

Yours truly,

Ed C. Jones
County Attorney

\lp

cc: Via Certified Mail No. P 332 282 202
    Mr. Joe Hendricks
    204 E. Lufkin Avenue #204
    Lufkin, Texas 75901

Hendricks Investigations
202 E. Lufkin Avenue # 204
Lufkin, Texas 75901
Ph: 409-634-0007
Fax: 409-634-0012

COPY

December 20, 1999

The Honorable John Cornyn
Texas Attorney General
P.O. Box. 12584, Capitol Station
Austin, Texas 78711-2548

Regarding: Public Information Request

Dear Attorney General Cornyn,

I have received from Angelina County Attorney Ed Jones a copy of the letter he sent to you asking for an opinion concerning the Texas Open Records Act.

I was hired by the family of Cory Wood to investigate the circumstances of his death. The Angelina County Sheriff's Department has ruled his death a suicide, but there are many discrepancies in their investigation. It is the family's desire to have an outside investigator review the case. Sheriff Kent Henson refused to release the report, despite the case being closed and an inquest having ruled this matter a suicide.

On December 1, 1999, Joy Brunner, the deceased's mother and I presented a formal demand for the report to Sheriff Henson.

Mr. Jones' asked for a clarification of the demand in a phone conversation on December 7, 1999. I delivered a written clarification to his office on December 9, 1999. His letter to you asking for an opinion is dated December 14, 1999.

It is my understanding that even with the pause in time for the clarification he requested, he should have asked for an opinion by December 12, 1999. Please inform me if you will be rendering an opinion in this matter or if Mr. Jones' request will be denied.

Sincerely,

Joe Hendricks, Tx. Lic. # A09586
Hendricks Investigations

February 23, 2000

Mr. Ed C. Jones
County Attorney
Angelina County
P O Box 1845
Lufkin, Texas 75905-1845

OR2000-0656

Dear Mr. Jones:

You ask whether certain information is subject to required public disclosure under chapter
552 of the Government Code. Your request was assigned ID# 132377.

The Angelina County Sheriff's Office (the "county") received a request for information
concerning the death of Cory Woods. You claim that the requested information is excepted
from disclosure under section 552.108 of the Government Code. We have considered the
exception you claim and reviewed the submitted information.

We remind you that section 552.108 is a discretionary exception so any information held by
a law enforcement agency or prosecutor that is not otherwise confidential by law may be
released to the public at anytime. Gov't Code § 552.007. Therefore, in this instance, the
Public Information Act does not prohibit the county from releasing the requested information
to the requestor.

Nonetheless, the county has established the applicability of section 552.108(a)(2). You
inform us that the case concluded in a result other than a conviction or deferred adjudication.
However, section 552.108 is inapplicable to basic front page information about this incident.
Gov't Code § 552.108(c). We believe such basic information refers to the information held
to be public in *Houston Chronicle Publ'g Co. v. City of Houston*, 531 S.W.2d 177 (Tex. Civ.
App. --Houston [14th Dist.] 1975), *writ ref'd n.r.e. per curiam*, 536 S.W.2d 559 (Tex. 1976).
Thus, with the exception of the basic front page information, you may withhold the requested
information from disclosure based on section 552.108(a)(2).

In addition, the information you submitted contains an autopsy report. Autopsy reports must be disclosed, in that they are expressly made public by the Code of Criminal Procedure. *See* Code Crim. Proc. art. 49.25, § 11. Therefore, the autopsy report must be released to the requestor.

This letter ruling is limited to the particular records at issue in this request and limited to the facts as presented to us; therefore, this ruling must not be relied upon as a previous determination regarding any other records or any other circumstances.

This ruling triggers important deadlines regarding the rights and responsibilities of the governmental body and of the requestor. For example, governmental bodies are prohibited from asking the attorney general to reconsider this ruling. Gov't Code § 552.301(f). If the governmental body wants to challenge this ruling, the governmental body must appeal by filing suit in Travis County within 30 calendar days. *Id.* § 552.324(b). In order to get the full benefit of such an appeal, the governmental body must file suit within 10 calendar days. *Id.* § 552.353(b)(3), (c). If the governmental body does not appeal this ruling and the governmental body does not comply with it, then both the requestor and the attorney general have the right to file suit against the governmental body to enforce this ruling. *Id.* § 552.321(a).

If this ruling requires the governmental body to release all or part of the requested information, the governmental body is responsible for taking the next step. Based on the statute, the attorney general expects that, within 10 calendar days of this ruling, the governmental body will do one of the following three things: 1) release the public records; 2) notify the requestor of the exact day, time, and place that copies of the records will be provided or that the records can be inspected; or 3) notify the requestor of the governmental body's intent to challenge this letter ruling in court. If the governmental body fails to do one of these three things within 10 calendar days of this ruling, then the requestor should report that failure to the attorney general's Open Government Hotline, toll free, at 877/673-6839. The requestor may also file a complaint with the district or county attorney. *Id.* § 552.3215(e).

If this ruling requires or permits the governmental body to withhold all or some of the requested information, the requestor can appeal that decision by suing the governmental body. *Id.* § 552.321(a); *Texas Department of Public Safety v. Gilbreath*, 842 S.W.2d 408, 411 (Tex. App.–Austin 1992, no writ).

If the governmental body, the requestor, or any other person has questions or comments about this ruling, they may contact our office. Although there is no statutory deadline for

---

[1] The Public Information Act's exceptions do not, as a general rule, apply to information expressly made public by other statutes. Open Records Decision No. 525 (1989).

contacting us, the attorney general prefers to receive any comments within 10 calendar days
of the date of this ruling.

Sincerely,

Rose- Michel Munguia
Assistant Attorney General
Open Records Division

RMM/jc

Ref: ID# 132377

Encl.   Submitted documents

cc: Mr. Joe Hendricks
        Hendricks Investigations
        204 East Lufkin Avenue #204
        Lufkin, Texas 75901
        (w/o enclosures)

OPEN RELEAS
633-7491
ED JONES

County Attorney

DENNIS JONES
Assistant County Attorney

JULIE CAHALANE
Assistant County Attorney

WILLIAM AGNEW JR.
Assistant County Attorney

OFFICE OF THE COUNTY ATTORNEY
ANGELINA COUNTY
Post Office Box 1845
LUFKIN, TEXAS 75902-1845

December 14, 1999

Area Code 409
Telephone 634-3927
Fax # 632-7096

Hot Check Division
Telephone 634-4004

DAVID PARISH
Investigator

VIA CERTIFIED MAIL NO. P 332 282 201
The Honorable John Cornyn
Texas Attorney General
P. O. Box 12584, Capitol Station
Austin, Texas 78711-2548

RE: PUBLIC INFORMATION OPINION REQUEST

Dear Attorney General Cornyn:

Within the last ten (10) business days, the Sheriff of Angelina County received a written request dated December 1, 1999 from Joe Hendricks requesting the following information:

"Please consider this letter a formal demand under the Texas Open Records Act, [Vernon's Texas Statutes and Codes: Annotated/Government Code. Title 5(a)552.221 et al] for the release of the case file concerning the death of Cory Woods.

Please include copies of any and all reports of the investigation, copies of any and all statements taken from witnesses or other individuals related to this matter, any and all photographs taken of the scene, and any and all evidence collected by your department."

It is the position of the Sheriff of Angelina County that the information sought is not subject to public disclosure because of the exception set forth in Section 552.108(a)(2) Texas Government Code because "it is information that deals with the detection, investigation, or prosecution of crime only in relation to an investigation that did not result in conviction or deferred adjudication;".

DEC 1 6 1999

COPY

I am submitting a copy of the request and certify that it was received on December 1, 1999.

I request that you review this special request and render an opinion in accordance with Section 552.301 through 552.306 of the Texas Government Code Annotated.

Yours truly,

Ed C. Jones
County Attorney

\lp

cc: Via Certified Mail No. P 332 282 202
    Mr. Joe Hendricks
    204 E. Lufkin Avenue #204
    Lufkin, Texas 75901

Hendricks Investigations
204 E. Lufkin Avenue # 204
Lufkin, Texas 75901
Ph: 409-634-0007
Fax:409-634-0012
Email: jh0007@lkc.net

COPY

December 1, 1999

Sheriff Kent Henson
Angelina County Sheriff

Re: Cory Wood

Dear Sheriff Henson,

Please consider this letter a formal demand under the Texas Open Records Act,
[Vernon's Texas Statutes and Codes; Annotated/Government Code. Title 5 (a) 552.221 et
al] for the release of the case file concerning the death of Cory Woods.

Please include copies of any and all reports of the investigation, copies of any and all
statements taken from witnesses or other individuals related to this matter, any and all
photographs taken of the scene, and any and all evidence collected by your department.

If any fees for copies of reports, statements or photographs are required, please contact
me at the above phone number and let me know so payment can be arranged for time of
release.

Thank you for your cooperation.

Sincerely,

Joe Hendricks, TX. Lic. # A-09586

Joy Brunner,
Mother of Cory Wood   (Deceased)

Hendricks Investigations
202 E. Lufkin Avenue # 204
Lufkin, Texas 75901
Ph: 409-634-0007
Fax: 409-634-0012

December 9, 1999

COPY

Mr. Ed Jones
Angelina County Attorney
P.O. Box 908
Lufkin, Texas 75901

Regarding: Clarification of request for case file concerning death of Corey Wood

Dear Ed,

In regard to our phone conversation of Tuesday, December 7, 1999, I am sending this letter clarifying my request for evidence in the matter.

As far as giving you a list of the physical evidence I wish to inspect, I do not know what evidence was collected. Because of not knowing what evidence was collected, how can I request to see specific items. Thus, my original request for "any and all evidence collected" by the Angelina County Sheriff's Department remains as is.

As to my request of the photographs taken of the death scene by the Sheriff's Department, I do want copies of all photographs. I will pay for the cost of copying the photographs.

Please confirm if the case file will be released by December 10, 1999, the tenth (10th) day following the presentation of the original demand to the Angelina County Sheriff's Department for release of the report.

Very Truly Yours,

Joe Hendricks, TX Lic. #A-0956
Email: jh0007@tcc.net

Melody Lowery

From:
To: william gates <blkl1121@earthlink.net>
Subject: Re: inquest letter
Date: Thursday, November 18, 1999 9:40 PM

> From: william gates <blkl1121@earthlink.net>
> To: misty tatum <mlowery@integrafin.com>
> Subject: inquest letter
> Date: Thursday, November 18, 1999 3:27 PM
>
TO WHOM THIS MAY CONCERN:

On the night of September 27, 1999, Corey Wood was visiting me at my house about 7:00 p.m. Our conversation consisted of Corey returning to his job off shore on the following Thursday, September 30th. He said that he was looking forward to going back and making the money, he just wished he had more time to spend with his friends and family. We also talked about me moving to Austin soon in hopes that when I did he would come and visit, often. Corey was in a great mood that night and seemed as happy as ever, full of fun and laughter always. Corey and I made plans that night to go out and eat on the following night September 28 since he would be returning to work soon, Tuesday was going to be our time together. He left my house at approximately 9:10 p.m and was going home.

Corey had told me to call him in about an hour or so after he left, just to talk. I called him at about 10:30 p.m. and he answered the phone. We only talked for about 5 minutes because I was going to bed. His mood was still the same as before and he reminded me to call him when I woke up the next morning, if he wasn't already at my house by that time. We were going to spend the day together and go out to eat that night of September 28, 1999.

Misty Tatum

ANGELINA COUNTY
Claude Marshall, Jr.
Justice of Peace Pct. 84
P. O. Box 31 • Zavalla, Texas 75980
(409) 897-2424

Melba Tinsley
Clerk

Concerning informal Inquest hearing
on 11-19-1999, after hearing all the
evidence presented by the D. A., Sheriff
office and the Family of Cory Wood.
This along with what the Autopsy
indicated and what I saw personally
at the sene, I made my decision.
Cause of death Contact gunshot wound to
the head and manner of death Suicide.
    I then Called the Funeral Home
and released the death Certificate.

Claude Marshall Jr.

VOLUNTARY STATEMENT
(Not Under Arrest)

I, **Melody Lowery**, am not under arrest for, nor am I being detained for any criminal offenses concerning the events I am about to make known to **Ron Brandon**. Without being accused of or questioned about any criminal offense, I, in the case I am about to state, I volunteer the following information of my own free will, for whatever purpose it may serve.

I am **45** years of age, and I live at **Shadowood Drive, Huntington TX.**

On Monday, 9-23-99 I left my residence at approximately 5:40 a.m. to drive my daughter to Huntington Middle School to meet with other students getting on a student council field trip to Galveston. As I was driving out my Avenue, I notice that both vehicles of our neighbors across the street were gone from home. Our neighbors at that time were Randy and Stephanie Watson. I thought it odd that Randy's vehicles were gone so early in the morning because Randy usually left for work shortly before I did. I did about the same time. I don't believe Stephanie was employed at that time. When I returned home at about 5:55 am I noticed Stephanie's car was back and parked in the usual spot. I went on for my day and started getting ready for work. When I left my house again about 8:00 a.m. to go to work I noticed Stephanie's youngest son's truck parked at her home and Randy's truck was still not there. I first didn't think more about it other than thinking maybe Randy was out of town. At about 11:30 am that same morning I received a call at work that Randy Watson had died by a gunshot but had no other details.

This statement, three pages, and pages of this statement... I have read... each copy of which I certify to be true and correct.

Witnessed by: _____ , date _____ date **19th** of **January** _____

Witness: _____ **Melody Lowery**

VOLUNTARY STATEMENT
(NOT UNDER ARREST)

I, _Patricia Shaw Alderman_ , am not under arrest, nor am I being detained for any criminal offenses concerning the events I am about to make known to _Ron Brandon._ Without being accused of or questioned about any criminal offenses regarding the facts I am about to state, I volunteer the following information of my own free will, for whatever purposes it may serve.

I am _45_ years of age, and I live at _Rt. 2 Box 1576 - Neal Rd (422-5545)_

On or About Sept. 28, 1999 I was taking my
daughter somewhere at about 5:45 to 6:00 in
and drove past the trailer at the end of
Neal Road. It was not yet daylight and I
noticed the kitchen light on and two dark
colored pick-ups there at the time. They was
fullo sized pick-ups.

I have read each page of this statement consisting of ___ page's, each page of which bears my signature and corrections, if any, bears my initials, and I certify that the facts contained herein are true and correct.

Date : _____ at 12:00 A. M. this 61 day of _____ 19__

WITNESS _____ _Patricia S. Alderman_
Signature of person giving Voluntary Statement

7-25-99

C.H. McCLURE, M.D., P.A.
300 N. JOHN REDDITT DRIVE
SUITE 5
LUFKIN, TEXAS 75904
(409) 639-3266

NOVEMBER 3, 1999

RE: COREY WOOD

COREY WOOD WAS SEEN IN MY OFFICE ON 09-24-99
WITH PHARYNGITIS AND TRACHEOBRONCHITIS. HE
WAS GIVEN KEFZOL 500 IM AND PLACED ON
DURICEF 500 AND TUSSI-ORGANIDAN DM, WHICH ARE
NON NARCOTIC COMPOUNDS. THERE WERE NO
SIGNS OF DEPRESSION. THERE WERE NO SIGNS
OF ANY ATTEMPT TO HURT HIMSELF OR ANYONE ELSE.

C. H. MCCLURE, M.D.

To Whom It May Concern:

On the night of Monday September 27, 1999 I arrived at my home at approximately 9:00 PM after having fall baseball practice in Lufkin with my son. Upon arrival I found Cory Wood and my daughter Misty Tatum standing in the driveway talking. As I started in the house I stopped and spoke to them for about five minutes. Cory was very up beat and spoke of all the good things that was going on in his life. He told me of his new house he was living in along with his job. He said he was going back in the next few days and wanted to come by and visit before he went back. Cory was a long time friend of my family and stopped by from time to time. He appeared very alert and clear-headed. It was very obvious he had direction in his life and things were going good for him. He will be missed.

Respectfully Submitted,

TEXAS DEPARTMENT OF PUBLIC SAFETY
5805 N. LAMAR BLVD. · BOX 4087 · AUSTIN, TEXAS 78773-0001

CRIME LABORATORY SERVICE MSC 0460
P.O. BOX 4143
AUSTIN, TEXAS 78765-4143
512/424-2105

DUDLEY M. THOMAS
DIRECTOR

THOMAS A. DAVIS, JR
ASST. DIRECTOR

COMMISSION
JAMES B. FRANCIS, JR.
CHAIRMAN
ROBERT B. HOLT
M. COLLEEN McHUGH
COMMISSIONERS

October 20, 1999

INV DAVID CASPER
ANGELINA CO SHERIFFS DEPT
113 2ND ST
LUFKIN TX 75902

SUBJECT: L-275374; Death; 09-28-99; Angelina County; Corey Adam Wood, victim

DATE RECEIVED: October 5, 1999

METHOD OF SUBMISSION: Certified mail

EVIDENCE SUBMITTED: Hand swabs from Corey Wood

REQUESTED ANALYSIS: Determine the presence of gunshot primer residue (antimony, barium and lead) on the swabs from Corey Wood.

RESULTS OF ANALYSIS: The hand swabs from Corey Wood are being returned without analysis. Victims of close range gunshot (including suicide victims) have obviously been in an environment of gunshot primer residue. More gunshot primer residue goes out of the weapon's barrel than escapes from near the handle. If the victim of a close range shooting attempts to grab the gun or instinctively uses their hands as a shield from the gunshot, significant amounts of gunshot primer residue can be left on the hands. Laboratory analysis cannot determine whether the deposition of gunshot primer residue was made in this manner or was the result of a self-directed firing.

DISPOSITION OF EVIDENCE: We are returning the evidence to you by U.S. Mail.

Thomas R. White, Criminalist V
Criminalistics Section

TRW/SKR:hs

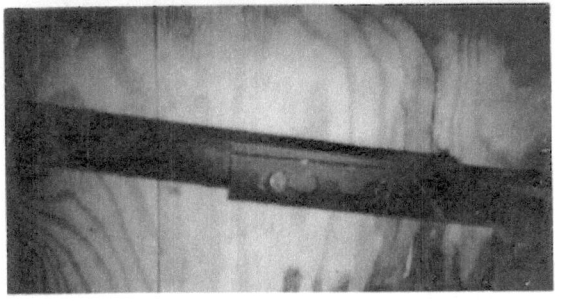

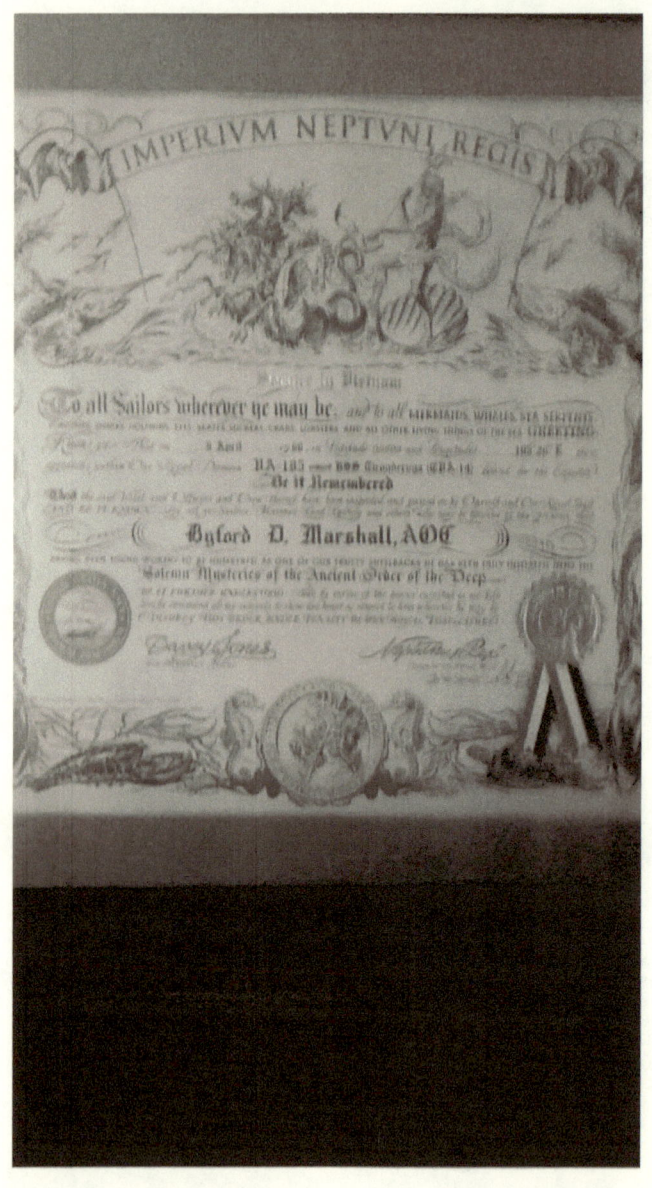

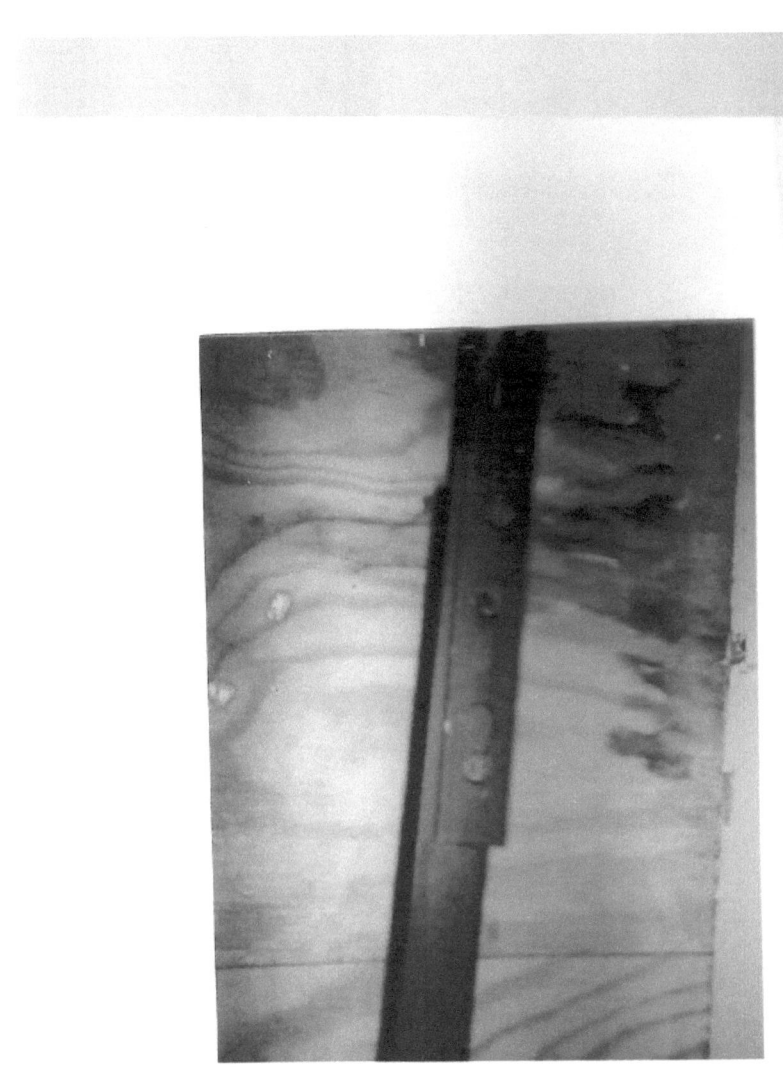

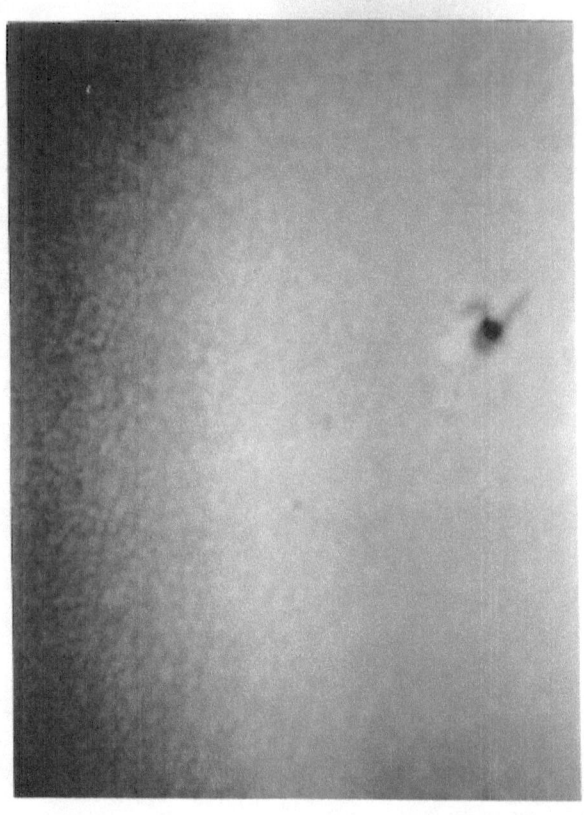

TEXAS DEPARTMENT OF PUBLIC SAFETY

CRIME LABORATORY SERVICE MSC 0460
P.O. BOX 4143
AUSTIN, TEXAS 78765-4143
512-424-2105
November 01, 1999

JUDGE CLARK E MARSHALL
JUSTICE OF THE PEACE
PT 1 BOX 15
UVALDA, Texas 78980

Laboratory Case Number	Agency Number	Offense Date
L 17004		09/28/99

Victim(s)   **Suspect(s)**

WEBB, Carey ALAN (Deceased)   None Listed

Investigation: Suicide or Accidental Death
County of Offense: Angelina (003)

Evidence Submitted
    October 19, 1999 AIRBORNE EXPRESS
        Blood from Carey Alan Webb (Deceased)

Results of Analysis
    Blood Alcohol: 0.16 grams per 100 milliliters

    Blood Drug: No drug detected

Blood Analysis: An enzymatic method (EMIT) was used to screen for six classes of drugs: amphetamines, barbiturates, benzodiazepines, cocaine and its metabolites, opiates, and propoxyphene. The detection cut off for most drugs of interest is 1 mg/L in blood.

The specimen will be retained for 90 days, then discarded unless other arrangements are made.

_____   _____
L. Dawn Cole   Dan Rice
Criminalist V, Toxicology   Criminalist III, Toxicology
Texas DPS Austin Laboratory   Texas DPS Austin Laboratory

Copy to: Dr. Bruce, Austin

Joy Brunner

December 3, 2000

Dear Sheriff Kent Henson,

There are many reasons to why my son Corey Wood did not commit suicide.

1. Corey had just received a 10-dollar a day raises the very day before he was found.

2. He had just purchased a new home, and had only lived in that home 1-day and 3 wks.

3. He had just told the girl he had loved all though high school the night before he loved her. He had offered her the money to move to Austin, and had made plans to visit her in the future.

4. Corey was studding to be a ship captain, and had already been behind the wheel of the vessel. He was talking to my Mother Dr. Yvonne Marshall about ettering the very night before.

5. He had made plans to meet his Sister in New Orleans for the turn of the centurey and was very excited about the New Year 2000.

6. Corey had a tooth capped only days before he was found.

7. He had just bought a new entertainment center, and had made plans to furnish his new home on his return from sea. The day before his death he called the furniture store he had purchased the entertainment center from and told the sales person he would have to come in after he got back and pick out his furniture. He had enough credit to furnish his whole house.

8. The very month he died he was planning on buying a new jeep. I have found his loan status only this week. It was in the papers he was found on.

9. The folder and papers he was found laying on were his bills. Not a late notice in the bunch, and all were paid for the month of September. He was planning on paying the month of November with my Mother the very next day. In his checking account he had $996.00 and $744.00 in a savings account. Hardly the reason that was planted in your department's investigation, that he was upset about money.

10. Corey had just purchased a new set of tires for his pick-up for around $1,000.00 only the week before he was found. I have spoken to the man he bought the tires from and he will testify that Corey was as happy with his life as he had ever seen.

11. I spoke to my son only 4 hours before he was supposed to have killed himself. No depression what so ever. I spoke of the Lord to my son. Told him not to worry one thing about our lives we were fine and we would walk the path the Lord chose for us.

12. Corey saw Dr. Mc Clure only just that Friday before he was found. I have a letter from him stating the frame of mind Corey was in. He was not going to hurt himself or anyone else.

Kent do you believe in the Lord our God? If you do believe, how can God be telling you and me two different things? I know I am praying every day for the strength to go on with life and all things that have happened to us. Our lives will never be the same again. God is here with me, and I know Corey is in Heaven. What do you know? You can say for sure with out doubt that Corey took his own life?

I have two children here on earth; one is grown and has a family of her own. She spoke to her brother only a week before he was found, she knows that Corey did not take his own life. She has stated that Corey may have taken someone else's life but never his own. She will always remember her brother as the fun loving person he was, and she feels like all of Corey's family and friends, someone took Corey's life from him, while he was asleep on the couch, you see Kent I have a witness that Corey was on the couch at 12:30. Your theory of Corey jumping off the couch at 5:30 and putting a gun up to the opposite side of his head is ridiculous. No one, No one takes their own life at the highest point in their life. You have not read that in any book in the world. I also know that every homicide psychologist in the world will tell you someone does not kill himself in the left side of his head if he is right handed. Did you know this? Lt. Galloway did not know if Corey was right handed are left-handed and did not know if Corey was shot in the left side of his head or the right.

Back to my children. Kent I have a 3 yr old, he is a blessing in all our lives. Corey loved him as he loved all of us, and only wanted the best for us. I will not let Corey's name in this town or in the world be left like this. You have 4 more years in office. You will hear from me on a regular basis. I will not I repeat I will not let you and your department do this to Corey, or my family.

This means nothing to you or your department, if you or all involved cared about Corey in the 1st place, this would not be happening. You and all involved will be held accountable for the investigation that was conducted on my son's death.

Kent you bet I am so angry. What gives you the right? You have known me for a long time, I thought you were brought up like I was, knowing right from wrong. I am not ever saying I have not ever been wrong, we both know that I have. I should not even have to go there, you know my life, I do not know yours, and would not have chosen to be here. I was placed here when my son was wrongfully accused of killing himself.

What are you going to do? Are you going to let the men that killed Corey go free? Isn't that what you chose your profession for, what are you going to do when these people kill again? And they will, maybe not here but the boy, is very sick, I spoke to him for the 1st time last week, his last words to me were Corey and God are the only two that know what happened down there and he did not want to speak to either one of them again for the rest of his life. I ask him if he meant God? He hung up. No I am sorry about Corey only anger toward Corey and me. This boy has never been back to see us Kent, this boy was in and out of our homes for 4 years, and he wagged Jenson around like his own. This is not normal behavior, for anyone.

The blood smeared down the side of this house. Do you really think I have made kids mad? Have I made you mad asking questions into the death of my son? Mad enough to smear blood down the side of a house? Only a hand full of people knew where Corey was found, and for sure where the end table was he was found lying on. The blood was there Kent.

I wanted you to take another look at Corey's life, and the life of the boy's that were down here. The Father of one of the roommates had forged 6800 dollars out of Corey's checking account. Corey came to me only 9 months before his death and said he thought the man was stealing his money. He also stated on his 21st birthday there would be we'll if I get home and do not have any money in my account. This was in the home of REV. and Marie Jones in La. Then he came to me and said he thought money was missing. I talked him out of killing the man, only because I thought it was only a few 100 dollars. Told him to take it as a life lesson and go on with his life to get away from these two men. Randy and Brian Wilson. Had I known this could have happened in a million years I would have confronted this man.

This man had something to do with the death of my son. The 911 call came in at 6:32 the morning of the 28th of September. Randy's car was gone from his home a 5:40 that very morning so was his wife's. I would like to know where they were, seems like plenty of time to stage a suicide and clean the scene. The 1st officer on the scene minutes before 7 that morning. The wife's car was back in the driveway by 6 and Heath her son was pulling in to the drive at that time. None of this was told to us about that morning by these people, that were supposed to have loved Corey so much, and none of them even bothered to show up for the inquest. We won't even get into the inquest. The very informal inquest.

These are issues I felt you and your department need to know.

Sincerely,

JOY BRUNNER
Signature

CHAPTER 3

The night of the 27th of September 1999 was unusually hot for September, it was one of those nights that people are up late, I was up, my mother Dr. Yvonne Marshall, my cousin Tish Bell, my best friend Rhonda Byers, all of us were on call waiting, beeping in, I was talking to my mother, Corey, and Rhonda, my cousin knocked on my mother's door around 10.00 pm that night, she had been going through my aunt's belongings and my mother said she nearly feel in her arms when she opened the door for her. My father B D Marshall a retired war veteran, (navy nuclear weapons expert) was out of town with another cousin that he drove a truck for picking up hay in west Texas, my mother was waiting up for their return, unbelievably my dad passed Corey's house.

At the time of his murder or close to it. My mother excused herself and helped my cousin, not before she said good night to Corey, they made plans for the next day with him, they exchanged "I love you" and "see you" in the morning.

Myself, Corey, and Rhonda continued our conversations, I remember Corey was upset at his roommates and he was also upset because I had separated from his stepdad, Rhonda and I laughed she said, "I wonder where he gets his aggression from."

"That would be me" and we laughed. I said goodbye to my friend and continued talking to Corey.

He had been cutting trees or a tree down in his yard, he had just purchased a new mobile home and was in the process of getting everything set up to go back on the tugboat, he was set to go back out the day after he died, with a 10 dollar a day raise and promotion that he received the day of his death.

Randy and Stephanie Wilson

Picture of Dad in uniform

In loving memory of BD Marshall (Mamps)

Corey's Family

CHAPTER 4

Corey was more upset with his roommates for the condition his house was in when he arrived unannounced, he called me and told me when he would be arriving and for me not to say anything to his roommates, so I did not tell them he was coming.

He walked into a mess, the home was only 3 months old, and he was not happy. He told me that night that everyone would be out when he got back from this tour, he would be gone 3 months, and that the things that were going on in his house would not be going on again, then he preceded to tell me about how the toilets had rings in them, he told Jeremy that if he ever saw his toilet in that shape again, he would put his head in it, then Corey told me what a no-good sob Brian was and that Jeremy would be getting married (he did to Jana Clark) so he would be gone, but he would tell Brian that he had to find another place to live when he got back, he did say he only let Brian stay for this tour, because Brian's dad (Randy Wilson) had married Heath Talbet's mother (Corey's best friend in high school) and Corey felt obligated to let him stay the 3 months but the sorry sob would be out in 3 months, Heath Talbert's mother is Stephanie Talbert Wilson,

I ask him Corey are these people able to hear what you are saying because you are really talking loud and bad about these people (guys) he went on about some other things like Brian having no respect, and other things Corey said he did not care

It was true and he was sick of them... Then he went into my separation, how he was going to go to my father in the morning and they would find my husband and bring him home, no one was going to treat me bad, Corey had been drinking and so things were exaggerated, but I calmed him down, we talked about choices in our lives, mine, his sister Darci, she was out of town working, and his little brother Jenson, he was not yet 2, I assured him we were going to be fine, and then we talked about God.

Corey ask me how did I know that God was real, could we just be worshiping like the Vikings and all the gods they worshiped

I got to witness to my son about God the night before he was killed, how we feel the Holy Spirit, how it is our faith that separates us from those that do not know God, and reminded him of the things in his life that he felt, and saw.

Corey was saved and baptized at the age of accountability, 13 in our religion, Baptist, I really don't remember all the things that were said but the Holy Spirit was with us, and we just knew, he agreed we planned to meet in the morning so I could cut his hair, and say our goodbye's before he went back on the boat, he worked for tidewater, the youngest anchor man in the fleet and would have been a ship's captain at 25, Corey was 22 years old not only was he the youngest but also had been awarded the best anchor man in the fleet. He loved his job. We said our good night's and I told him to call me when he got up.

CHAPTER 5

Jenson was little and would have me up early, and he may want to sleep in so it would be best for him to call me, I got to tell my son about God and how much I loved him hours before he was killed.

Corey was calm and falling asleep on the couch he was already half asleep when we hung up, he was asleep. We were at peace.

That same morning Jenson was up, he was going to be 2 on October 5, 1999. I remember I was laying on the couch, Jenson sitting on me, and we were singing an old black folk song. Jenson loved it. I saw Jenson walking in the rain, he was holding Corey's hand never be the same, and I would put all our names in it, Jenson would tell me who to put in next, it was our game.

The phone rang and it was my sister-in-law, she was asking about me and Roland, my husband. I guess she had heard we were separated before I could even respond. A sheriff's car pulled into the driveway, I remember laughing and saying oh I hope they are not here to get me, and I laughed and made some stupid joke. I walked out on the porch, Buford was the deputy's name, and he was from Huntington. I had been to prayer meetings at his parent's house.

I asked if it was Corey, in my mind I thought there may have been a confrontation and Corey may have hurt one of the roommates. I was never prepared for his answer, he told me Corey was dead, from a self-inflicted gunshot wound. I said suicide, no way.

I remember running through the house, pulling my hair, I don't remember screaming, but I had asked my sister-in-law to hold on. She later told me I screamed and then she was at my house. I fell down in the living room and Buford comforted me. The whole time I was trying to wrap my mind around Corey being dead, and self-inflicted that was not possible. I then went into denial I did not believe it was Corey, had to be one of his roommates. I kept asking are you sure, my parents arrived some time. I met them on the porch and my dad broke down and I knew it was true. I ask my mother if it could have been because we were fighting, she knew about the separation and said no way, Corey was a grown man, and he did not commit suicide. She said she had worked suicide hotlines and Corey showed no signs of suicide then or before in his life. I told you she is a Dr. A christen psychologist, also at the time she had her forensic psychologist license, she was a forensic psychologist, and my mind shattered into darkness at that time.

I called the funeral home and ask to see Corey, I was told he was already on an autopsy table. I did not want an autopsy but was told it was procedure and I had no choice. Then I called the pathologist and told him Corey wanted to donate his organs. I was told he had been dead too long, and they could salvage nothing. I went to my parents', my husband had come home, and he drove me to my parents where people were already gathering.

As soon as I got there my dad met me at the door and said he had already talked to tidewater, and I needed to take care of the insurance. Corey had told me just two weeks before that he had upped his insurance and laughed that if he got hurt, I would be a rich lady. I responded you better be careful and ware that harness or whatever holds you on that boat.

CU. TDI

AIG Insurance

844-930-0370 (Fax)

Sharon Joy Brunner
2101 Church Street #305
Galveston, TX 77550
409-224-0715

RE: Policy BSC8052554

To Whom It May Concern:

I am sending you all the letters I have received in regards to this policy. I am also attaching a chronological diary and supporting documents.

I was told that when the death certificate was amended, that the accident and health and life insurance policies would be paid in full.

Of course, this still has not happened.

In 2001 all of this could have been rectified, through Mr. Robert Bull's investigation.

During that time, even though Mr. Bull's report stated that my son, Corey Wood, did not commit suicide, AIG upheld the decision due to suicide. AIG did not honor their own investigator. (Robert Bull)

Another point in question, is that AIG performed their own autopsy and came to a conclusion, without any forensic evidence, mainly, my son, Corey Wood's body.

Even after the death certificate was amended, it was denied.

None of this makes sense. There was a smaller claim paid out, and I was told repeatedly by Carol Leverette, that after the death certificate was amended, that the claim would be paid out.

This has been devastating to our family. It seems that even though all the points of question have been clarified (i.e not a suicide) AIG, as a company, will not uphold the policy.

Please contact me if you have more questions that need to be clarified.

Sincerely,

Sharon Joy Brunner

125

DATE	DESCRIPTION	Dispute / Facts	
November December 1998	Copies of checks written/ stolen from Corey's account by Randy Wilson before murder - 1 check written to the county attorney , Kirby	Randy Wilson license revoked. His son was Corey's roommate. Randy wrote checks on Corey's account and used his ATM card. NEVER charged.	
9/1/1997	TDI - disiplinary actions revoking license and fining agency	Randy Wilson license revoked. His son was Corey's roommate. Randy wrote checks on Corey's account and used his ATM card. NEVER charged.	
3/10/1998	Randy Wilson signature on tax return	Copy obtained to compare signatures on fraudulent checks	
9/29/1999	Death Certificate of Corey Adam Wood	Original before ammended	
1/10/2001	Interview - DA Clyde Harrington, investigator Ron Brandon	Interview notes with Joy conflict with Robert Bull's interview and report	
1/19/2001	AIG request police reports, crime scene photos, autopsy photos, ME report, interview of Dr. James Bruce	see letter	
2/16/2001	AIG requesting reports again. *Angelina County has declined to reply to requests*	see letter	
5/24/2001	AIG Claims specialist unable to interview Vincent Smith. *Angelina County Sherrif's office declined to furnish requested* autopsy microscopic glass slides. ME rerport, ballistic report, the photo of weapon, dimensions of weapon, due to exception under the OPEN RECORDS ACT of Texas Government Code. Awaiting independent forensic pathologist.	see letter	
6/20/2001	Formost Insurance Acknowledgement of claim 682-1485 for Property (Trailer)	Because this was a crime scene, it was not cleaned to not destroy evidence. Trailer was repossessed June 11, 2003. Joy attended court for the repossession with Randy Wilson (salesman, financed through Bombardia Capital). While on the stand, it was brought up that Randy Wilson endorsed a referral check made out to B.D. Marshal for a referral for sale of the trailer.	

		Constable Beuford ? From Angelina County repeatedly called Bombardia Capital, requesting when the trailer was being picked up with crime scene still intact. Bombardia Capital stated they have this on audio tape.	
	CONT		
1/22/2001	AIG received independent forensic pathology report. Currently being reviewed.	Report was inclosed. Where is copy?	
	There was actually 2 reports, 2 different reports of shift change, and conflicting information. The original reports were lost in 2005 in Ms. Brunners house when it was burnt down.		
7/19/2001	AIG claimed denied due to suicide.	see letter	
1/20/2001	AIG received appeal request. To be reviewed by ERISA quarterly.	see letter	
1/31/2001	AIG appeals commity holding claim pending info from Grand Jury Decision. Independent forensic pathologyis opinion included in this letter.	see letter	
6/3/2002	AIG - appeal still under investigation. Awaiting evidence from lab	see letter	
1/25/2002	AIG - enclosed statement from Angelina County District Attorney Investigator, **Ron Brandon**	Where is copy?	
1/25/2002	AIG - Appeals committee upheld denial of claim. Concluded suicide / self - inflicted injury	Start ammending death certificate	
1/10/2003	**Granddaughter was murdered 6/11/2003**	This was retaliation, murdered by a person in this group. Felicia Pizzel	
1/24/2005	**Sharon Joy Brunners home was burnt down**	Angelina County Fire Marshal had NO record. The fire marshall from Austin had to report it in 2005	
1/19/2005	Judgement for defendents Wilson, Wilson, Talbert, Holders, Boles		
5/14/2012	American Forensics		
7/5/2012	Chartis o/b/o National Union Fire Insurance acknowledgement of appeal. Company paid $30, 000.00 to Joy Brunner	*1 claim acknowledged and PAID, why do the other policies deny claim?*	
1/28/2012	Chartis denied appeal. Reviewed by ERISA 9/25/2002		

3/24/2014	AIG Appeal denied with ammended death certificate. Death can not be proved it was an accident.	It was proven not a suicide. So how does this get paid?	
9/24/2014	AIG denial revisieted. "Could not be determined" is still not grounds for an accidental death claim.		
7/25/2017	*Initial investigation mishandled resulting in loss of evidience.* Letter from William Campbell, retired CSI Investigator		
7/26/2017	Ferral Law Firm - Deny civil case against AIG.		
8/21/2018	Request to AIG to reopen claim		
Robert Bull	Private Investigator for AIG, stated not a suicide. AIG did not use conclusion		
Peter Lloyd	Rep from Tidewater insurance. There is only 1 claim that will pay. Others will be denied because it was listed as suicide. Although the sherrif stated it was an accident. Joy was instructed by Peter Lloyd to appeal the claim. Private Investigator, ROBERT BULL (AIG) delcared this was not self inflicted. AIG did not take his conclusion.		
	AIG will not send the report to Joy from Robert Bull, they refused. He verbally told her that he concluded not self inflicted. 2000 /2001		

Name: **Wood, Corey A.**
Account: 521360000

Page: 2
File: A813085-01

Ed C. Jones, Angelina County Attorney   Complete   Enclosed

District Attorney Herrington   Pending

LAW ENFORCEMENT CONTACT

ANGELINA COUNTY SHERIFF'S JAIL
LUFKIN, TX
936-634-3331
01/30/01

A call was made to the jail. The sargent stated the jail hours
were from 1:00 P.M. to 5:30 P.M. daily, Monday through Friday.

On afternoon of 02/01/01, direct contact was made at the Angelina
County Jail and access to the prisoner was denied because the
specific hours of the visit were not given over the telephone.

CHIEF DEPUTY CASPER
ANGELINA SHERIFF'S OFFICE
LUFKIN, TX
02/01/01

A request was made to see the sheriff, Kent Henson, however, he
was not available. Chief Deputy Casper finally came out and
stated that he handled everything for the sheriff. It was
explained that the insurance company had requested that a
conversation be made directly with the sheriff. Chief Deputy
Casper stated if that was done, the sheriff would just turn
everything back over to the chief deputy. He was asked to
provide detailed information as to why they refused to allow
access to the records regarding the death of the insured.

After a long conversation with Chief Deputy Casper, it was
finally decided that he would recheck on whether or not the
records could be released. During the conversation, he stated he
personally was the one who gave the orders not to release the
records. He would not, or could not, give a reason for this
decision.

"Committed to Consistent Quality Service"

Name: **Wood, Corey A.**   Page: 2
Account: 521360000   File: A813085-01

Ed C. Jones, Angelina County Attorney   Complete   Report of 3-9-01

District Attorney Herrington   Canceled

Ed C. Jones, Angelina County Attorney   Complete   Report of 03-22-01

LAW ENFORCEMENT CONTACT

ANGELINA COUNTY SHERIFF'S OFFICE
LUFKIN, TX
936-634-3331
03/23-04/02/01

This source states that Vincent Smith is still in jail. However, he
cannot receive incoming telephone calls, though he can make outgoing
telephone calls at certain times for certain limited lengths of
time.

As it was not deemed prudent to discuss the Corey Wood case over the
sheriff's telephone, a name and telephone number was not left. On
April 2, 2001, the jail stated that Mr. Smith had been released and
was no longer incarcerated. They had no forwarding address.

Robert F. Bull, HIA, ALHC, CFE
Claims Consultant

blw

International Claims Specialists

Date:	06/20/02	**Account No:**	521360000
Name:	Wood, Corey A.	**Account Name:**	AIG Life Companies
Add:	Rt. 3 Box 7020	**File Number:**	BSC 8052554
	Huntington, TX 75949	**Requestor:**	Carol Leverette
		Phone Number:	N/S
		Nature of Loss:	

Emp:	N/S		
DOB:	12/15/76		
Type of Inv:	Limited Death	**Regional Office:**	Dallas, Texas
Dates of Inv:	06/19/02	**Phone Number:**	1-800-725-2167
Status of Report:	Partial	**Date of Next Report:**	07/04/02

INVESTIGATIVE SUMMARY

Source	Status	Reference
Ron Brandon, Angelina County District Attorney's Office	Pending	

DISTRICT ATTORNEY

RON BRANDON, INVESTIGATOR
ANGELINA COUNTY DISTRICT ATTORNEY
ANGELINA COUNTY COURTHOUSE
LUFKIN, TX 75902-1845
936-632-5090 - PHONE
06/19/02

This source states he is still awaiting the state lab to finish their work. He does again state that he will call when it is completed.

Robert F. Bull, HIA, ALHC, CFE
Claims Consultant

jlw

"Committed to Consistent Quality Service"

Name: **Wood, Corey A**.   Page: 2
Account: 521360000   File: BSC 8052554

He also states has not received any completed reports on the State lab work,
which he has requested.

Robert F. Bull, HIA, ALHC, CFE
Claims Consultant

jlw

"Committed to Consistent Quality Service"

International Claims Specialists

Date:	07/01/02	**Account No:**	521360000
Name:	Wood, Corey A.	**Account Name:**	AIG Life Companies
Add:	Rt. 3 Box 7020	**File Number:**	BSC 8052554
	Huntington, TX 75949	**Requestor:**	Carol Leverette
		Phone Number:	N/S
		Nature of Loss:	

Emp:	N/S		
DOB:	12/15/76		
Type of Inv:	Limited Death	**Regional Office:**	Dallas, Texas
Dates of Inv:	06/28/02	**Phone Number:**	1-800-725-2167
Status of Report:	Partial	**Date of Next Report:**	07/24/02

INVESTIGATIVE SUMMARY

Source	Status	Reference
Ron Brandon, Investigator, Angelina County District Attorney's Office	Pending	

DISTRICT ATTORNEY

RON BRANDON, INVESTIGATOR
ANGELINA COUNTY DISTRICT ATTORNEY
ANGELINA COUNTY COURTHOUSE
LUFKIN, TX 75902-1845
936-632-5090
06/28/02

This source states that he has still not heard from the state lab. He anticipates it will be several months still. He states he will call when he gets this.

Next report will not be until 7/24/02.

Robert F. Bull, HIA, ALHC, CFE
Claims Consultant

pg

RECEIVED
JUL 08
AD&D UNIT

"Committed to Consistent Quality Service"

International Claims Specialists

Date:	07/15/02	**Account No:**	521360000
Name:	Wood, Corey A.	**Account Name:**	AIG Life Companies
Add:	Rt. 3 Box 7020	**File Number:**	BSC 8052554
	Huntington, TX 75949	**Requestor:**	Carol Leverette
		Phone Number:	N/S
		Nature of Loss:	

Emp:	N/S		
DOB:	12/15/76		
Type of Inv:	Limited Death	**Regional Office:**	Dallas, Texas
Dates of Inv:	6/28;7/3,12/02	**Phone Number:**	1-800-725-2167
Status of Report:	Partial	**Date of Next Report:**	07/29/02

INVESTIGATIVE SUMMARY

Source	Status	Reference
Ron Brandon, Angelina County District Attorney's Office	Complete	Enclosed

DISTRICT ATTORNEY

RON BRANDON, INVESTIGATOR
ANGELINA COUNTY DISTRICT ATTORNEY'S OFFICE
ANGELINA COUNTY COURTHOUSE
LUFKIN, TX 75902
936-632-5090
06/28, 07/03, 07/12/02

RECEIVED

JUL   02

AD&D UNIT

Attachment "A" is the original signed statement of Ron Brandon. Mr. Brandon stated on the phone that Corey Wood's mother continues to make statements in the community, such as that there is soon going to be arrests made and that she has won a court case. She has a court case in a civil action concerning the death of her son that was thrown out of the Angelina County Court. She replaced it in the San Antonio courts and is telling people that she won the case just because it is still in the courts. The court case has not been heard and this source states that he feels sure that the case will be thrown out of the San Antonio courts also because there is no basis for it.

"Committed to Consistent Quality Service"

International Claims Specialists

Date:	07/09/02	**Account No:**	521360000
Name:	Wood, Corey A.	**Account Name:**	AIG Life Companies
Add:	Rt. 3 Box 7020	**File Number:**	BSC 8052554
	Huntington, TX 75949	**Requestor:**	Carol Leverette
		Phone Number:	N/S
		Nature of Loss:	

Emp:	N/S		
DOB:	12/15/76		
Type of Inv:	Limited Death	**Regional Office:**	Dallas, Texas
Dates of Inv:	06/28, 07/03/02	**Phone Number:**	1-800-725-2167
Status of Report:	Partial	**Date of Next Report:**	08-01-02

INVESTIGATIVE SUMMARY

Source	Status	Reference
Ron Brandon, Investigator, Angelina County District Attorney's Office	Pending	

DISTRICT ATTORNEY

RON BRANDON, INVESTIGATOR
ANGELINA COUNTY DISTRICT ATTORNEY'S OFFICE
ANGELINA COUNTY COURTHOUSE
LUFKIN, TX 75902
936-632-5090
06/28/02, 07/03/02

RECEIVED
JUL 12 2002
A&H CLAIMS
ROCKWOOD

Calls were made to this source. This source stated that he is still awaiting the results from the state lab on two small items which he has sent to them. He again reiterates that it sometimes takes three to four months or more to get the results on non-rush requests.

The statement which Ron Brandon had given by phone was faxed to him because he was not going to be in his office to receive it by regular mail. He signed it and faxed it back, therefore, there is not an original. He agreed to sign the original and the form has been sent to him for signing. This is anticipated by July 18, 2002.

"Committed to Consistent Quality Service"

RECEIVED
JUL 12 2002
A&H UNIT

Name: **Wood, Corey A**.   Page: 2
Account: 521360000   File: B5C 8052554

Follow up will not be made again until 8/1/02 regarding the lab results.

Robert F. Bull, HIA, ALHC, CFE
Claims Consultant

pg

"Committed to Consistent Quality Service"

Name: **Wood, Corey A.**
Account: 521360000

Chief Deputy Casper then requested that a call be made to him the end of the next week and he would give the reason or be able to release the records.

The call was made and he was not available. A second call request was left on his voice mail.

ATTORNEYS

ED C. JONES, COUNTY ATTORNEY
ANGELINA COUNTY
P. O. BOX 1845
LUFKIN, TX 75902-1845

An attempt was made to personally talk to the county attorney. He was not available. **Attachment "A"** is a copy of the documents previously provided.

DISTRICT ATTORNEY HERRINGTON
ANGELINA COUNTY
P. O. BOX 908
LUFKIN, TX 75901
02/01/01

An attempt was made to interview the district attorney, Herrington, however, he also was not available as he was in court hearings.

Robert F. Bull, HIA, ALHC, CFE
Claims Consultant

pg

"Committed to Consistent Quality Service"

```
Name: Wood, Corey A.                                    Page: 4
Account: 521360000                              File: A013095-01
```

ATTACHMENTS

Attachment "A" - Copy of the duplicate information which was sent
                 through the mail by the county attorney

137

International Claims Specialists

Date:	07/24/02	**Account No:**	521360000
Name:	**Wood, Corey A.**	**Account Name:**	AIG Life Companies
Add:	Rt. 3 Box 7020	**File Number:**	BSC 8052554
	Huntington, TX 75949	**Requestor:**	**Carol Leverette**
		Phone Number:	N/S
		Nature of Loss:	

Emp:	N/S		
DOB:	12/15/76		
Type of Inv:	Limited Death	**Regional Office:**	Dallas, Texas
Dates of Inv:	07/24/02	**Phone Number:**	1-800-725-2167
Status of Report:	Partial	**Date of Next Report:**	08/07/02

INVESTIGATIVE SUMMARY

Source	Status	Reference
Ron Brandon, Angelina County District Attorney's Office	Completed Pending	Report of 07/15/02

DISTRICT ATTORNEY

RON BRANDON, INVESTIGATOR
ANGELINA COUNTY DISTRICT ATTORNEY'S OFFICE
ANGELINA COUNTY COURTHOUSE
LUFKIN, TX 75902
936-632-5090
07/24/02

RECEIVED

JUL 2 9 2002

Ann Grady
ROCKWOOD

This source states he still has not received the laboratory reports from the state lab. He does not have any idea when they will be received, but it usually takes four to six months.

Robert F. Bull, HIA, ALHC, CFE
Claims Consultant

pg

"Committed to Consistent Quality Service"

PAGE 1 OF 1

DATE: 5/13/200_

NAME: Ron Brandon, District Attorney Investigator

ADDRESS: Angelina County DA's office, Lufkin Tx 759__

01 My name is Ron Brandon, Investi-
02 gator for the Angelina District Attorney. I
03 have been working on this case for 1½ yrs
04 There is nothing new, not any physical
05 evidence other than the Sheriff's initial report.
06 Norma came in confused. No indication
07 of a struggle over the gun. I even had a
08 Crime Scene Unit out of Houston come out
09 examine the scene. They said everything
10 consistent with a self inflicted wound, no
11 fight. Sheriff investigated, Tx Ranger looked at
12 it, & I had a hearing + the Pathologist report
13 all shows - self inflicted gun shot wound.
14 There is no other evidence. I'm waiting for
15 2 little pieces of evidence from the lab - don't expect
16 anything out of it. I told you I have done
17 all I can do.   Ron Brandon
18 _____ Ron BRANDON, Investigator
19 _____ Angelina Sheriff's Dept
20 _____ DA office Lufkin, Tx
21 _____
22 _____

International Claims Specialists

Date:	10/04/02	**Account No:**	521360000
Name:	Wood, Corey A.	**Account Name:**	AIG Life Companies
Add:	Rt. 3 Box 7020	**File Number:**	BSC 8052554
	Huntington, TX 75949	**Requestor:**	Carol Leverette
		Phone Number:	N/S
		Nature of Loss:	

Emp:	N/S		
DOB:	12/15/76		
Type of Inv:	Limited Death	**Regional Office:**	Dallas, Texas
Dates of Inv:	10/04/02	**Phone Number:**	1-800-725-2167
Status of Report:	Final		

INVESTIGATIVE SUMMARY

Source	Status	Reference
Ron Brandon, Angelina County District Attorney's Investigator	Completed Completed	Report of 07/15/02 Enclosed

DISTRICT ATTORNEY

RON BRANDON, INVESTIGATOR
ANGELINA COUNTY DISTRICT ATTORNEY'S OFFICE
ANGELINA COUNTY COURTHOUSE
LUFKIN, TX 75902
936-632-5090
10/04/02

This source called stating that he had received back the reports from the Texas State Crime Lab and they have found nothing. He had sent in a baseball bat because the mother alleges that her son was beaten with a baseball bat. There is nothing that they can find that would substantiate him being beaten with a baseball bat.

He also sent in swabs from the wall in the hallway, the bedroom, the back bedroom and the lampshade. There was blood only found on the lampshade and it was not high impact like that would be from a gunshot wound.

"Committed to Consistent Quality Service"

They did a DNA on the blood. It did not match the sample of the insured's blood that the local pathologist had on file.

Robert F. Bull, HIA, ALHC, CFE
Claims Consultant

pg

International Claims Specialists

Date:	11-07-01	Account Number:	521360000
Name:	Wood, Corey A.	Account Name:	AIG
Add:	Rt. 3, Box 7020	File Number:	B5C 8052554
	Huntington, TX 75949	Requestor:	Carol Leverette
		Phone Number:	
		Nature of Loss:	GSW

Emp:	N/S		
DOB:	12-15-76		
Type of Inv:	Limited Death Claim	Regional Office:	Dallas, Texas
Dates of Inv:	11-06-01	Phone Number:	1-800-725-2167
Status of Report:	Final	Date of Next Report:	

INVESTIGATIVE SUMMARY

Source	Status	Reference
District Attorney Herrington	Complete	Enclosed

DISTRICT ATTORNEY

DISTRICT ATTORNEY HERRINGTON
ANGELINA COUNTY COURTHOUSE
LUFKIN, TX 75902-1845
936-632-5090
936-637-6462
11-06-01

Spoke to District Attorney Herrington stated this case has not gone to a grand jury nor has anyone been indicted. The case is not what he would consider open and it is not closed. He would consider it more inactive. If he had to choose between open and close, he would say it was closed unless something comes up. The following is a synopsis of what the District Attorney stated during the phone call this date.

This source stated the Angelina County Sheriff answered a call in a small town close to Lufkin called Huntington, Texas. In a trailer house, they found Corey Wood dead, along with a 22 rifle and the scene seemed to be an apparent suicide. The case was closed as a suicide. The Justice of the

"Committed to Consistent Quality Service"

Name: **Wood, Corey A.** Page: 2
Account: 521360000 File: B5C 8052554

Peace ruled on the death certificate it was suicide. The mother of Corey Wood, Joy Bruner, asked the D. A. to look into it. There were two to three other people present sleeping and did not wake up when the gun apparently went off. When they did wake up in the morning, they found Corey dead. There is one odd thing. There seems to be a time lapse of approximately one hour between the time they found the body and the time they called law enforcement.

When the sheriff arrived, the place was very clean, which was odd since they all had been up drinking and partying early into the morning. If there was one thing he wishes the sheriff's office had done, it would have been to keep control of the site longer.

Ms. Bruner keeps coming up with what she thinks are witnesses and she thinks there is a cover up. She feels Corey was shot on the couch and then rearranged. This source had an investigator and a Texas Ranger go to Dallas to interview a supposed witness who said he had nothing to tell them.

At present, they have no solid lead to show it was not suicide. The deceased had no valid reason that they could find to commit suicide. This, however, does not mean that he did not commit suicide. This source states he does not know if it's suicide or not. At this point, he would consider it 95% being suicide. He told the mother, Joy Bruner, if she wanted him to look into it, not to talk to anyone and not do any investigation by herself, but she continued to do the investigation and because of this, no one would talk to the district attorney's people. He feels that possibly the mother, as a parent, might have some feelings of guilt. He states he has done all that he can do at this time. Unless someone has a guilty conscience and talks to the district attorney, there is nothing that he can do.

Robert F. Bull, HIA, ALHC, CFE
Claims Consultant

pg

143

International Claims Specialists

Date:	05/15/02	**Account Number:**	521360000	
Name:	**Wood, Corey A.**	**Account Name:**	AIG Life Companies	
Add:	Rt. 3 Box 7020	**File Number:**	BSC 8052554	
	Huntington, TX 75949	**Requestor:**	**Carol Leverette**	
		Phone Number:	N/S	
		Nature of Loss:		

Emp:	N/S		
DOB:	12/15/76		
Type of Inv:	Limited Death Claim	**Regional Office:**	Dallas, Texas
Dates of Inv:	05/10, 13/02	**Phone Number:**	1-800-725-2167
Status of Report:	Final	**Date of Next Report:**	

INVESTIGATIVE SUMMARY

Source	Status	Reference
Joy Bruner	Complete	Enclosed
Ron Brandon, investigator	Complete	Enclosed

NEXT OF KIN

JOY BRUNER
RT. 3 BOX 7020
HUNTINGTON, TX 75949
05/10, 05/13/02

After several attempts on 05/10 and 05/13, Ms. Bruner was contaced. This source states that she is residing in Corey's old house. She talks of new found evidence, that she personally met with four sheriff's deputies just before Christmas of 2001 and they stated that a Jeremy Watts had stated that he had shot Corey Bruner and that Corey did not commit suicide. The sheriff, however, did not take the statement.

The confession was that "they" were fighting over a gun when it went off. Jeremy was one of Corey's roommates. The Sheriff's Department would not take the confession. She states she has proof that another roommate, Brian

---

"Committed to Consistent Quality Service"

THE EMPTY GRAVE

Name: **Wood, Corey A.**   Page: 2
Account: 521360000   File: B5C 8052554

Wilson, and his dad, Randy Wilson, did not call the authorities for an hour
after the shooting.

Brian and Randy Wilson were taking money from Corey's accounts up to the day
before the shooting. They were being helped by a bank teller named Shelly
Matthews. She was allegedly helping to debit Corey's account, as someone in
the bank had to help without their signature being on the signature card.
They did it with checks, ATM machine and debiting the account.

Joy Bruner stated she called the F.D.I.C. about them taking the money and
they are investigating. She states that they also admitted this to the
District Attorney's investigator, Ron Brandon. The District Attorney is
Clyde Herrington, but Mr. Herrington for some reason did not want this
information to "come to light".

There is supposed to be a fragment of a bullet at the pathologist's office,
a Dr. R. Bruce in Lufkin, Texas and a full-fledged bullet at the Sheriff's
Department that they showed to the judge who ruled in Corey's death and
ruled it a suicide. That means that there were two bullets and not one
bullet as the sheriff's deputies stated. These four deputies gave Ms.
Bruner aluminal that she sprayed down the back of the hallway and found
blood spots everywhere.

She states she has a lawsuit that she has brought in Angelina County that
she is handling as her own attorney because she cannot afford an attorney.
The case has been moved to San Antonio and she cannot locate the case
number. She is suing Stephanie Wilson, Brian Wilson, Randy Wilson, Keith
Talbert, Jeremy Holder and Melinda Bowles.

Jeremy Holder and Melinda Bowles told the sheriff that they were there when
Corey was shot but did not hear a shot or anything. Jeremy Holder called
Brian Reese after Corey was shot, but before the police were called. Jeremy
Holder told Brian Golden that he had shot Corey. Brian Golden was a
classmate of Corey's. Two other girls came to the house, a Jana Clark, who
is now Jeremy's wife, and Stephanie Durham, who has disappeared and not been
seen since the shooting.

It looks like a bullet hole in the ceiling in the living room. It had
spackled over.

Brian Wilson pawned his guns last week, a pistol and a high-powered rifle.
She believes that Brian Wilson is the shooter. Jeremy said all three,

"Committed to Consistent Quality Service"

145

Jeremy Holder, Brian Wilson and Corey, were fighting over the gun and the gun went off.

Corey had been monitoring his balances in his checking and saving accounts and found over $6,500.00 missing.

They changed Corey's boots and they cannot find Corey's shirt that he was wearing when he was shot. Mrs. Bruner has the evidence that the District Attorney gave to the crime scene lab. She stated she gave everything to a medical investigator, Karen Bransteder, who stated that there is no way Corey could have killed himself. Her phone number is 512-473-7641.

Ron Brandon is the Assistant District Attorney that Joy Bruner has been working with. The District Attorney says there were no pictures of the autopsy; however, Ron Brandon says that there are. She states that the Texas Attorney General gave them all permission to give Joy Bruner all of the evidence.

Joy Bruner is upset because she is shown as the informant on the death certificate and she thinks this means that she told them that this was a suicide. She is trying to get that changed now.

She has a State Representative that is helping to get the corpse's remains exhumed. Her mother is in forensic sciences.

The above information was provided by Ms. Joy Bruner.

DISTRICT ATTORNEY

RON BRANDON, INVESTIGATOR
ANGELINA COUNTY DISTRICT ATTORNEY
ANGELINA COUNTY COURTHOUSE
LUFKIN, TX 75902-1845
936-632-5090 – PHONE
936-637-2818 – FAX
05/13/02

Attachment "A" is the statement of Investigator Brandon.

Robert F. Bull, HIA, ALHC, CFE/Claims Consultant/jlw

"Committed to Consistent Quality Service"

Name: **Wood, Corey A.**   Page: 4
Account: 521360000   File: B5C 8052554

ATTACHMENTS

Attachment "A" -   Statement of Ron Brandon, Angelina County District
                    Attorney investigator, Lufkin, Texas

"Committed to Consistent Quality Service"

International Claims Specialists

Date:	08/26/02	**Account No:**	521360000
Name:	Wood, Corey A.	**Account Name:**	AIG Life Companies
Add:	Rt. 3 Box 7020	**File Number:**	BSC 8052554
	Huntington, TX 75949	**Requestor:**	Carol Leverette
		Phone Number:	N/S
		Nature of Loss:	

Emp:	N/S		
DOB:	12/15/76		
Type of Inv:	Limited Death	**Regional Office:**	Dallas, Texas
Dates of Inv:	08/23/02	**Phone Number:**	1-800-725-2167
Status of Report:	Partial	**Date of Next Report:**	10-15-02

INVESTIGATIVE SUMMARY

Source	Status	Reference
Ron Brandon, Angelina County District Attorney's Office	Complete Pending	Report of 07/15/02

DISTRICT ATTORNEY

RON BRANDON, INVESTIGATOR
ANGELINA COUNTY DISTRICT ATTORNEY'S OFFICE
ANGELINA COUNTY COURTHOUSE
LUFKIN, TX 75902
936-632-5090
08/23/02

This source states that they still have not received the lab reports, but they will notify this claims consultant as soon as they are received. This source still states that they have no way of knowing exactly when it will be received or when the laboratory test will be performed, but it still takes four to six months in order to get reports.

This source will be contacted again in approximately 45 days to obtain an updated status.

Robert F. Bull, HIA, ALHC, CFE/Claims Consultant/bgj

"Committed to Consistent Quality Service"

Name: **Wood, Corey A.**   Page: 3
Account: 521360000   File: B5C 8052554

ATTACHMENTS

Attachment "A" - Signed statement

149

CHAPTER 6

Corey and I were moving Darci's things to his new house while she was out of town. We were at the red light by beards and mall on the loop headed to his house in Huntington on 844. I made the call and this is when I was told by the insurance man at Tidewater, that the sheriff's department had already called and found out about his insurance and that they were going to rule Corey's death as a suicide, but that he did not believe that Corey would committed suicide, he had like I said just sat down with Corey and gone over his insurance with him, he told me that the investigation into Corey's death was not detailed and it made him suspicious that they would call, Peter Lloyd, of all names that was his name, he told me in detail how to appeal the insurance that only a very small policy would pay, only because it was over two years old, but to appeal it and the insurance company would have to send an investigator down to investigate, and since the sheriff's office had closed theirs in about 30 minutes the time it took to pick Corey up, that they would do an intense investigation, and they did Robert bull was the investigators name. After his investigation he told me no way my son committed suicide, but he could only write that in the report. He could not tell me what the insurance company would do, well AIG was who I worked with for years, and who did not go by their investigator's findings. They went by the death certificate and suicide was ruled on that, it took over 10 years to get that changed.

Ammended Death Certificate

TEXAS DEPARTMENT OF STATE HEALTH SERVICES

DAVID L. LAKEY, M.D.
COMMISSIONER

P.O. Box 149347 ♦ Austin, Texas 78714-9347
1-888-963-7111 ♦ http://www.dshs.state.tx.us
TDD: 512-458-7708

November 04, 2015

SHARON J BRUNNER
632 OAK HILL RD
HUNTINGTON TEXAS 75949

RE: COREY ADAM WOOD
     Died 09/28/1999
     ANGELINA
Cert 126370
Req. N300849 11/4/2015 $0.00

Dear Customer:

Thank you for contacting the Vital Statistics Unit. We have received and processed your request regarding the record identified above.

Enclosed is a full size certified copy (s) of the record as presently on file in our office with the official "raised" State of Texas seal.

My telephone number and email address are listed below my name if you need any further assistance. Please do not hesitate to contact me.

Sincerely,

RONDA COOK
AMENDMENTS SPECIALIST
Vital Statistics
Phone: 512-776-2546
Email: RONDA.COOK@DSHS.STATE.TX.US

An Equal Employment Opportunity Employer

Ammended Death Certificate

Only to find out that the insurance company that I delt with for all those years was not even the company that held the policy.

DATE	DESCRIPTION	Dispute / Facts	
November December 1998	Copies of checks written/ stolen from Corey's account by Randy Wilson before murder - 1 check written to the county attorney , Kirby	Randy Wilson license revoked. His son was Corey's roommate. Randy wrote checks on Corey's account and used his ATM card. NEVER charged.	
9/1/1997	TDI - disciplinary actions revoking license and fining agency	Randy Wilson license revoked. His son was Corey's roommate. Randy wrote checks on Corey's account and used his ATM card. NEVER charged.	
3/30/1998	Randy Wilson signature on tax return	Copy obtained to compare signatures on fraudulent checks	
9/29/1999	Death Certificate of Corey Adam Wood	Original before ammended	
1/10/2001	Interview - DA Clyde Harrington, Investigator Ron Brandon	Interview notes with joy conflict with Robert Bull's Interview and report	
1/19/2001	AIG request police reports, crime scene photos, autopsy photos, ME report, Interview of Dr. James Bruce	see letter	
2/16/2001	AIG requesting reports again. *Angelina County has declined to reply to requests*	see letter	
5/24/2001	AIG Claims specialist unable to interview Vincent Smith. *Angelina County Sheriff's office declined to furnish requested* autopsy microscopic glass slides, ME report, ballistic report, the photo of weapon, dimensions of weapon, due to exception under the OPEN RECORDS ACT of Texas Government Code. Awaiting independent forensic pathologist.	see letter	
6/20/2001	Formost Insurance Acknowledgement of claim 682-1483 for Property (Trailer)	Because this was a crime scene, it was not cleaned to not destroy evidence. Trailer was repossessed June 11, 2003. Joy attended court for the repossession with Randy Wilson (salesman, financed through Bombardia Capital). While on the stand, it was brought up that Randy Wilson endorsed a referral check made out to B.D. Marshal for a referral for sale of the trailer.	

	CONT	Constable Beuford ? From Angelina County repeatedly called Bombardia Capital, requesting when the trailer was being picked up with crime scene still intact. Bombardia Capital stated they have this on audio tape.	
1/22/2001	AIG received independent forensic pathology report. Currently being reviewed.	Report was inclosed. Where is copy?	
7/19/2001	There was actually 2 reports, 2 different reports of shift change, and conflicting information. The original reports were lost in 2005 in Ms. Brunners house when it was burnt down. AIG claimed denied due to suicide.	see letter	
7/20/2001	AIG received appeal request. To be reviewed by ERISA quarterly.	see letter	
7/31/2001	AIG appeals commity holding claim pending info from Grand Jury Decision. Independent forensic pathologyis opinion included in this letter.	see letter	
6/3/2002	AIG - appeal still under investigation. Awaiting evidence from lab.	see letter	
7/25/2002	AIG - enclosed statement from Angeline County District Attorney Investigator, Ron Brandon	Where is copy?	
7/25/2002	AIG - Appeals committee upheld denial of claim. Concluded suicide / self - inflicted injury	Start ammending death certificate	
7/10/2003	Granddaughter was murdered 6/11/2003	This was retaliation, murdered by a person in this group. Felicia Pizzel	
7/24/2005	Sharon Joy Brunners home was burnt down	Angelina County Fire Marshal had NO record. The fire marshall from Austin had to report it in 2006	
1/18/2005	Judgement for defendents Wilson, Wilson, Talbert, Holders, Boles		
1/14/2012	American Forensics		
2/5/2012	Chartis c/b/o National Union Fire Insurance acknowledgement of appeal. Company paid $30, 000.00 to Joy Brunner	1 claim acknowledged and PAID, why do the other policies deny claim?	
1/26/2012	Chartis denied appeal. Reviewed by ERISA 9/25/2002		

3/24/2014	AIG Appeal denied with ammended death certificate. Death can not be proved it was an accident.	It was proven not a suicide. So how does this get paid?	
9/24/2014	AIG denial revisieted. "Could not be determined" is still not grounds for an accidental death claim.		
7/25/2017	Initial investigation mishandled resulting in loss of evidence. Letter from William Campbell, retired CSI investigator.		
7/26/2017	Ferrel Law Firm - Deny civil case against AIG.		
3/21/2018	Request to AIG to reopen claim		
Robert Bull	Private Investigator for AIG, stated not a suicide. AIG did not use conclusion		
Peter Lloyd	Rep from Tidewater insurance. There is only 1 claim that will pay. Others will be denied because it was listed as suicide. Although the sherrif stated it was an accident. Joy was instructed by Peter Loyd to appeal the claim. Private investigator, ROBERT BULL (AIG) delcared this was not self inflicted. AIG did not take his conclusion.		
	AIG will not send the report to Joy from Robert Bull, they refused. He verbally told her that he concluded not self inflicted. 2000 /2001		

AFFIDAVIT

STATE OF TEXAS

COUNTY OF ANGELINA

BEFORE ME, THE UNDERSIGNED NOTARY PUBLIC, ON THIS DAY PERSONALLY APPEARED JOY BRUNNER, WHO BEING BY ME DULY SWORN ON HER OATH DEPOSED AND SAID.

1. I AM JOY BRUNNER PRO SE. THE ATTORNEY OF RECORD FOR PLAINTIFF IN THE ABOVE-ENTITLED AND NUMBERED CAUSE UNDER OATH AM OVER THE AGE OF 18 YEARS. HAVE NEVER BEEN CONVICTED OF A CRIME, AND AM OTHERWISE COMPETENT TO MAKE THIS AFFIDAVIT. THE FACTS DATED IN THIS AFFIDAVIT ARE WITHIN MY PERSONAL KNOWLEDGE AND ARE TRUE AND CORRECT.

2. I MAKE THIS AFFIDAVIT IN SUPPORT OF NOTICE OF LIMITATION OF APPEAL.

3. NONE OF THE DEFENDANTS CALLED FOR HELP FOR THE DECEASED, COREY WOOD FOR AN HOUR AFTER HE WAS SHOT. CALLS WERE MADE TO FAMILY AND FRIENDS BEFORE ANY CALL FOR HELP WAS MADE. BEFORE THIS HOUR. IN PREPARING THIS CAUSE FOR TRIAL I MADE THE FOLLOWING INVESTIGATION.

   a. THE DAY OF COREY WOOD, DECEASED, DEATH I JOY BRUNNER SPOKE TO STEPHANIE WILSON, DEFENDANT. SHE STATED SHE WAS AT HOME AND HAD RECEIVED A PHONE CALL FROM BRIAN WILSON, DEFENDANT, ONE OF COREY'S ROOM MATES AND HER STEP-SON. SHE STATED THAT HER HUSBAND RANDY WILSON WAS ON HIS WAY TO PICK UP BRIAN HIS SON TO TAKE HIM TO WORK, HE HAD TO BE AT WORK AT 7:00AM THE MORNING OF SEPT. 28TH 1999. SHE STATED SHE WAS ON THE PHONE WITH HER MOTHER WHEN THE CALL CAME IN. THAT SHE HAD TO CALL HER SON. ROBERT HEATH TALBERT BACK FROM OUT OF TOWN TO TELL HIM OF COREY'S DEATH. STEPHANIE NEVER SAID SHE HAD BEEN AT COREY'S HOME THAT MORNING. SHE STATED TO ME SHE HAD BEEN HOME, AND AS THE EVENTS HAPPENED THAT MORNING SHE WOULD NOT HAVE HAD TIME TO GO TO COREY'S HOUSE WITHOUT MY PARENTS OR SOMEONE SEEING HER.

   LATER IN THE DAY RANDY, STEPHANIE, AND BRIAN ARRIVED AT MY PARENTS HOME. THEY LIVE 2 MILES NORTH OF COREY'S HOME. TO GET TO COREY'S YOU HAVE TO PASS THEIR HOME. STEPHANIE STATED IN MY PARENTS HOME IN FRONT OF FAMILY AND FRIENDS, THAT AS SHE FLEW BY MY PARENTS HOME GOING TO COREY'S. STEPHANIE'S CAR WAS SEEN GONE FROM HER HOME AT 5:40 THE MORNING OF COREY'S DEATH. A SWORN AFFIDAVIT FROM MELODY LOWERY IS ON FILE, AND STATES THESE FACTS OF BOTH STEPHANIE AND RANDY WILSON'S CARS ARE GONE FROM THEIR HOME.

   I HAVE MADE ATTEMPTS TO CONTACT AND QUESTION STEPHANIE WILSON. SHE HAS REFUSED TO COOPERATE.

   b. RANDY WILSON HAD FORGED 6300 DOLLARS OUT OF COREY'S CHECKING ACCOUNT. THE LAST CHECK WAS FORGED ONLY 9 MONTHS BEFORE HIS DEATH. THE CHECKS AND SIGNATURE CARD ARE ON FILE. AT THIS TIME I HAVE SUBPOENAED RECORDS FROM THE SAVINGS ACCOUNT IN ANOTHER BANK THAT RANDY HAD ACCESSED TOO. THESE ARE PENDING.

   RANDY MET THE SHERIFF DEPARTMENT AND STATED THAT COREY DID NOT HAVE ANY

FAMILY AROUND HERE, AND WAS FIGHTING WITH HIS MOTHER IS WHY HE COMMITTED SUICIDE. THAT COREY WAS HAVING MONEY PROBLEMS AND THAT IS WHY HE WAS SO UPSET. COREY WOOD RECEIVED A 10 DOLLAR A DAY RAISE AND A PROMOTION ONLY THE DAY BEFORE HIS DEATH, AND HAD 1700 DOLLARS IN HIS CHECKING AND SAVINGS ACCOUNT COMBINED. I AM COREY'S MOTHER AND HE WAS NOT FIGHTING WITH ME.

RANDY'S CAR WAS ALSO SEEN AWAY FROM STEPHANIE'S HOME AT 5:40. RANDY HAS STATED TO MANY PEOPLE THAT COREY COMMITTED SUICIDE AND USED A PILLOW TO MUFFLE THE SOUND OF THE SHOT. THERE WAS NO PILLOW.

I HAVE A SWORN AFFIDAVIT FROM PATRICE SHAW ALDERMAN, THAT TWO FULL SIZE DARK PICK UP WAS PARKED AT COREY WOOD'S, ALONG WITH COREY'S PICK UP, A DARK NAVY, Z-71, HOME ON THE MORNING OF SEPTEMBER 28TH 1999, AT 5:45AM. RANDY DROVE A FULL SIZE DARK GREEN PICK UP. NO OTHER VEHICLES BESIDES COREY WOOD'S WERE SUPPOSED TO BE THERE ACCORDING TO RANDY WILSON, BRIAN WILSON, AND JEREMY HOLDER. MRS. ALDERMAN ALSO STATES THE LIGHT IN THE KITCHEN WAS ON AT THIS TIME. JEREMY'S STATEMENT SAYS HE TURNED THIS LIGHT OFF AT 5:30AM THE MORNING ON SEPT. 28TH 1999. JEREMY STATES HE LEFT FOR WORK AT 5:30AM.

THE CALL FOR HELP DID NOT GO OUT UNTIL 6:53AM. THE CALL WAS MADE DIRECTLY TO THE ANGELINA COUNTY SHERIFF DEPARTMENT.

c. BRIAN WILSON WAS COREY WOOD'S ROOM MATE. THE STATEMENT HE MADE TO SHERIFF DEPARTMENT IS INCONSISTENT WITH TIMES. AT THIS TIME I HAVE NOT BEEN ABLE TO QUESTION BRIAN. I DID CALL AND TRY OVER THE PHONE AND WAS TOLD, THE ONLY PEOPLE THAT KNEW WHAT HAPPENED TO COREY WAS COREY AND GOD AND HE HOPED HE NEVER SAW EITHER ONE OF THEM AGAIN.

BRIAN HAS STATED THAT HE AND HIS GIRL FRIEND, MELINDA BOLES, WERE ASLEEP AT THE TIME COREY WAS SHOT AND DID NOT HEAR A THING. THIS WITNESS IS WILLING TO TESTIFY TO THIS.

AT THIS TIME I HAVE SUBPOENAED BRIAN WILSON'S STATEMENT FROM THE SHERIFF'S DEPARTMENT. I HAVE READ THE STATEMENT. HE STATES HE WENT INTO COREY'S ROOM TURNED OFF A LIGHT AND ON THE WAY OUT NOTICED COREY SLUMPED OVER THE END TABLE BY THE BED, BLOOD WAS ON HIS BACK. HE THOUGHT HE HAD JUST GOT HIS ASS BEAT. AT SOME POINT HE TURNED THE LIGHTS OFF IN THE HOUSE.

THE SHERIFF OF ANGELINA COUNTY HAS REFUSED TO RELEASE THE CASE FILE.

d. JEREMY HOLDER IS THE OTHER ROOMMATE. JEREMY CALLED A BRIAN REESE'S HOME THE MORNING OF SEPTEMBER 28TH 1999, SOON AFTER COREY WAS SHOT AND STATED THAT THEY WERE PLAYING RUSSIAN RULET. COREY NEVER KNEW WHAT HIT HIM. BRIAN REESE STATES THAT COREY DID NOT EVEN KNOW THIS WAS GOING ON. HE DID NOT EVEN KNOW ANY ONE WAS IN THE ROOM WITH HIM. BRIAN REESE STATES THAT COREY DID NOT COMMIT SUICIDE, AND JEREMY HOLDER CALLED HIS HOME BECAUSE JANA CLARK WAS STAYING THERE, THIS IS JEREMY'S WIFE NOW. JANA CLARK AND STEPHANIE DURUM DROVE DOWN TO COREY'S HOUSE AFTER THE CALL WAS MADE AND WOULD NOT LET HIM. BRIAN REESE COME BECAUSE BRIAN WILSON WAS A TIME BOMB WAITING TO EXPLODE. BRIAN REESE TOLD ME THAT BRIAN WILSON SHOT COREY WOOD.

BRIAN REESE HAS ALSO STATED THAT HE DID NOT BELIEVE JEREMY HOLDER'S STORY OF PLAYING RUSSIAN RULET.

Sharon Joy Brunner
2101 Church Street #305
Galveston, TX 77550

03/21/2018

AIG
PO Box 25987
Shawnee Mission, KS 66225

RE: Insured – Corey Wood, Policy# BSC8052554
        Policy Holder – Tidewater, Inc
        Claim # - 645-088586
        Date of Loss – 09/28/1999

To Whom It May Concern:

I am filing a formal complaint in regards to the above claim of my son, Corey Wood. I have appealed the original decision and was denied September 25, 2002. I believe that there are extenuating circumstances to this case and it should be reviewed again.

Corey was murdered and his death was originally reported as a suicide. He has an amended death certificate that I have submitted to you in the past.

I have reviewed all the reports from AIG's investigator, Robert Bull and still have not received the final conclusion. I have requested it, but it still, to this day, 17 years later, have not received it. I have spoken to Mr. Bull directly, and he verbally concluded to me that my son's death was indeed, NOT suicide.

For the last 15 years, I have also been in communication with your (now retired) claims adjuster, Carol Leverlet. She informed me that when a death certificate is amended, that both policies, A & H and the life insurance would be paid in full at the time of the receipt. I sent the amended death certificate in 2015.

In 2001 / 2002 all of this could have been resolved with the assistance of Mr. Bull's report, who identified Corey's death as not a suicide

In September of this year, my son has been gone 18 years. I have never stopped communicating with your company trying to appeal to you to do the right thing to release the final investigative report and accept the amended death certificate.

Corey's death has been devastating for our family, and the daily pain of his loss is unbearable. It is disappointing that we have to continually have to ask AIG to honor his policy, particularly when it is clear that is such a vast difference between suicide and MURDER.

Sincerely,

Sharon Joy Brunner

Sharon Joy Brunner

cc: Kent Sullivan, Texas Department of Insurance PO Box 149104 Austin, TX 78714-9104

Derek Stone
Claims Examiner
Accident & Health Claims
Olathe Claims Processing Center

CHARTIS
on behalf of
AIG Life Insurance Company

September 28, 2012

Sharon Joy Brunner
239 County Road 046
Jasper, TX 75951-8329

RE:	Corey Wood
Policy Number:	BSC 8052554
Group:	Tidewater Inc.
Claim Number:	645-088586
Date of Loss:	September 28, 1999

Dear Sharon:

We have received the paper file from closed file storage as mentioned in our previous correspondence. The file was obtained in response to your July 2, 2012 request for the remainder of accidental death benefits from the above mentioned policy.

We reviewed the documentation and you exercised your appeal rights in 2001 after the original denial of your claim. The claim was reviewed by the ERISA Appeals Committee and denied on September 25, 2002. Your administrative remedies have been exhausted and no further action will be taken.

This does not preclude you from seeking legal remedy.

Sincerely,

Derek Stone

Derek Stone
AD & D Claims Examiner

Chartis
PO Box 25987
Shawnee Mission KS 66225
www.chartisinsurance.com

CHAPTER 7

I also hired a PI, for a second opinion, Joe Hendricks of Hendricks Investigations. When I buried Corey, I was told the ruling was going to be accident through the whole funeral we were led to believe the findings were changed to accident, only to be told after we buried Corey, that he committed suicide and for me to go home I did not know my son, this was told to me by the investigating deputy that was the chief deputy's son and only 22 years of age, he was so inexperienced he could not work the camera, so there are no crime scene photos, in deputy Casper's defense, he did call for help on Corey's case and was told he could handle it, this would not be true he could not.

The day after we buried Corey, I went to the sheriff's office to make my statement. I was one of the last people to talk to Corey. No statement was taken. I was told my son committed suicide, for me to go home, and that I did not know my son. I stated to Deputy Casper, investigator of Corey's case, same age as Corey, I said you don't even know Corey. He dropped his head and said with distaste, I could see it on his face, oh I knew Corey Wood, I played baseball with him.

Now Corey was a great baseball player for Huntington, he was a great athlete, he played baseball, and was scouted. But due to eyesight he was not picked, Corey could throw a baseball at 97 miles an hour. He also played basketball, the most valuable player. And ran track and was really good at that too. The fastest runner in the county or whatever district that's it district anyway.

This young officer had played against Corey, from a rival school, in these small towns they take these sports seriously. I could see we were going to have a problem, I knew this sheriff's department was not honest, I just had no idea how corrupt and how far up this would go, and how many people would cover and be involved in Corey's death.

At this time, I was still in denial and believed Corey had accidentally been shot, by his own hand. He was in a small space by his bed, I thought he may have grabbed the 22 rifle, that is the weapon that was lying beside Corey to his left. I was only told this, but to this day I have not seen the two pictures of the whole crime scene, when I said there were no pictures, there were two. One of Corey slumped down in that little space and a picture of the shell casing, there were no other bullets in the rifle, it was a 22 Mosburg lever action, like the rifleman uses. We were also told he was shot in the left temple, he was right-handed.

The 3rd PI I contacted by phone, was up in Dallas, cannot remember his name, but he really made me feel well. The hair on the back of my neck stood up on the phone with him, I told him what I knew of Corey's death, and he ask was he right-handed. What side of his head was he shot in, I said left, and he said there's no way did my son kill himself, and was I on a landline, i was on the battery operated, he told me not to use it again, he gave me his name, and license number like he was talking to someone other than me on the line. Wished me luck and got off the phone.

The day of Corey's death he was coming to get a haircut from me, and he was meeting my mother, she was going to take over his bills and anything he had to pay while he was out on the boat, he would be gone to Mexico for 3 months.

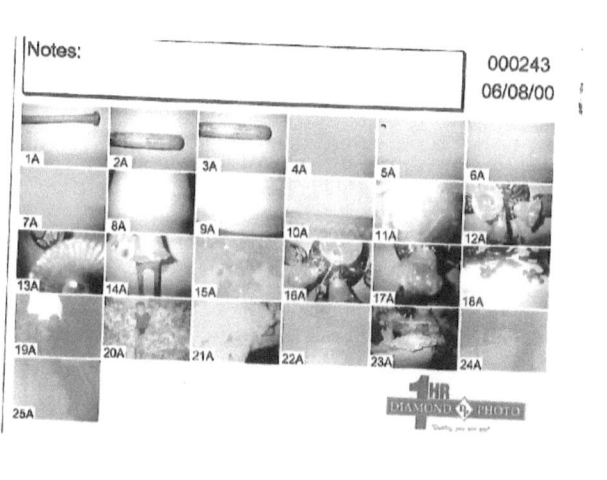

Page one

To whom It may Concern:

Please answer the following questions, and send back. These are questions we, the family of Corey Wood, have:

1.) Why was there no blood test done?

2.) Why weren't Corey's hands tested for powder burns?

3.) Why were we told these test were done?

4.) What were the circumstances leading to the Conclusion of Suicide?

5.) Why wasn't the entry to the crime scene, the day after Corey's death, Recorded?

6.) Why was Corey's Grand father told the case was Closed?

7.) Was the case closed on the 25th of Sept?

8.) Was the crime scene left un locked?

9.) Why was this entry not investigated?

10.) How many times did the investigater return to Crime scene?

11.) Was there any photographs or finger prints taken at Crime scene?

12.) If none were taken, was the reason, to save the County money?

13.) How many statements were Recorded?

14.) How many people were told their statement would

15.) How many self inflicted gun shootings are investigated in this manner?

16.) How many self inflicted gun shootings have you investigated?

17.) Did investigator go to crime scene?

18.) How long did investigator stay at crime scene?

19.) How long did Judge stay at crime scene?

20.) When did both arrive? When did they leave? (Times)

21.) What time was Dr Bruce called?

22.) Did ambulance transport Corey?

23.) Where was Corey transported 1st?

24.) What time was autopsy performed?

25.) What tests where preformed?

26.) Under who's instruction?

27.) Where was the autopsy sent?

28.) Was the autopsy sent anywhere?

29.) Who are the investigating officers?

30.) Was there an autopsy performed?

31.) Who was present for autopsy?

32.) Who performed autopsy?

33.) How was pretiminary report evaluated?

34.) What was the evidence?

35.) Where is the evidence.

36.) What was the procedure at crimescene?

37.) How many hours have been spent on this

39.) Have you already signed death certificate?

40.) What are the reasons for your assumptions, as to what happened to Corey Wood?

41.) How have you determined suicide?

42.) Was there a suicide note?

43.) Why do you assume Corey and His Mother (myself) were fighting?

44.) Where did this information come from?

45.) Did Corey's appearance ~~appearance~~ influence your Ruling?

46.) Did anything in Corey's house influence this Ruling?

47.) When did you come to your Conclusion?

48.) Have you talked to the owner of the gun?

49.) Did you know the owner said to his son, "why did you take that old gun up there?" You know that old gun has a History of miss firing?

50.) Why were Grand parents not Contacted sooner?

51.) Did the investigator or sheriff's department tear Corey's room apart?

52.) Why was the rest of house not searched?

53.) Why was tattooing so important until Autopsy Report came back? Now sort ring is.

54.) Why was Corey's mother's statement not given to Judge?

55.) Where is Corey's mother's statement?

56.) How did David Casper know Corey? When?

About Corey himself
1) Dreams goals
2) Accomplishments - new house...
3) everyday life   money in bank -
4) Achievements   Curess the...
                        people the...

5) New two days before
   Newtooth (Corp)

God
1) Act of God
2) You are seeking a woman that
   has been carved in the palms
   of our Lord.
3) Only by the Grace of God do
   we stand before you.
   We ask in the name of our God
   Almighty that you know the
   truth.
4) This was an Act of God. Corey is
   in Heaven. He did not murder himself
   to get there. God took Corey.
   Noone heard the shot. Corey went
   peacefully. And we buried Corey
   with pride... G ...

This is Joy ~~Behaees~~ Brunner

Don't Know the date:

Suicide
1) warning signs
2.) Myths
3) talked to people - John DODO Mac. Gail
Corey had no signs of suicide - of murdering
himself.

Q

· Autopsy
1.) No certain diagnoses
2.) Consistent means (bought -   (talk about
3) 2nd opinion is to reopen case.   indiscrepencies
Autopsy means nothing - final   (tattoo - with
decision is for police - what they   pendat)
find by talking to people that
had last spoken to Corey.
4.) No tatooing on head. Around wound
soot could have been from dirty
gun. depending on last time cleaned.
5.) Coreys stomach was empty. He
had been asleep for the 4 hrs.
1 - 5
6.) Corey was healthy,

Letters from Corey's friends and agitos
1.) Silvestre

Questions about investigation
1) Questions already ask?
2) ask new questions
3) tell about how many people
shoot themselves in the side
of the head [left] side, with
rifle. I have talked to many
people in law enforcement
FBI and Texas Rangers - they said
they had never heard of it. Would almost
be impossible (Do Not give up, blood-luck)

Blood splatter
1) pictures
2) are you an expert.
3) Line Called 3 - Lehman? 's
then Jean Padlette Sutton
La - Jimmy Barnhill
Aikaith - Max Courtney
I also spoke to Jamie Bofuerte.
Blood splatter is very intense
work, takes takes days to
determine. Have to recreate
crime scene. Cannot
just look at it.

Corey and I spoke of God the morning of his passing. Of how wonderful our lives were when we walked the Lord's path.

I told Corey that was the path I was going to walk. Of how when we were in Church. Our lives were so much better. So much more at peace. These are the things I talked about with my son before he met the Lord.

I would not change any of that conversation for the world. I felt so loved and so protected when I went to bed. I thought Corey was safer than he had ever been. He was asleep on the couch in his own home. I knew he loved us, with all his heart. And only wanted the best for his family.

No I would not change the events leading up to Corey's passing.

I killed Corey instead.

Corey is waiting on us. We will all die. All of us. We don't know how are when. We can only hope we will go as fast and as peaceful as Corey. This was not a tragity. It was an Act of God. God is the only one with this power. To give life and to take you home.

We Corey's family cash again please. Change this evening.

Page one

To whom It May Concern:

Please answer the following questions, and send back. These are questions the family of Corey Wood, have:

1) Why was there no blood test done?
2) Why weren't Corey's hands tested for powder burns?
3) Why were we told these test were done?
4) What were the circumstances leading to the conclusion of Suicide?
5) Why wasn't the entry to the crime scene, the day after Coreys death, Recorded?
6) Why was Coreys Grand father told the case was closed?
7) Was the case closed on the 28th of Sept?
8) Was the crime scene left unlocked?
9) Why was this thing not investigated?
10) How many times did the investigater Return to crime scene?
11) Was there any photographs or finger prints taken at crime scene?
12) If none were taken, was the reason, to save the county money?
13) How many statements were Recorded?
14) How many people were told their statement would

15.) How many self inflicted gun shootings are investigated in this manner?

16.) How many self inflicted gun shootings have you investigated?

17.) Did investigator go to crime scene?

18.) How long did investigator stay at crime scene?

19.) How long did judge stay at crime scene?

20.) When did both arrive? When did they leave? (Times)

21.) What time was Dr Bruce called?

22.) Did ambulance transport Corey?

23.) Where was Corey transported 1st?

24.) What time was autopsy performed?

25.) What tests where preformed?

26.) Under who's injunction?

27.) Where was the autopsy sent?

28.) Was the autopsy sent anywhere?

29.) Who are the investigating officers?

30.) Was there an autopsy performed?

31.) Who was present for autopsy?

32.) Who performed autopsy?

33.) How was preliminary report evaluated?

34.) What was the evidence?

35.) Where is the evidence?

36.) What was the procedure at crime scene?

37.) How many hours have been spent on this

39) Have you already signed death Certificate?

40) What are the reasons for your assumptions, as to what happened to Corey Cool?

41) How have you determined suicide?

42) Was there a suicide note?

43) Why do you assume Corey and his Mother (myself) were fighting?

44) Where did this information come from?

45) Did Coreys ~~appearance~~ appearance influence your ruling?

46) Did anything in Coreys house influence this ruling?

47) When did you come to your conclusion?

48) Have you tested to the owner of the gun?

49) Did you know the owner said to his son, "why did you take that old gun up there?" You know that old gun has a history of miss firing?

50) Why were Grandparents not Contacted sooner?

51) Did the investigator or sheriff's department tear Corey's room apart?

52) Why was the rest of house not searched?

53) Why was tattooing so important until Autopsy Report came back? How scot ping is.

54) Why was Corey's mothers statement not given to Judge?

55) Where is Corey's mothers statement?

56) How did Daniel Casper know Corey? When?

him to come get hair cut
and help me clear out
just shop product.
Plans with me Plans with
Misty and Plans with my
Mother- She had just taken
Over Corys Bills while he was
Out. as a matter of fact my
mom found the checks that
Randy Wilson wrote out of Corys
acct and signed them. Come to
find out 6500 dollars worth. Yes
It is coverd by FDIC and has never
been paid or resolved Criminally.
- Checks are in Case file -

Ron Brandon - on Sept 24, 2002,
He did allow a blood spec.? Some
People they used - out of county - the
SO office had already Sealed
these items #1, #5 - In evidence
room in plastic for 4mos and two.
more after I found out they were not
in a lab. Went to the 4 mos. that

The Lamp shade had Corey's
hair and piece of scalp on
it. As I would clean - bugs
here die and stick to things I
wiped one time - then went
back later - long? when I
went back it was Corey's hair
and part of his scalp. I But him
to sleep the night he was killed.
he was asleep he had worked all
day clearing and was drinking
Southern Comfort. He told me - and
I could tell he was feeling
it. The Lamp was at that end
of the couch - 1st I noticed
blood splatter on walls in
the dining room. I realized
we had the bat while I was
talking to the attorney general
Roland over heard me and
he Shuck Willis get a bat
out of Brian's room, while
Randy was down there with

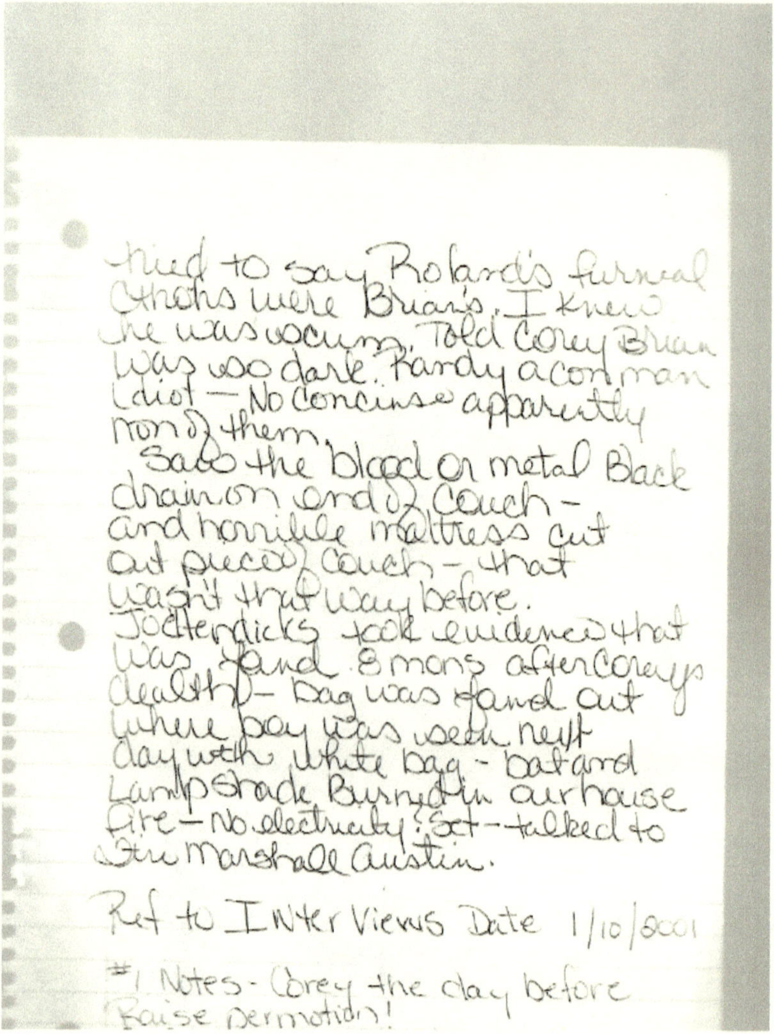

tried to say Roland's furneal
Cothohs were Brian's, I knew
he was wong, Told Corey Brian
was too dark. Hardy a con man
idiot — No Concinse apparently
non of them.
Said the blood on metal Black
chain on end of Couch —
and horrible mattress cut
out pieces couch — that
wasn't that way before.
Jockersticks took evidence that
was found. 8 mons after Coreys
death) — Bag was found cut
where boy was seen next
day with white bag — bat and
Lamp shade Buring in our house
fire — No electricity? Set — talked to
Stev Marshall Austin.

Ref to INter views Date 1/10/2001

#1 Notes - Corey the day before
Bause dermotion!

time for the girls at KTER
they had the Red Light and
they were stopped and given a
ticket before they got to my
house - I bloor went down the
hall - on the wall to small
bathroom just outside Jeremy
and Brian's rooms - they Roommates

Have affidavits? of Spraying.

Tammmy Wolmac - made me
get up and fight for Corey.
She was fitng for her son.
   She was there - When my mind
Was tiing to make sense of all
of this - the spraying - it was some
thing - my mind was tiing to
shut that out, and we did the
test on the Chicken blood - Scary
Corey was Daying at the end of
the hall - we all saw that.
In brite green - we forgot
the red light. Refer to spirit -

today 8/11/11

have pictures of this and
but - all evendes - blood
that was under the bed.

I moved well my family
moved us in Corey's new home -
I went and looked and said
no way - but thought and prayed
about it all well along time
and my answer was - if some
thing happened to Roland I would
have to come home and get
in the same bed - Material things
only mean comfort - we are
allowed to have that.
        So we moved in on my mom's
birthday Oct 9 - Jensons is Oct 5
we buried Corey on Oct 1 1999
He was asking us about millenium
and thought Darci was too far
away in New York - She didn't
make it - Corey was killed. all

we are 2 payments behinde -
so we did - then Because Corey
was chearsed - well it cyud not
be done either way - we had already
been sitting or had decided to
move - Brooke - was still apparent
on walls down hall,
you went crazy when told we would
have to move - eviction - so ran
to bed - throw myself in wanted
to put the pillow over my head and
hide - well the Lord spoke to me
and told me to take it to court
I would have Randy in Court.
And I did - he lost it on the stand
so gunned I killed Corey by my
Actions - He was let go. But
not until he was proven a
liar - That felt good and
the jury pooled - wrote me
letters and told me not to
give up. Randy walked out
of the court crying - pants in the
crack of his ass !!! That really

back really - The day or night
we were told to expect - or they
thought - the phone rang and
I got a hang up - I told myself
Do not be so paranoid - well!
I did that * and Lo, and
behold- Cavarian Book my answered -
Health Talbert - worked and managed
that store in Lufkin. He had interest
in this?

The day after - trailer moved
out on my property - Bailey Boo Boo
murdered the next morn - I was
homeless and could not take
her. Babysit.

Also Constable Howard
called Continually wanting to
know when trailer would be
moved. I finally ask him who
all was involved in this besides
my mortgage company and me.
The mortgage company told me
to tear down the walls of the
place. I just could not bring

180

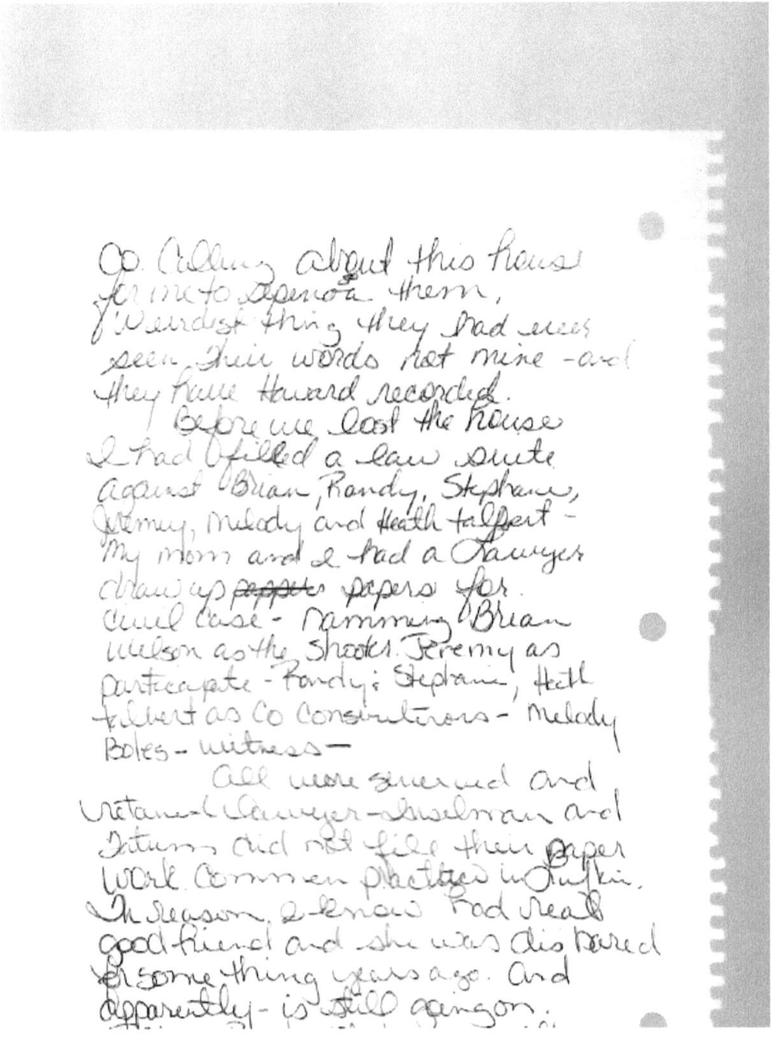

OO. telling about this house
for me to spend a them,
"Weirdest thing they had ever
seen. their words not mine - and
they have Howard recorded.
Before we lost the house
I had filled a law suite
against Brian, Randy, Stephanie,
Jeremy, Melody and Heath talbert -
My mom and I had a lawyer
draw up papers papers for.
civil case - naming Brian
Wilson as the Shooter. Jeremy as
participate - Randy; Stephanie, Heath
talbert as Co Constructions - Melody
Boles - witness -
All were served and
retained lawyer - Isselman and
Jturns did not file their paper
work. Common practices in Lufkin.
In reason, I know had real
good friend and she was disbarred
for something years ago. And
apparently- is still going on.

Core Legal – the other two –
null and void – not worth any
thing – Saturn... did not even
respond until the *assigning* of
the Judgment – They all
signed and agreed not to pay
me any thing – and they would
not sue me. But they did agree
they did all *said* they did.
Pay all court cost – Charges out
the Rear-end – that made me
feel good too. Pay day – Any way –
find pray for it to be justice for
Corey and how we Serve/is Bailey.
Refer to Spirit-Book – God has really done
all of this and I am so grateful
to have Children in heaven and the
power of the Lord to make a difference
for good –
    Tarot Cards were found
Laying out on Corey's dresser. By
the time I found them they
were Stacked – and I just Burned
them in the fire; Now I *laugh*

I really thought they were
harous - knowing when
not to babble - of course
this had nothing to do with
real health - only God, Jesus
Holy Spirit can home for you
in health. And health is used
for greater good of Gods people -
breathing it be knowledge - flesh
or spirit. When you are stuck
with guilt is hurt - unmovable -
And with health always comes
guilt and sorrow. Pray for
grace - a comforting grief
Sometimes you see both good
and evil - choose good.
I guess what I'm trying to
say I have seen strange things -
the Power of God ~~and~~ ~~want to~~ ~~his~~ words
~~But~~ ~~and~~ full of peace - Love
And forgiveness. Powerful stuff.
Only way - why would you
or anyone choose - false happy
ness. God will provide you peace

I try to be thank ful - praise
ing - daily - frankly for peace.
Asking for protection. The
strange stuff that already happened
or happing - the woman found
under bridge in Dublin name either
Yvonne Joy or Joy Yvonne -
Mine and my moms name. Her
last name is bybee - I tell
Jenson that when I say goodbye
bye bye bee - So the flesh and
the spirit run parallel would
that be paralell or parallel -
key to spirit Book -

Jeremy Holders step mom was
called to be a jurior on the trailer
duration. We all Stopped that - Should
we have left her on? Then Wes one of
Danes boy friends was also called
I found out in yail he was dead his
heart blew up. He told danie about it
and even came by her house. Cannot
recall Wes's last name. He was the 1st one

184

Steele magnolia's - went to Natchdch
and stayed in Bed & Breakfast with
my best friend - Kate Candel. In Church
when girl was married - Saw a fleeting
glance J Roland - then saw Barb again
on holiday -

2 ambulances called to Corey's house
on morn he was killed. Boy
with blond hair in 1st ambulance -?
Still do not know - Maybe our
but 2 ambulance run sheets -

When picked up Ems report - Steve mcccol
well I called and ask for it, 1st - he
said there is something on here that
makes no sense and before he gave it
to me it would have to go to the city
attorney - Sherray - his office was
with Ralyn Deaton and Brother Ryers -
Steve said that about some thing
being amiss - I told him that all
the bizzare things that were
happening I would not be surprized

handcuffs - Sat down right
behind Deaton (Ryan) he jumped
really about 10 ft over by the
judge - not with his back to me -
the judge even nodded to me. and
the rest of the court was a witness.
last encounter.

Although ~~Ray~~ Ryan Deaton's
dad and partner - was Randy's lawyer
for the trailer matter. He told me
well the guy (Randy) was a mobil home
salesman - what that means? I
took it like he was comparing him
to a used car sales man they all had
jokes -

Going to file on the two that
did not respond -

Eddie Matthews 1st to arrive
on scene — almost 7 mm - 658 -
name.....num/dispatch sheet.
Secured Crime Scene -
another officer was with him -
talked to Corey the day before -
kissed him about coming off shore
with him and make some real
money. Corey was buying some
thing to eat + he had worked in
yard all day - hee-work work.

SO shows up - Every one up to
the Sherrif crif who knows who all.
Kent never went in the Crime
Scene - ~~street~~.

I did not go down there to
house - only know what documents
say and Mom.

Bubu Buford came and told
me in Central where I was
Living with Roland and Jenson.

187

Yvonne Marshall, Ph.D.
Route 2 Box 348 • Huntington, Texas 75949 • Phone: (409) 422-5342

November 20, 1999

RE: Reference Line I.D. No. 132377

To Whom It May Concern:

I am writing this letter after the inquest on Friday November 19,1999, because I was not allowed to make a statement with Judge Marshall.

I was under the impression the inquest would be recorded and I would be able to speak and give my statement on behalf of Corey A. Wood, my grandson, who died on September 28, 1999 from a 22 caliber rifle gunshot wound to his head at his residence in Huntington, Texas. At the inquest, Judge Marshall stated no statement or letter would be read. Therefore, I have not of this date been able to tell, or state, that I spoke with Corey on the night of September 27th around 10:30 p.m. We talked for about an hour. I knew Corey well: my husband B. D. and I helped our daughter (Joy) raise Corey. I was also Corey's Head Start teacher. I have a Master's degree in Early Childhood and Child Development, as well as a Doctorate in psychology and counseling. Corey and his sister Darci were both evaluated and assessed during my college studies. Corey had high self-esteem, very good social skills, attitude, good thoughts about himself, and enjoyed his school years. He played all sports and had a great desire to go far in life. Corey had no emotional problems during his childhood or as an adult of 22 years. He loved life and was planning for his future.

Corey called me on the night of September 27, 1999, talking about his Mom and Stepfather (Roland) having words about his Stepfather's drinking and not coming home. I told him I knew about this, because I had visited my daughter that day. Corey said he was coming the next morning to get his grandfather B.D. and go talk to Roland about going back home to his Mom and little brother Jenson, and if he had to, he would kick Roland's butt. Yes, Corey was mad about his Stepfather leaving his Mom and Jenson, but he was going to talk to Roland the next morning. Corey was a 22 year old young man—involved with his own life, making plans for his future. He had a good job, a 4-wheel drive truck, and a brand new mobile home. Corey did not want to kill anyone, least of all himself.

Hendricks Investigations
204 E. Lufkin Avenue # 204
Lufkin, Texas 75901

COPY

Please consider this letter a formal demand under the Texas Open Records Act. [Vernon's Texas Statutes and Codes; Annotated/Government Code. Title 5 (a) 552.221 et al] for the release of the case file concerning the death of Cory Woods.

Please include copies of any and all reports of the investigation, copies of any and all statements taken from witnesses or other individuals related to this matter, any and all photographs taken of the scene, and any and all evidence collected by your department.

If any fees for copies of reports, statements or photographs are required, please contact me at the above phone number and let me know so payment can be arranged for time of release.

Thank you for your cooperation.

Sincerely,

_____
Joe Hendricks, TX. Lic. # A-09586

_____
Joy Brunner,
Mother of Cory Wood (Deceased)

Hendricks Investigations
204 E. Lufkin Avenue # 204
Lufkin, Texas 75901
Ph: 409-634-0007
Fax: 409-634-0012
Email: h0007@tlcc.net

COPY

December 1, 1999

Sheriff Kent Henson
Angelina County Sheriff

Re: Cory Wood

Dear Sheriff Henson,

Please consider this letter a formal demand under the Texas Open Records Act.
[Vernon's Texas Statutes and Codes; Annotated/Government Code. Title 5 (a) 552.221 et
al] for the release of the case file concerning the death of Cory Woods.

Please include copies of any and all reports of the investigation, copies of any and all
statements taken from witnesses or other individuals related to this matter, any and all
photographs taken of the scene, and any and all evidence collected by your department.

If any fees for copies of reports, statements or photographs are required, please contact
me at the above phone number and let me know so payment can be arranged for time of
release.

Thank you for your cooperation.

Sincerely,

_____
Joe Hendricks, TX. Lic. # A-09586

_____
Joy Brunner,
Mother of Cory Wood   (Deceased)

Hendricks Investigations
202 E. Lufkin Avenue # 204
Lufkin, Texas 75901
Ph: 409-634-0507
Fax: 409-634-0012

December 9, 1999

COPY

Mr. Ed Jones
Angelina County Attorney
P.O. Box 908
Lufkin, Texas 75901

Regarding: Clarification of request for case file concerning death of Corey Wood

Dear Ed,

In regard to our phone conversation of Tuesday, December 7, 1999, I am sending this letter clarifying my request for evidence in the matter.

As far as giving you a list of the physical evidence I wish to inspect, I do not know what evidence was collected. Because of not knowing what evidence was collected, how can I request to see specific items. Thus, my original request for "any and all evidence collected" by the Angelina County Sheriff's Department remains as is.

As to my request of the photographs taken of the death scene by the Sheriff's Department, I do want copies of all photographs. I will pay for the cost of copying the photographs.

Please confirm if the case file will be released by December 10, 1999, the tenth (10th) day following the presentation of the original demand to the Angelina County Sheriff's Department for release of the report.

Very Truly Yours,

Joe Hendricks, TX Lic. #A-0956
Email: jh0007@lcc.net

191

County Attorney

DENNIS JONES
Assistant County Attorney

JULIE CAHALANE
Assistant County Attorney

WILLIAM AGNEW JR.
Assistant County Attorney

OFFICE OF THE COUNTY ATTORNEY
ANGELINA COUNTY
Post Office Box 1845
LUFKIN, TEXAS 75902-1845

December 14, 1999

Area Code 409
Telephone 639-3929
Fax # 639-3905

Hot Check Division
Telephone 634-9995

DAVID PARISH
Investigator

VIA CERTIFIED MAIL NO. P 332 282 201
The Honorable John Cornyn
Texas Attorney General
P. O. Box 12584, Capitol Station
Austin, Texas 78711-2548

RE: PUBLIC INFORMATION OPINION REQUEST

Dear Attorney General Cornyn:

Within the last ten (10) business days, the Sheriff of Angelina County received a written request dated December 1, 1999 from Joe Hendricks requesting the following information:

"Please consider this letter a formal demand under the Texas Open Records Act, [Vernon's Texas Statutes and Codes; Annotated/Government Code. Title 5(a)552.221 et al] for the release of the case file concerning the death of Cory Woods.

Please include copies of any and all reports of the investigation, copies of any and all statements taken from witnesses or other individuals related to this matter, any and all photographs taken of the scene, and any and all evidence collected by your department."

It is the position of the Sheriff of Angelina County that the information sought is not subject to public disclosure because of the exception set forth in Section 552.108(a)(2) Texas Government Code because "it is information that deals with the detection, investigation, or prosecution of crime only in relation to an investigation that did not result in conviction or deferred adjudication;".

DEC 1 6 1999

COPY

I am submitting a copy of the request and certify that it was received on December 1, 1999.

I request that you review this special request and render an opinion in accordance with Section 552.301 through 552.306 of the Texas Government Code Annotated.

Yours truly,

Ed C. Jones
County Attorney

\lp

cc: Via Certified Mail No. P 332 282 202
    Mr. Joe Hendricks
    204 E. Lufkin Avenue #204
    Lufkin, Texas 75901

Hendricks Investigations
202 E. Lufkin Avenue # 204
Lufkin, Texas 75901
Ph: 409-634-0007
Fax: 409-634-0012

December 20, 1999

COPY

The Honorable John Cornyn
Texas Attorney General
P.O. Box. 12584, Capitol Station
Austin, Texas 78711-2548

Regarding: Public Information Request

Dear Attorney General Cornyn,

I have received from Angelina County Attorney Ed Jones a copy of the letter he sent to you asking for an opinion concerning the Texas Open Records Act.

I was hired by the family of Cory Wood to investigate the circumstances of his death. The Angelina County Sheriff's Department has ruled his death a suicide, but there are many discrepancies in their investigation. It is the family's desire to have an outside investigator review the case. Sheriff Kent Henson refused to release the report, despite the case being closed and an inquest having ruled this matter a suicide.

On December 1, 1999, Joy Brunner, the deceased's mother and I presented a formal demand for the report to Sheriff Henson.

Mr. Jones' asked for a clarification of the demand in a phone conversation on December 7, 1999. I delivered a written clarification to his office on December 9, 1999. His letter to you asking for an opinion is dated December 14, 1999.

It is my understanding that even with the pause in time for the clarification he requested, he should have asked for an opinion by December 12, 1999. Please inform me if you will be rendering an opinion in this matter or if Mr. Jones' request will be denied.

Sincerely,

Joe Hendricks, Tx. Lic. # A09586
Hendricks Investigations

February 23, 2000

Mr. Ed C. Jones
County Attorney
Angelina County
P O Box 1845
Lufkin, Texas 75905-1845

OR2000-0656

Dear Mr. Jones:

You ask whether certain information is subject to required public disclosure under chapter 552 of the Government Code. Your request was assigned ID# 132377.

The Angelina County Sheriff's Office (the "county") received a request for information concerning the death of Cory Woods. You claim that the requested information is excepted from disclosure under section 552.108 of the Government Code. We have considered the exception you claim and reviewed the submitted information.

We remind you that section 552.108 is a discretionary exception so any information held by a law enforcement agency or prosecutor that is not otherwise confidential by law may be released to the public at anytime. Gov't Code § 552.007. Therefore, in this instance, the Public Information Act does not prohibit the county from releasing the requested information to the requestor.

Nonetheless, the county has established the applicability of section 552.108(a)(2). You inform us that the case concluded in a result other than a conviction or deferred adjudication. However, section 552.108 is inapplicable to basic front page information about this incident. Gov't Code § 552.108(c). We believe such basic information refers to the information held to be public in *Houston Chronicle Publ'g Co. v. City of Houston*, 531 S.W.2d 177 (Tex. Civ. App. --Houston [14th Dist.] 1975), *writ ref'd n.r.e. per curiam*, 536 S.W.2d 559 (Tex. 1976). Thus, with the exception of the basic front page information, you may withhold the requested information from disclosure based on section 552.108(a)(2).

In addition, the information you submitted contains an autopsy report. Autopsy reports must be disclosed, in that they are expressly made public by the Code of Criminal Procedure.[1] *See* Code Crim. Proc. art. 49.25, § 11. Therefore, the autopsy report must be released to the requestor.

This letter ruling is limited to the particular records at issue in this request and limited to the facts as presented to us; therefore, this ruling must not be relied upon as a previous determination regarding any other records or any other circumstances.

This ruling triggers important deadlines regarding the rights and responsibilities of the governmental body and of the requestor. For example, governmental bodies are prohibited from asking the attorney general to reconsider this ruling. Gov't Code § 552.301(f). If the governmental body wants to challenge this ruling, the governmental body must appeal by filing suit in Travis County within 30 calendar days. *Id.* § 552.324(b). In order to get the full benefit of such an appeal, the governmental body must file suit within 10 calendar days. *Id.* § 552.353(b)(3), (c). If the governmental body does not appeal this ruling and the governmental body does not comply with it, then both the requestor and the attorney general have the right to file suit against the governmental body to enforce this ruling. *Id.* § 552.321(a).

If this ruling requires the governmental body to release all or part of the requested information, the governmental body is responsible for taking the next step. Based on the statute, the attorney general expects that, within 10 calendar days of this ruling, the governmental body will do one of the following three things: 1) release the public records; 2) notify the requestor of the exact day, time, and place that copies of the records will be provided or that the records can be inspected; or 3) notify the requestor of the governmental body's intent to challenge this letter ruling in court. If the governmental body fails to do one of these three things within 10 calendar days of this ruling, then the requestor should report that failure to the attorney general's Open Government Hotline, toll free, at 877/673-6839. The requestor may also file a complaint with the district or county attorney. *Id.* § 552.3215(e).

If this ruling requires or permits the governmental body to withhold all or some of the requested information, the requestor can appeal that decision by suing the governmental body. *Id.* § 552.321(a); *Texas Department of Public Safety v. Gilbreath*, 842 S.W.2d 408, 411 (Tex. App.–Austin 1992, no writ).

If the governmental body, the requestor, or any other person has questions or comments about this ruling, they may contact our office. Although there is no statutory deadline for

---

[1] The Public Information Act's exceptions do not, as a general rule, apply to information expressly made public by other statutes. Open Records Decision No. 525 (1989).

contacting us, the attorney general prefers to receive any comments within 10 calendar days of the date of this ruling.

Sincerely,

Rose- Michel Munguía
Assistant Attorney General
Open Records Division

RMM/jc

Ref: ID# 132377

Encl. Submitted documents

cc: Mr. Joe Hendricks
       Hendricks Investigations
       204 East Lufkin Avenue #204
       Lufkin, Texas 75901
       (w/o enclosures)

OPEN RECORDS
633-7691
ED JONES

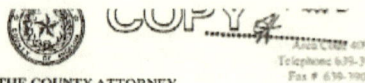

County Attorney

DENNIS JONES
Assistant County Attorney

JULIE CAHALANE
Assistant County Attorney

WILLIAM AGNEW JR.
Assistant County Attorney

OFFICE OF THE COUNTY ATTORNEY
ANGELINA COUNTY
Post Office Box 1845
LUFKIN, TEXAS 75902-1845

Area Code 409
Telephone 639-3929
Fax # 639-3905

Hot Check Division
Telephone 634-5904

DAVID PARISH
Investigator

December 14, 1999

VIA CERTIFIED MAIL NO. P 332 282 201
The Honorable John Cornyn
Texas Attorney General
P. O. Box 12584, Capitol Station
Austin, Texas 78711-2548

RE: PUBLIC INFORMATION OPINION REQUEST

Dear Attorney General Cornyn:

Within the last ten (10) business days, the Sheriff of
Angelina County received a written request dated December 1, 1999
from Joe Hendricks requesting the following information:

"Please consider this letter a formal demand under the Texas
Open Records Act, [Vernon's Texas Statutes and Codes;
Annotated/Government Code. Title 5(a) 552.221 et al] for the
release of the case file concerning the death of Cory Woods.

Please include copies of any and all reports of the
investigation, copies of any and all statements taken from
witnesses or other individuals related to this matter, any and all
photographs taken of the scene, and any and all evidence collected
by your department."

It is the position of the Sheriff of Angelina County that the
information sought is not subject to public disclosure because of
the exception set forth in Section 552.108(a)(2) Texas Government
Code because "it is information that deals with the detection,
investigation, or prosecution of crime only in relation to an
investigation that did not result in conviction or deferred
adjudication;".

I am submitting a copy of the request and certify that it was received on December 1, 1999.

I request that you review this special request and render an opinion in accordance with Section 552.301 through 552.306 of the Texas Government Code Annotated.

Yours truly,

Ed C. Jones
County Attorney

\lp

cc: Via Certified Mail No. P 332 282 202
    Mr. Joe Hendricks
    204 E. Lufkin Avenue #204
    Lufkin, Texas 75901

Hendricks Investigations
204 E. Lufkin Avenue # 204
Lufkin, Texas 75901
Ph: 409-634-0007
Fax:409-634-0012
Email: jh0007@kcc.net

COPY

December 1, 1999

Sheriff Kent Henson
Angelina County Sheriff

Re: Cory Wood

Dear Sheriff Henson,

Please consider this letter a formal demand under the Texas Open Records Act,
[Vernon's Texas Statutes and Codes; Annotated/Government Code. Title 5 (a) 552.221 et
al] for the release of the case file concerning the death of Cory Woods.

Please include copies of any and all reports of the investigation, copies of any and all
statements taken from witnesses or other individuals related to this matter, any and all
photographs taken of the scene, and any and all evidence collected by your department.

If any fees for copies of reports, statements or photographs are required, please contact
me at the above phone number and let me know so payment can be arranged for time of
release

Thank you for your cooperation.

Sincerely,

_____
Joe Hendricks, TX. Lic. # A-09586

_____
Joy Brunner,
Mother of Cory Wood   (Deceased)

Hendricks Investigations
202 E. Lufkin Avenue # 204
Lufkin, Texas 75901
Ph: 409-634-1907
Fax: 409-634-0012

December 9, 1999

COPY

Mr. Ed Jones
Angelina County Attorney
P.O. Box 908
Lufkin, Texas 75901

Regarding: Clarification of request for case file concerning death of Corey Wood

Dear Ed,

In regard to our phone conversation of Tuesday, December 7, 1999, I am sending this letter clarifying my request for evidence in the matter.

As far as giving you a list of the physical evidence I wish to inspect, I do not know what evidence was collected. Because of not knowing what evidence was collected, how can I request to see specific items. Thus, my original request for "any and all evidence collected" by the Angelina County Sheriff's Department remains as is.

As to my request of the photographs taken of the death scene by the Sheriff's Department, I do want copies of all photographs. I will pay for the cost of copying the photographs.

Please confirm if the case file will be released by December 10, 1999, the tenth (10th) day following the presentation of the original demand to the Angelina County Sheriff's Department for release of the report.

Very Truly Yours,

_____
Joe Hendricks, TX Lic. #A-0956
Email: jh0007@lcc.net

ANGELINA COUNTY
Claude Marshall, Jr.
Justice of Peace Pct. #4
P. O. Box 31 • Zavalla, Texas 75980
(409) 897-2424

Melba Tinsley
Clerk

Concerning informal Inquest hearing on 11-19-1999, after hearing all the evidence presented by the D. A., Sheriff office and the Family of Cory Wood. This along with what the Autopsy indicated and what I saw personally at the scene, I made my decision. Cause of death Contact gunshot wound to the head and Manner of death Suicide.

I then called the Funeral Home and released the death Certificate.

Claude Marshall Jr.

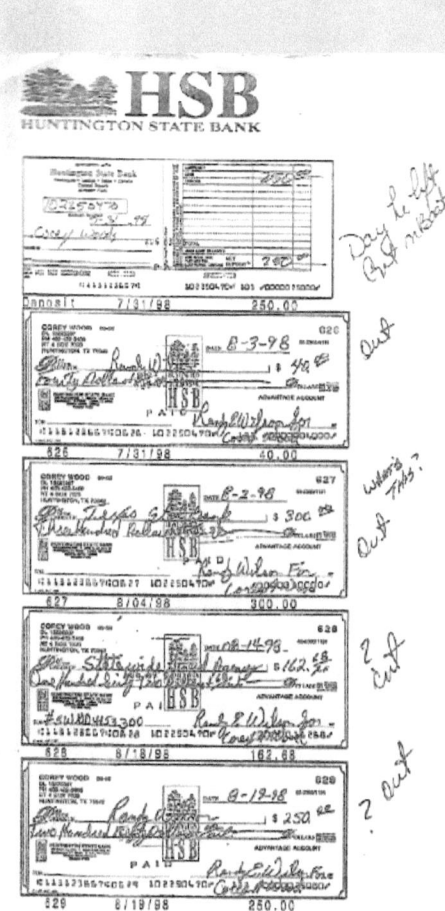

OFFICE OF THE GOVERNOR

RICK PERRY
GOVERNOR

July 18, 2002

Ms. Joy Brunner
Route 2, Box 159-D
Huntington, Texas 75049

Dear Ms. Brunner:

Thank you for taking the time to share your concerns with the Office of the Governor.

Please note that, according to constitutional provisions, Governor Perry has no jurisdiction over the judicial system, an independent branch of government. Any attempt to address court-related action would therefore best be directed through legal and judicial channels.

In addition, please note that district attorneys are locally elected. They are independent officials who have the jurisdiction to determine the cases that they will pursue. Therefore, you may consider continuing to work with that office.

You may also consider obtaining legal counsel. For your information, the State Bar of Texas operates a lawyer referral service, for which information is enclosed.

Sincerely,

Dede Keith
Deputy Director of Administration and Constituent Services
Office of the Governor

DK:dww

Enclosure

Angelina County Sheriff's Office
P.O. Box 908, Lufkin TX. 75902 Phone: 936-632-...

Inq-Info:
KENT HENSON   INCIDENT/OFFENSE REPORT   Page:

Incident ID: 34287   Case # 9910090   Off Date: 08/29/1998 Time: 04:53   Location Type:
Status : .. C: (24427541)   # Premises:

------------------------------ INITIAL CALL INFORMATION ------------------------------
Initial Call Reported By:
  WILSON,VERNON   Received On: (Date
  T 2 BOX 9288   Date: 08/29/1998
  HUNTINGTON, TX 75949   Time: 04:53am
  4235431   Note: PHONE

Nature of Call : UNADEATH-UNKNOWN DEATH

------------------------- INCIDENT/OFFENSE INFORMATION -------------------------
Offense/Incident Location: Area of Off:
  FM 844/REAL RD   Beadle/Grid:
  FM 844/REAL RD
  HUNTINGTON, TX 75949

Officer/Unit Assigned........ Date...... Disp. Arr. Clear. Fetal.   Disposition..................
  DKT (TORRES, WILLIE)   08/29/1999 04:53 05:07 05:47 05:54   OFFENSE REPORT

Investigator Assigned : WDC (CAPPY, WILLIAM DAVID)

--------------------------- DESCRIPTION OF PROPERTY ---------------------------
Category.... Property Class..... Descriptio................................ Tot Miis.. Value...... Disposition..........
  EVIDENCE   RIFLE   22 CALIBER MOSSBERG 800/BOLT #PT79XXX .22 LIVE $150.00 EVIDENCED LOCALLY
                                ACTION RIFLE

  Total Value of Property $150.00

--------------------------- COMPLAINANT/VICTIM INFORMATION ---------------------------
PID..... Name of Victim/Complainant.... Description....... Address.............. Phone....... Injury Typ.......
  030262   WOOD, COREY ADAM   W M 030 165 12/09/70 GT. 2 BOX 908/REAL RD. H(409)422-6631
                                                              CORNER REAL RD. & FM 8 W
                                                              HUNTINGTON, TX 75949

-- DETAILS --
  Ref to : E ON FM 844 200 GO TO R (REAL RD) MOBILE HOME ON LEFT (GREY SINGLE WIDE ON LEFT

------------------------------   ------------------------------
REPORTING OFFICER   APPROVED BY

Hendricks Investigations
204 E. Lufkin Avenue # 204
Lufkin, Texas 75901
Ph: 409-634-0007
Fax:409-634-0012
Email: jh0007@irc.net

COPY

December 1, 1999

Sheriff Kent Henson
Angelina County Sheriff

Re: Cory Wood

Dear Sheriff Henson,

Please consider this letter a formal demand under the Texas Open Records Act,
[Vernon's Texas Statutes and Codes; Annotated/Government Code. Title 5 (a) 552 221 et
al] for the release of the case file concerning the death of Cory Woods.

Please include copies of any and all reports of the investigation, copies of any and all
statements taken from witnesses or other individuals related to this matter, any and all
photographs taken of the scene, and any and all evidence collected by your department.

If any fees for copies of reports, statements or photographs are required, please contact
me at the above phone number and let me know so payment can be arranged for time of
release.

Thank you for your cooperation.

Sincerely,

_____
Joe Hendricks, TX. Lic. # A-09586

_____
Joy Brunner,
Mother of Cory Wood (Deceased)

contacting us, the attorney general prefers to receive any comments within 10 calendar days of the date of this ruling.

Sincerely,

Rose- Michel Munguía
Assistant Attorney General
Open Records Division

RMM/jc

Ref: ID# 132377

Encl. Submitted documents

cc: Mr. Joe Hendricks
Hendricks Investigations
204 East Lufkin Avenue #204
Lufkin, Texas 75901
(w/o enclosures)

OPEN RECORDS
633-7691
ED Jones

Hendricks Investigations
202 E. Lufkin Avenue # 204
Lufkin, Texas 75901
Ph: 409-634-0007
Fax: 409-634-0012

December 9, 1999

COPY

Mr. Ed Jones
Angelina County Attorney
P.O. Box 908
Lufkin, Texas 75901

Regarding: Clarification of request for case file concerning death of Corey Wood

Dear Ed,

In regard to our phone conversation of Tuesday, December 7, 1999, I am sending this letter clarifying my request for evidence in the matter.

As far as giving you a list of the physical evidence I wish to inspect, I do not know what evidence was collected. Because of not knowing what evidence was collected, how can I request to see specific items. Thus, my original request for "any and all evidence collected" by the Angelina County Sheriff's Department remains as is.

As to my request of the photographs taken of the death scene by the Sheriff's Department, I do want copies of all photographs. I will pay for the cost of copying the photographs.

Please confirm if the case file will be released by December 10, 1999, the tenth (10th) day following the presentation of the original demand to the Angelina County Sheriff's Department for release of the report.

Very Truly Yours,

_____
Joe Hendricks, TX Lic. #A-0956
Email: jh0007@lcn.net

Hendricks Investigations
202 E. Lufkin Avenue # 204
Lufkin, Texas 75901
Ph: 409-634-0007
Fax: 409-634-0012

December 20, 1999

COPY

The Honorable John Cornyn
Texas Attorney General
P.O. Box. 12584, Capitol Station
Austin, Texas 78711-2548

Regarding: Public Information Request

Dear Attorney General Cornyn,

I have received from Angelina County Attorney Ed Jones a copy of the letter he sent to you asking for an opinion concerning the Texas Open Records Act.

I was hired by the family of Cory Wood to investigate the circumstances of his death. The Angelina County Sheriff's Department has ruled his death a suicide, but there are many discrepancies in their investigation. It is the family's desire to have an outside investigator review the case. Sheriff Kent Henson refused to release the report, despite the case being closed and an inquest having ruled this matter a suicide.

On December 1, 1999, Joy Brunner, the deceased's mother and I presented a formal demand for the report to Sheriff Henson.

Mr. Jones' asked for a clarification of the demand in a phone conversation on December 7, 1999. I delivered a written clarification to his office on December 9, 1999. His letter to you asking for an opinion is dated December 14, 1999.

It is my understanding that even with the pause in time for the clarification he requested, he should have asked for an opinion by December 12, 1999. Please inform me if you will be rendering an opinion in this matter or if Mr. Jones' request will be denied.

Sincerely,

Joe Hendricks, Tx. Lic. # A09586
Hendricks Investigations

HENDRICKS INVESTIGATIONS

Contract For Services

THIS AGREEMENT is made on *NoveMbeR 8, 1999*_____, in Angelina County Texas between Joe Hendricks, of Hendricks Investigations, hereinafter referred to as "investigator", and *Sharon Joy Brunner*_____, hereinafter referred to as "client".

In consideration of the promises made herein, the parties agree as follows:

I.
PURPOSE OF INVESTIGATION

1.01 The client retains the investigator to investigate the facts and circumstances as follows: *THE Death of Client's Son;*

Cory Wood

II.
INVESTIGATOR'S FEES AND EXPENSES

2.01 In consideration of services rendered by the investigator, client agrees to pay the investigator the following amount: a non-refundable retainer of $250.00 in advance. Charges for investigation service shall be at the rate of $30.00 per hour. Client agrees to pay all charges over and above the retainer fee upon receipt of invoice. Unpaid fees shall accrue interest at the rate of 18% per annum. Investigator may withhold reports, conclusions, and work product if any invoice remains more than 30 days past due.

III.
COVENANTS AND AGREEMENTS

3.01 Client warrants that he or she has not committed, been arrested for, charged with, or convicted of any violent crime against the subject of the investigation, including but not limited to any crime of domestic violence.

3.02 Client has not been convicted of any violent crime against any person within the last ten years.

3.03 The results of investigation, and any reports or information provided, will not be used by the client for any illegal purpose.

3.04   Client agrees to indemnify, defend, and hold harmless Investigator from any and all damages to persons or property resulting from the breach of the covenants contained herein.

IV.
REPRESENTATIONS

4.01   It is understood and agreed that the investigator can not warrant or guarantee the outcome of the investigation, and that the investigator has not represented to the client that the investigator will discover any or all information desired by the client.

V.
TEXAS LAW TO APPLY

5.01   This agreement shall be constructed under and in accordance with the laws of Texas.

5.02   This agreement shall be binding on the parties.

I certify and acknowledge I have had the opportunity to read this agreement. I further state I have voluntarily entered this agreement fully aware of it's terms and conditions.

Signed on this ____8TH____ day of _November_ , 1999

Sharon Joy Brunner
Client

Joe Hendricks
Joe Hendricks, Tx. Lic.#A-09586
Hendricks Investigations

C.H. McCLURE, M.D., P.A.
500 N. JOHN REDDITT DRIVE
SUITE 5
LUFKIN, TEXAS 75904
(409) 639-3266

NOVEMBER 3, 1999

RE: COREY WOOD

COREY WOOD WAS SEEN IN MY OFFICE ON 09-24-99
WITH PHARYNGITIS AND TRACHEOBRONCHITIS. HE
WAS GIVEN KEFZOL 500 IM AND PLACED ON
DURICEF 500 AND TUSSI-ORGANIDAN DM, WHICH ARE
NON NARCOTIC COMPOUNDS. THERE WERE NO
SIGNS OF DEPRESSION. THERE WERE NO SIGNS
OF ANY ATTEMPT TO HURT HIMSELF OR ANYONE ELSE.

C. H. MCCLURE, M.D.

Sheriff uses exemption to avoid giving family investigative records into death

Reported by Paul Adrian
News of Texas Correspondent
May 09, 2000

It seemed like Corey Wood had a limitless future.

At 22, he worked on a tugboat and got a healthy paycheck. His boss said Wood could have made a career out of the job. He was training to be a ship's captain.

For three months at a time, he worked in the gulf near Mexico City. Then, on three-week breaks, he came home to Huntington near Lufkin and visited family and friends. It was during a break in September of last year that Wood's future ended.

Corey's mother, Joy Brunner, struggles daily to understand what happened to her son.

She visits his grave, kisses a baseball pendant her son once wore, and asks the tombstone, "What do I do about all this?"

Unfortunately, Brunner can't find an easy answer.

She is one of a growing number of family members in Texas cut off from police investigative records into deaths.

Brunner wants the records because she believes they will help her better understand what happened to her son.

On Monday, Sept. 27, 1999, Corey Wood was preparing to return to his job. He planned to fly to Mexico midweek and was hanging out in the evening with some friends and roommates at his new home.

Wood had purchased a mobile home the last time he was home, but only got to sleep in it one night. It was on the September break that he first really got to live in it, although only for three weeks. His mother said Wood had made plans at a local store to purchase furniture and already had bought a stereo for the living room.

During the break, Brunner said Wood also purchased pricey tires for his Chevy extended cab pickup truck and he paid a dentist to put a cap on a tooth. Brunner said her son cared a lot about how he looked, what he drove and where he lived.

On that Monday night, Corey talked by phone to both his grandmother and mother.

He told his grandmother, Yvonne Marshall, he was going

Twenty-two-year-old Corey Woods was studying to be a ship captain before his death six months ago.

Angelina County Sheriff Kent Henson refuses to release Woods' death investigation files to his family...

And his mother, Joy

"He had gotten his raise that day. He was making good money," Marshall said. "And he would come back and have a good Christmas with the family."

Wood also told his grandmother that she and his grandfather should enjoy their retirement and not worry about the family.

"He said he would be making the money," Marshall said. "He could take care of his mom. He could take care of his little brother. He could take care of his sister, if needed, because he could take care of the family, like Mamps (Wood's grandfather) took care of him."

Wood spoke to his mother later in the evening.

"We just talked about my husband and myself," Brunner said. "We talked about the Lord, living a life with the Lord. We talked about drinking. We talked about the every day things that we talked about."

Wood also made plans with his mother to get a haircut from her the next morning.

But he wouldn't keep the appointment.

After hanging up with Corey at one in the morning, Brunner went to sleep. The next morning a deputy from the Angelina County Sheriff's Department drove into her front yard.

"As soon as he walked up I said, 'Oh my God, its Corey.' And he said, 'Yes.' And I said, 'Oh God. What is it?'" Brunner's eyes glistened as she remembered. "He said, 'It's a self-inflicted gun wound.'"

At about the same time that Brunner's world crumbled, Justice of the Peace Claude Marshall had the task of viewing the death scene and determining how Wood died. Although he would eventually depend on a report from the sheriff and the pathologist to make his ruling, he would also depend on what he saw at the scene.

Marshall said Corey Wood was sitting on the edge of his bed facing the wall. His head was slumped over a small table that served as a nightstand. He had been shot in the left temple. The weapon used appeared to be the .22-rifle that Wood still clutched in his right hand. There was no note.

"What I saw would appear to be suicide," Marshall said. "But I have not been around that many suicides. I've seen some. They've had some here in town before when I was a judge."

Within a few days, Marshall received the sheriff's report and the pathologist's report. He concurred with both and ruled Wood's death a suicide. About a month later, at the district attorney's request, he held an inquest in his court that the family attended.

"I listened to all the evidence that was presented by every party and after hearing that evidence, I didn't change my ruling," Marshall said. "I still ruled it suicide."

For the family, the bad news turned bizarre the day after Wood died.

A neighbor said he saw someone run from the yard around Corey's home to the woods across the street. That person was carrying a white kitchen trash bag with something in it. Later in the day, Corey's grandfather and a friend went into the home and found that the dead man's bedroom had been ransacked.

"I called the sheriff's department and talked to the investigator," B.D. Marshall said. "They said the case is closed. They wouldn't even come down here."

A couple of months after Wood's death, his grandmother made another disturbing find. She discovered that a friend, who had paid Wood's bills while he was at sea, had written checks to himself on Wood's account. She said it added up to about $6,500.

The friend claimed that Wood knew about the money taken out of the account. The Huntington Police Department started an investigation into the $6,500, which is still open. So far, no charges have been brought against the friend.

Wood's mother doesn't believe him.

"Sixty-five hundred dollars is a lot of money and if Corey had known it, he would have confronted him," she said.

Perhaps the strangest thing to occur since Wood's death happened about one month ago.

Brunner said she was working in her garden, outside Wood's home, when she smelled something awful. She looked around and discovered a stain on the mobile home. She said someone had smeared blood on an outside wall at the exact location where her son's body was found inside the home. She thinks it was a warning to her to stop asking questions about Wood's death.

But accepting the suicide ruling is not something Brunner can do.

"For Corey to jump up off the couch, snap completely out of his mind out of a dead sleep, and run into his room and blow his head off because his life is going so wonderful is just not the answer," Brunner said.

She wanted a second opinion. So, Brunner hired private investigator Joe Hendricks. He had been a lawman for 14 years prior to becoming a private eye.

"I gave her an estimate of reviewing the report for about three hours, talking to the investigating officers, and then giving her a second opinion," Hendricks said.

But it wouldn't be nearly that easy.

Hendricks asked Angelina County Sheriff Kent Henson to see his department's report, some of the witness statements and evidence collected at the scene.

The sheriff refused.

He used a new exemption in the Texas Open Records Act. The exemption gives police agencies the discretion whether or not to release an investigative file when that investigation did not result in a conviction or deferred adjudication. Since this investigation resulted in a finding of suicide, no one was convicted. It qualified. The sheriff kept his files.

When appealed, the attorney general's office reminded the sheriff that the records could be released to the public at any time. But the attorney general did not force him to release the records.

"If this was a good, thorough, proper investigation, why are they hiding behind a one sentence exception in the Open Records Act?" Hendricks asked.

According to the attorney general's office, Wood's family is not alone in being cut off from investigations into suicides.

"Access to suicide reports is an issue that comes up frequently," spokeswoman Andrea Horton, of the attorney general's office, said.

But because of the exemption, it's left up to law enforcement agencies to decide whether to release the investigative reports.

State representative Sylvester Turner co-sponsored the exemption to the Open Records legislation when it was written in 1997.

"The wording was not intended, in my view — and I was one of the ones who carried the bill in the house — was not intended to cover this scenario," Turner said.

Turner said the exemption was written to protect people investigated by police departments, who were ultimately found innocent, and not convicted. He said it was never meant to deny family's access to suicide investigations.

"That is a totally different scenario than what we intended in the spirit," Turner said. "And let me just even go one step further. I think it's outside the wording of the law itself."

The News of Texas tried to get Sheriff Henson to explain why he won't release the records to Joy

Brunner. But despite many attempts, the sheriff repeatedly denied any explanation.

At one point, he referred inquiries to Angelina County Attorney Ed Jones. But Jones could not answer why the records were not being released either, saying that although he represents the sheriff's office, he cannot respond to questions about Henson's policy. He said only Henson could do that.

After a recent interview, Henson still didn't answer the question. He never told the News of Texas why he wouldn't let Brunner see the evidence that led the detectives to believe her son committed suicide.

Private investigator Hendricks thinks he knows why. He thinks the investigation was incomplete.

"A suicide is so easy and so convenient. So much less work, so much less paperwork, so much less time," Hendricks said. "But Joy Brunner doesn't buy it. At this point, I don't buy it, because I don't have all the facts."

Half a year has passed since Brunner's son died. And each day, her need for answers grows.

"We just need more. We need more," Brunner said. "And the longer it goes, the stronger we get, and the more that we want. I want to see every bit of that file."

She is prepared to wait, even if it means waiting for the law to change, which could happen in the next legislative session. Turner said he will bring up this issue in January, and hopes some rewording will make it clear to law enforcement agencies that suicide reports cannot be kept from families.

No matter how tough it might be, Brunner thinks seeing the files about her son's death will help her better understand what happened to her son.

RELATED LINKS

Texas Open Government
http://http://www.oag.state.tx.us/opinopen/opengovt.htm

Sample Open Records request
http://http://www.ma.utexas.edu/users/guilfoyl/ora.html

Friday, May 12 2000 at 02:39 PM

Subject: Consealed suicide records :
In the case of Corey Woods, and others in such cases it is easy to point the finger at local authorities,and offices to vent frustration and discust. However, it does not change the fact they are not operating outside the law.If you want to be cnstructive, and make a difference, you must help change the laws. Remember actions speak louder than words. Words are spoken but seldom heard and absorbed ;actions cannot be forgotten when they bring resolve to such passionate issues. If you want to make a difference contact your local congressman or other members of the Texas legislature and have such laws repealed or changed. This is something you can really do to make a difference. Also pray for those who inforce the laws, and please respect and obey the laws yourself.

– "T" from Bald Hill

Friday, May 12 2000 at 01:18 PM

Subject: Stuff it, Jill!
The reason nobody ran against him is that they'd have
wound up dead or worse! The only way anyone'll ever
replace Hitler Henson is for him, his deputy, and that
homo brat of his to all get killed at the same time. Until
then, Huntington's a police state!

– Hank A. from Huntington

Friday, May 12 2000 at 12:24 PM

Subject: Files
Will someone please tell me what kind of man would
keep such important records and information from a
grieving mother? I thought that all police files/records
were public information anyway.?.

– James from Zavalla

Friday, May 12 2000 at 12:10 PM

Subject: The Law
I think it is a disgrace to the family for the Sheriff not
to turn over the files and allow the family to understand
all they can about this tragedy. They need to have
closure to be able to go on with their lives. Even if the
files say that he did committ suicide, then at least they
can come to terms with it, and continue living. You
need to show some compassion for the people in your
county!

– Bettie from Wells

Friday, May 12 2000 at 11:55 AM

Subject: Cover your own........tracks
Personally I think all of you who are bad-mouthing the
sheriff and other small town law enforcement should
first find out the whole story before showing your
ignorance all over the Internet. Obviously Mr. Henson
is doing a good job because NO ONE contested him in
the last election. Everyone around this area is a lot of
talk but not much action. If you have a problem with
the way the law is enforced you should go to the proper

other people form bad opinions about innocent,
hardworking people like Mr. Henson!

– Jill from Lufkin area

Friday, May 12 2000 at 11:53 AM

Subject: Suicide Files
As I sit here and read all of these responses, I realize
that I am not the only person in Angelina County that
feels "used and abused" by the Sheriff and all of his
mishaps. Anyone who reads these articles will certainly
know how much disgrace he has caused the ACSO and
the unfortunate citizens who elected him. All I have to
say know is that if he (Sheriff Henson) has read any of
these responses, then he will surely turn over the files
to Mrs. Brunner to end this entire fiasco. Maybe this will
also make him change his unfortunate ways as well.
And if not, there's always another election!

– Jonathon from Homer

Friday, May 12 2000 at 11:13 AM

Subject: To Educated Citizen
I would like to say first of all that the comment about
Mrs.Brunner being a case for show and tell only proves
one thing, that obviously you are not very educated or
you would know that name-calling only shows your
ignorance. Now, of course people of your kind are
going to attack Mrs.Brunner, there are bruised egos
and jobs to be jeopardized over this matter. The main
fact that you need to think about is, that if you had a
child that was dead, and there was disputing evidence
as to how your child died, you would be curious to
know more yourself. Most people assume that this is a
parental instinct. She has a right to know and that will
be proven soon enough. Mrs.Brunner's past has no
bearing on any of this and for you to take time out to
try to hurt her for no apparent reason, just goes to
show how shallow of a person you are. So step on into
those biblical shoes yourself and learn a little empathy.

– Stephanie from Lufkin

Friday, May 12 2000 at 10:27 AM

Subject: I miss corey
Let me start by saying I come to this page after
hearing somthing that not only affanded me but the
people who were there for Corey. This all started along
time back when corey was a little on the wild side but
nothing ever really bad just being a kid. I was older
than corey and felt if anything could help him out of his
wild side, needless to say we became great friends
along with about six of us who still stay in touch. The
comment made in the article of money missing and
checks wrote out in high numbers is crazy . Why do
you think he left them with his checkbook and not you
(mother) it's because corey trusted the friends to take
care of him and that's just what they did. I know the
friends pretty damn well and if for one moment you
really think "the friends" would do this you need to be
investigated for smoke-n-crack. To all who really knew
Corey and have been there with him in the tough times
and the good ones we miss you and love you man c-
men

– friend from huntington

Friday, May 12 2000 at 08:55 AM

Subject: The File
I saw the newscast of the plight of the dead man's
family. I commend Mrs. Brunner for demanding
answers from the Sheriff. I am puzzled by the Sheriff's
refusal to release the file to the family. Has the Sheriff
given a reason he will not release it? Is there
something in the case file he thinks would harm the
family of Mrs. Brunner?? I do not know Mr. Hendricks
personally, but I know several police officers in Lufkin.
One of them told me that Joe Hendricks is a very
intelligent and methodical detective who worked for the
Lufkin PD back in the 80's before going to work for the
Missouri State Police. He went on to say that he too
disagrees with the Sheriff not releasing the file. If it
were me questioning the death of my son, I can assure
you I would be on Sheriff Hanson's doorstep daily
demanding answers.... I will contact my state
representative about changing this law.

– Stuart from Port Neches

Thursday, May 11 2000 at 11:55 PM

Subject: Corey, the law, and the file
Sorry , I wasn't through voicing my opinion. At the inquiry, they didn't want to hear anything. They held it to try to make her stop asking questions. Well, all of Corey friends are still asking questions and will never stop!!! There are so many questions that there are no answers to. Joe, you are a very nice person and you are the only one who has tried to help Corey's family. Now this news article has tried to help find the truth and law enforcement won't even try to help them. I know that a daughter loves her father and only wants to see his good and he may be a very good father but that doesn't excuse him from what he has done to this family. And all of you that want to talk about Mrs. Brunner and her son don't know diddly. I have known them for 15 years and they are wonderful, loving,caring people. You should be ashamed and YOU ARE A CASE OF REAL SHOW AND TELL. How petty to try to hurt someone who is already facing the most horrible thing that could ever happen to a mother. You should all be screaming for the sherrif to help her. He can release those files and if you read the story you know that the exemption was never meant to be used the way they are using it. So why won't they give it up unless they are hiding something. I pray daily that Corey's family will have the strength to continue and that their enemies will be defeated. It is their right to see the file and to know anything and everything concerning Corey. I love this family and Corey and we will never forget what has been done to him. Thanks, txn and all who write in support.

– Rhonda from Lufkin

Thursday, May 11 2000 at 06:28 PM

Subject: the truth
I would like to say that I knew Corey Wood and his family. I also am very familiar with Sheriff Henson and his department. First, Corey had been involved in some altercations with the law but nothing that is of the nature as to be held against him. I know for a fact that it was not drug related. Corey was a very nice young man that seemed to understand that his past was behind him and seemed to be doing what he needed to bring himself success in life. Secondly, Sheriff Henson's tenure has brought disgrace to what once was a respectable position in Angelina County. To Donald from Diboll, not only was the investigator the Chief Deputy's son, he also has another son that is currently a patrol deputy with the department. For all of those

223

law from jailer to patrol deputy. In my book, this is
indeed nepotism, if not by the letter of the law then by
the spirit of the law. All three of the above mentioned
positions were given to these family members without
any consideration for other employees who had more
seniority and qualifications. I personally know that the
majority of ACSO employees are honest, hard working
people and if asked in private, feel as I do. And my
feelings are that the ACSO currently exists for the
benefit of the Sheriff, his top henchmen and their
family members. Ms.Brunner, do not give up your fight
to obtain the report. Sheriff Henson knows that this
investigation was not handled properly and is afraid to
turn over the file because he knows of the civil liability
that he will face. In closing, I would like to say that I
have never seen the ACSO in such a condition of
mismanagement. It is my desire that a good, morale,
ethical and Christian person take charge of this
cesspool and bring much needed relief to the
employees of ACSO as well as the good citizens of
Angelina County.

– local peace officer x from lufkin

Thursday, May 11 2000 at 02:56 PM

Subject: On leaving real names
1) "Dorb", let's see you leave your full name first. 2) In
this situation, nobody in their right mind would leave
their real name, especially when you're dealing with
someone who's becoming an accessory to murder by
concealing evidence. Until retaliation is punishable with
death by extreme torture, protect yourselves! Use a
handle as you would a condom!

– R. E. Post from Huntington

Thursday, May 11 2000 at 02:53 PM

Subject: Ashhole..er..Ashley
Your dad is a slimball. He's probably the most corrupt
cop in the history of Texas' big list of small corrupt
towns. He may not have actually pulled the trigger to
kill this kid, but it's obvious as hell that he botched the
investigation, and now he's going out of his way to
cover his ass. What the people of this state need to do
is to lobby their congressmen to impose new laws to
ELIMINATE small town cops who pull the same sort of
h#! as your worthless father has. I've lived in
Huntington for all of my 52 odd years, and the worst

becoming sherrif. News of Texas should run an
investigative report on all the small town sheriffs so
everyone can find out just how bad off the situation is
across the state. We like to laugh about Judge Roy
Bean, but the reality isn't funny at all!

  R. E. Post from Huntington

Thursday, May 11 2000 at 02:21 PM
Subject: To Educated Citizen....
It is not my intent, nor will it ever be, to make this a
personal issue between anyone and myself. If you
know me personally (as you say you do) then I invite
you to call me or come to my office and talk with me
about this case. It is apparent to me that you are not
aware of all the facts surrounding Cory's death. My
office number is (936) 634-0007 and the address is
204 E. Lufkin Ave suite 204. I look forward to hearing
from you, who knows..we may be able to shed a little
light on both sides of the issue.

 — Joe Hendricks from Lufkin, Texas
jhendricks@hendricksinvestigat
www.hendricksinvestigation.com

Thursday, May 11 2000 at 01:55 PM
Subject: Sheriff's Office
I would like to respond to all the comments I'm reading
about the suicide files. It's obvious to me and several
other people in Angelina County that the Sheriff's Office
is not as it used to be. I can remember a time when
the sheriff had good christian morals, and stood up for
what was right and made good, honest decisions. That
is not true today. This is why I believe that Mrs.
Brunner should not give up the fight against Sheriff
Henson, because in the end, good will rise above all
evil. And that's exactly what has become of the
sheriff's office. Just ask most of the employees who
unfortunately have to work under such corrupt rules.
One of the main reasons I truly believe he will not turn
over the suicide files are because he is trying to protect
the investigator who made the report. I say this
because he is none other then the chief deputy's son.
There is alot of nebotism going on at the sheriff's
department, and until someone takes a stand against
them, I unfortunately see no end in sight. I will add
that I pray for Sheriff Kent Henson and all the
employees at the Sheriff's Office daily because we all
know they need it. God bless.

– Donald from Diboll

Thursday, May 11 2000 at 12:36 PM

Subject: To Miss Educated
Apparently you are not that smart or you would know
that this is about Corey and NOT his mother, or Joe,
they did their job. So if you have anything else to say
you might want to leave your name.

– Darel from Huntington

Thursday, May 11 2000 at 11:52 AM

Subject: Knowledge vs. Stupidity
I personally know Mrs. Brunner, Sheriff Kent Hanson,
ALL of the Angelina County Sheriff's Department
Investigators and Deputies, Private Eye Joe Hendricks
and knew Mrs. Brunner's son, Corey. Mrs. Brunner, I
should tell you now that I agree with one of the other
Angelina County residents that commented on this
article earlier. You will probably regret ever going
public with your story. The reason you are making such
an issue over this is to prove to yourself and others
that you are attempting to be a " concerned Mother".
How concerned for Corey were you all the nights you
never came and for days he nor his sister knew of your
whereabouts, due to bouts of alcoholism and drug
abuse? Your mother even stated in the article that
Corey expressed to her that he wanted to take care of
his grandparents as they took care of him as a child.
Mrs. Brunner you could be an object for "show and tell"
in the Psychology class at college. Give it up while you
are ahead. Private Eye Joe Hendricks, the only reason
you are making those comments in favor of Mrs.
Brunner is because she is probably your only source of
income right now and you would most certainly hate to
mess that up. I can't imagine YOU wanting to compete
with the wisdom and knowledge of ANY of our local law
enforcement entities. Remember Joe, you were once
employed by one of them. As for Sheriff Henson and
this team of Investigators and Deputies, I think you are
all doing a fine job. I don't think any other department
anywhere in this great State of Texas would have came
up with a different finding. People in the Bible were
never tormented by Satan as long as they were living
in sin, but when they came out of sin and began living
for God, that is when their troubles began. ACSO staff,
put yourself in those Biblical folks shoes. When you do

Love all of you.

– Educated Citizen from Huntington, Texas

Thursday, May 11 2000 at 11:38 AM

Subject: My dad is not corrupt!
To Corey's sister, I never said one negative word
toward your brother. I do know that my father would
give your mother those files if she really wanted them.
As for mr. henry we'll see who will be the first to help
you when you have a problem.

– Ashley from lufkin

Thursday, May 11 2000 at 10:39 AM

Subject: From a sisters point of view
First off Ashley if your father is not showing the files
because he is keeping the family from risk,then you are
stupid,because if this was a suicide then I don't think
we have anything to worry about, because the person
killing, is dead so, your concern for my family is nothing
but bluff. As for your father and all those involved can
kiss my foot, they did not do their job, and did not
want to do their job. They came in here with two other
people here, when Corey was found,and they weren't
even investigated, so do not tell me your father did his
job, . As for Long Duck Dong you have shown that you
are exatley like your name a big Dong. Apparently you
never knew my brother or you would know that he was
never picked up for drugs, so from me to you KISS MY
FOOT and since you are kissing Foot kiss COREY'S
because you are disrespecting him after he is gone. I
loved my brother very much and I feel neither one of
you knew him,so shut your mouths.

– Darci from Huntington

Thursday, May 11 2000 at 09:35 AM

Subject: Cory Wood
Ashley, In 1983 I was hired by then Sheriff Sammy
Leach as a Angelina County deputy sheriff. My training
officer was none other than your father, Kent Henson.
Seventeen years later, Kent is still my friend, and
though we disagree on this issue I have not lost any of
the respect I have for him. Kant and I have spoken
about this matter, we just havent reached agreement.
Nothing I say or do is meant to be insulting or
disrespectful of Sheriff Henson. As for my opinion, the
family should be allowed to see the report. As far as
the accusation by "Long Duck Dong" of Cory having
been arrested for drug offenses, I challenge you to
show me the evidence of those arrests....I checked
police records and did not find one single arrest for a
drug offense, I dont think you know much about Cory
at all!!

– Joe Hendricks from Lufkin, Texas
jhendricks@hendricksinvestigat
www.hendricksinvestigation.com

Thursday, May 11 2000 at 09:18 AM

Subject: What is the big deal?
He should give the poor family the records! Haven't
they been put through enough? If it was an actual
suicide, then let them see the report! Give them some
well needed rest. They have to mourn for their son. If
they read the report, that should give them the peace
of mind that they need to get started with the mourn
for their son! What kind of a person will put people who
have lost a child through additional pain???

– Cynthia Salazar from Seguin/Tx
CIN71@webtv.net

Thursday, May 11 2000 at 08:17 AM

Subject: What is the big deal?
He should give the poor family the records! Haven't
they been put through enough? If it was an actual
suicide, then let them see the report! Give them some
well needed rest. They have to mourn for their son. If
they read the report, that should give them the peace
of mind that they need to get started with the mourn
for their son! What kind of a person will put people who
have lost a child through additional pain???

– Cynthia Salazar from Seguin/Tx
CIN71@webtv.net

Wednesday, May 10 2000 at 09:54 PM

Subject: opinions
I would like to make a brief comment on the suicide
ruling. I personally believe that Mr. Kent Henson is as
corrupt as they come. Not only is his entire department
in shambles, but he has to hide behind laws to keep
from exposing himself and other officers, whom I
personally feel have no business wearing a badge or
carrying a gun, out of the line of fire. One day, all the
people of Angelina County will understand exactly what
I mean. And I pray everyday that someone with
administrative skills and dignity and descent christian
morals will run against Kent Henson, because when
that glorious day finally arrives, I will do all I can to see
that man elected. In the mean time, Mrs. Brunner, do
not give up. Fight everyday with all you have until you
win! Do not let Kent Henson beat you or your son. May
he rest in peace.

-- henry from huntington

Wednesday, May 10 2000 at 09:34 PM

Subject: Who's going to suffer?
Mrs. Brunner, You are probably going to wish you
would have never started this on the Internet, and I do
not mean that as a threat or anything. Mr. Henson is
not the one is going to suffer from this. You and your
family will though because the truth and lies about your
son and his death are going to hurt the most. Instead
of bringing up the bad memories, let him rest in peace.
If it was not a suicide, then be happy that he is in a
better place than he would have ever been here on this
earth.

-- Juliet from Lufkin

Wednesday, May 10 2000 at 08:35 PM

Subject: My Opinion!
So, far the investigation rules it was a SUICIDE. My dad
has never refused to to help ANYONE, and the people
of Angelina County know that! Who knows, maybe the
reason my dad is keeping the files, is because he does
not want information to get out because it will put the
family at risk. I do not know where you are from Mr.
Hendricks, but here in East Texas, the law enforcement
does not hide things. Maybe they do where you are
from but not here. If you are calling my father a lazy,

JOY BRUNNER

Wednesday, May 10 2000 at 06:13 PM

Subject: In it for the INSURANCE MONEY!
Exactly who does Mrs. Brunner think she is. Let's tell
the whole story if we are going to tell one- why don't
we Mr. Henson is not withholding those records
because he is mean -he is doing his job. If you wanted
him to arrest the child molestor next door you would
want him to follow the books to a "t" to make sure that
that child molestor stayed in jail. It seems when law
enforcers have to their job we turn our backs on them.
I live in the Huntington area and maybe Mrs. Brunner
does not WANT to know the truth. With all due respect,
I know her son was arrested several times for drug
abuse and other offenses. I think Mrs. Brunner should
sweep her own door step. Mr. Henson is a good
christian man. He is undeserving of any ill comments
that have been made about him. He has done an
excellent job running that Sheriff's Department and I
dare Mrs. Brunner to do in a week what he does in one
day. This is absolutely ridiculous- I mean no one even
opposed the man for re-election. That must say
someting!!! If anything I have said offends Mrs.
Brunner or her family .....think of Mr. Henson and his
family.

– Long Duck Dong from Lufkin

Wednesday, May 10 2000 at 03:25 PM

Subject: Smalltown Cops
Are inherently lazy. If they could get away with a lame
explanation of "act of God", they'd not only use it,
they'd have it as a check box on the autopsy report.
You betcher sweet ass that if ol' Henson had turned up
dead like that, they'd have every expert pulled in from
across the country to analyze the evidence.

– Homer S. from Springfield

Wednesday, May 10 2000 at 02:37 PM

Subject: what to do
i would give it to her cause she needs that evidence

– ? from ?
?
?

Wednesday, May 10 2000 at 04:10 AM

Subject: suicide investigation
Having had a nephew who committed suicide several
years back, I can certainly understand the parent's
need to know exactly what the circumstances were
surrounding their son's death. Oftentimes even an
autopsy report is released, and can answer some of the
questions. I don't think the open records act should
restrict access to a parent when an investigation is
done on a suicide. Even with the open records act, if a
person is investigated, found guilty as charged, they
should still be able to obtain a copy of the record. After
all—just because a law enforcement agency
investigates an incident, doesn't always mean, they
have all the facts collected. They are human and do
and can make mistakes as well. Give the lady the
records sheriff henson...don't be obstinate because of a
legal restraint or your position in law enforcement.

– jim walker from palestine, texas
lbgally@yahoo.com

Tuesday, May 09 2000 at 06:35 PM

Subject: RE: Sheriff Kent Henson
Let's try putting the shoe on the other foot. Would you
just stand back and accept what was being said or
would you be fighting to see the records. I personally
think that Joy Brunner should get what she is asking
for. I sure do hope that legislature gets changed. I
can't believe you just don't want to do the paperwork.
Maybe you should be out of that job!!! How cruel can
one be.

– Veronica from Altus

Tuesday, May 09 2000 at 06:00 PM

Subject: suicide -v- accident
Please I need some help and really don't know where
to go from here. I lost my oldest son on 8-14-99. I
need some help with the Medical Examiner-Dr.Tommy
Brown and the Justice of the Peace-Burl Thomas.
Mr.Brown has ruled his accident as a suicide. I have no
doubt that this is not what happened. The detective
and the ranger on duty that night has told us that it
was an accident but that they had to wait for the
Medical Examiner's ruling. No one knows there own
children like a mother knows them. His friends were
giving him a going away party (he was leaving for San

nothing about(he was raised hunting) at this party. Richard went to the gun and everyone told him to unload it. Richard unloaded the gun and then dried fired it. After a few minutes, Richard was laying in the middle of the bed with a couple on his left (this couple was playing a game on a laptop) and there was this guy sitting to his right (they were talking). Richard was just playing with the trigger and the gun went off. They said that he was talking earlier about shooting himself (this is where I know my son, he has ALWAYS had to be Mr.Tough Guy) Richard thought that the gun was EMPTY. I need someone to please help and work with me on this. I swear that he did not take his own life. PLEASE I AM BEGGING FOR SOMEONE TO HELP ME. Please don't just throw this in the trash. I am not a very intelligent person and just don't know where to go from here. I won't give up on this. I know my son better than anyone else in this world. This just another small town, scratching each other's back's not caring about their people's feelings.

– **Theresa Broussard** from Cleveland, Texas 77327
r-taylor@txucom.net

Tuesday, May 09 2000 at 12:26 PM
Subject: RE: Sheriff Henson
I'm from Huntington. Heaven help you if you've gotten a speeding ticket in Huntington, because if you don't go to jail, you're bound to have to pay the ticket twice -- once to clear the ticket, and a second time because they'll lose the record of your having paid and then claim you forged the receipt if you show that as evidence. Thankfully, my scholarship to UT came through, because I'm kissing this @s#!hole and its corrupt sheriff goodbye!

– **Kelly (Withheld)** from Huntington
(Withheld: Henson surfsi)

Tuesday, May 09 2000 at 12:20 PM
Subject: Bull@S#!!
Yet another small town Nazi sheriff trying to cover up his own tracks. The bastard or one of his Gestapo Barney Fifes was probably in on the scam, and probably pulled the trigger himself! The sooner these small towns are absorbed by larger cities, the sooner we can put these Nazi bastards in their place - either in jail where they can get buggered by rapists, or six foot under where they can share the worm dirt with the people they murdered!

– Gestapo Non Grata from Wemberly

Tuesday, May 09 2000 at 11:50 AM

Subject: family rights
I hope that our legislature does change this law. I feel
it is the family's right to view the police dept.'s records.

– pwilliams from Marquez
pwilliams@esc6.net

⊕ back to previous

✉ e-mail this story to a friend

© 2000 The News of Texas

CHAPTER 8

~

Randy and Stephanie Wilson, Brian Wilson's father and Corey's best friends, Heath Talbert's mother, they both are very involved in the theft of money missing and Stephanie signed a certified check from an insurance fraud that was discovered years into our investigation of Corey's death. She signed the check as Corey's mother, me. This is a small community that we are a part of, my cousin was my mail carrier and Stephanie's mail carrier mentioned that he had met Corey Wood's mother she signed a certified check. She got that money, and it was on its way or in the works at the time of Corey's death.

Texas state insurance fraud division found this insurance fraud and come to find out it was from the president of the bank's insurance company in town.

This story is about the injustice of Corey's death and how it was handled and the players that conspired to murder and cover up said Murder...

Corey and Heath Talbert.
Heath was pulling into his mother's drive way the morning of Corey's
murder. She told me he was called but was already on the road out of
town. Which was a lie. Heath's mother signed my name and pretended
to be me to receive the insurance fraud check. Stephanie talbert Wilson.

I am not sure I am ready to write this story; I have rage that is so deep, will I be able to move on from here? I must give God the glory and point out how God defeated the devil in this spiritual warfare. Vengeance is mine sayth the Lord our God...I do not know how to quote scripture, but I do recognize God's word, work, and plan. Plan is in hindsight, plain as day and always worth praise...

Around the time Stephanie Wilson Talbert forged an insurance fraud check using my identity, my mother was given Corey's banking information. Randy Wilson had been taking care of paying his bills prior to his death, Corey had come to me in 1998, it was around Christmas, I remember because he had taken me to the best department store in Lufkin and bought me my Christmas present.

Lots of fun I picked out a valure suit, not much. He was sitting on my couch and said he thought these people were stealing his money. I did not ask how much, just that money was not worth killing these people over, get your money away from them in short get away from them in general, ever met some people that you feel like you have to wipe off, when you leave them. He said ok. I told him to give his money to my day, really, he wanted me to take over his money, I was not very good still not, with my own and did not want to get his messed us plus I was managing two businesses and a personal account, my regret is that I did not put my boy's in the truck and confront this family.

I did call Stephanie, I kept her on the phone for over an hour, you would have thought the dumb bitch would have caught the drift that I would watch her die, as it turns out, and if it goes like it has, she will meet the lord on one of our birthday's, she didn't or she was to far into their scam she could not back out, at the time of the phone call I thought I would kill someone that messed or killed one of my kids, i believed that, and now have a real hard time letting these People live. God has taken many of them on our birthdays. That is a whole another journey.

HUNTINGTON STATE BANK
Member FDIC

April 29, 2002

John P. Misiewicz
Acting Regional Director
FDIC
1910 Pacific Avenue, 20th floor
Dallas, TX 75201

RE: 2000 Complaint from Joy Brunner

Dear Mr. Misiewicz

You have requested the bank provide FDIC with the bank's position regarding a missing ATM tape Ms. Brunner refers to in her letter and also to alleged unauthorized debits made from Mr. Wood's account during September 1999.

The bank's procedure for the video surveillance is a to place the tape in a rotation with 16 tapes before they are reused. The tapes are locked in the vault and the keys are under the control of the Information Systems Officer. When there is a request for a tape, the tape is then taken out of rotation. The Information Systems Officer said no one asked him to locate the tape and review it for September 27, 1999. No tapes in 1999 were reported as missing.

There were 3 ATM transactions totaling $140.00 withdrawn from Cory Woods account on Sept 27, 1999, the day before his death. The ATM requires the customer to enter his personal identification number (PIN) before a withdrawal of funds can be made from his account. A review of his September 1999 statement, did not find any unauthorized transactions. There were no transactions on the account following the death of Cory Woods on September 28, 1999.

Enclosed is a copy of Cory Wood's statement and withdrawals for September 1999.

I hope that this information will be useful to you in resolving any remaining issues concerning Cory Woods account with Huntington State Bank. If I can be of further service, please call me (936 633-5103).

Sincerely,

Janey Longacre
Internal Auditor

Enclosure

HUNTINGTON STATE BANK
MEMBER FDIC

HUNTINGTON	LUFKIN	ETOILE	ZAVALLA	CENTRAL
P.O. BOX 1090 • 208 HIGHWAY 69 SOUTH	2120 SOUTH FIRST ST.	HIGHWAY 103 EAST	250 MAIN ST.	3592 NORTH US HWY 69
HUNTINGTON, TEXAS 75949	LUFKIN, TEXAS 75901	ETOILE, TEXAS 75944	ZAVALLA, TEXAS 75980	LUFKIN, TEXAS 75904
(409) 639-5566	(409) 639-5566	(409) 639-5566	(409) 897-9023	(409) 639-5566

ABA 113123667

```
              COREY WOOD
              RT 4 BOX 7020            STATEMENT PERIOD
      3       HUNTINGTON TX 75949      LAST      ENDING
                                       9/26/99   10/28/99

                                          PAGE    1

                                       SS# 451 61 3497
```

```
        ACCOUNT     PREVIOUS  --- CREDITS --- --- DEBITS ---  TOTAL    PRESENT
        NUMBER      BALANCE   COUNT   AMOUNT COUNT   AMOUNT    FEE      BALANCE
     DDA 102250470  1177.88                     7    1177.88          *CLOSED ACCT*

        CHECK      DATE    AMOUNT   CHECK     DATE   AMOUNT DATE       BALANCE
        NUMBER                      NUMBER
                                    TRANSACTIONS
     CHECKING       102250470

                                       DAYS IN THIS CYCLE       32

     ********* CHECKS **********
              9/27      60.00 MDB                            9/27      973.99
     208 HWY 69              HUNTINGTON  TX
              9/27      60.00 MDB                            9/28      966.76
     208 HWY 69              HUNTINGTON  TX
              9/27      20.00 MDB                            10/15       0.00
     208 HWY 69              HUNTINGTON  TX
              9/27      13.89 MDB
     2215 SOUTH FIRST STUS     LUFKIN   TX
              9/27      50.00 CCK      10/15   966.76 CLO
        590* 9/28       7.23 CK

     ********* DEPOSITS **********
```

HUNTINGTON STATE BANK

MEMBER FDIC

HUNTINGTON	LUFKIN	ETOILE	ZAVALLA	CENTRAL
P.O. BOX 1090 • 300 HIGHWAY 69 SOUTH	2120 SOUTH FIRST ST	HIGHWAY 103 EAST	250 MAIN ST	3592 NORTH US HWY 69
HUNTINGTON, TEXAS 75949	LUFKIN, TEXAS 75901	ETOILE, TEXAS 75944	ZAVALLA, TEXAS 75980	LUFKIN, TEXAS 75904
(409) 829-5566	(409) 639-5566	(409) 639-5580	(409) 897-8023	(409) 639-5566

ABA 113123667

```
              COREY WOOD                    STATEMENT PERIOD
              RT 4 BOX 7020                 LAST      ENDING
       12     HUNTINGTON TX 75949           8/24/99   9/26/99

                                            PAGE    1

                                            SS# 451 61 3497
```

ACCOUNT NUMBER	PREVIOUS BALANCE	--- CREDITS --- COUNT	AMOUNT	--- DEBITS --- COUNT	AMOUNT	TOTAL FEE	PRESENT BALANCE
DDA 102250470	3727.42	2	1979.67	43	4529.21	7.00	1177.88

CHECK NUMBER	DATE	AMOUNT	TRANSACTIONS CHECK NUMBER	DATE	AMOUNT	DATE	BALANCE
CHECKING		102250470					

DAYS IN THIS CYCLE   33

********** CHECKS **********

	DATE	AMOUNT		DATE	BALANCE
TRAN FEE	8/26	1.15 DM		8/26	3359.89
TRAN FEE	8/26	1.15 DM		9/02	2959.89
TRAN FEE	8/26	1.15 DM		9/07	3906.09
TRAN FEE	8/26	1.15 DM		9/08	2706.09
TRAN FEE	8/26	1.15 DM		9/09	2239.09
TRAN FEE	8/26	1.15 DM		9/10	1639.09
TRAN FEE	8/26	1.15 DM		9/16	1537.09
TRAN FEE	8/26	1.15 DM		9/17	1337.09
336 OFICINA CEN	8/26	108.58 MDB VERACRUZ, MEX		9/20	837.09
BANAMEX	8/26	108.58 MDB MEX		9/21	1429.43
BANAMEX	8/26	54.29 MDB MEX		9/22	1327.03
336 OFICINA CEN	8/26	21.72 MDB VERACRUZ, MEX		9/23	1184.88
336 OFICINA CEN	8/26	21.72 MDB VERACRUZ, MEX		9/26	1177.88
BANAMEX	8/26	21.72 MDB MEX			
BANAMEX	8/26	10.86 MDB MEX			
BANAMEX	8/26	10.86 MDB MEX			
MULTIBANCO COMERMEX	9/07	21.67 MDB BCO INVERLAT			
TRAN FEE	9/07	1.15 DM			
	9/07	1.15 DM			

PLEASE SEE NEXT PAGE

241

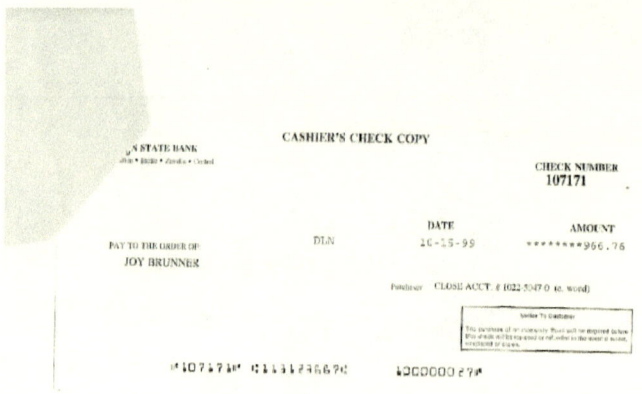

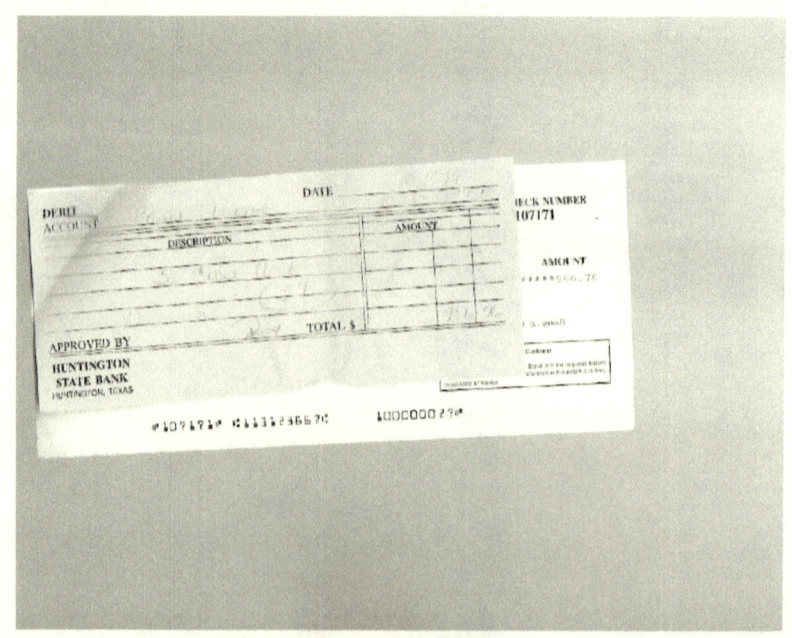

CHAPTER 9

Stephanie Talbert Wilson: mother of Heath Talbert, stepmother to Brian Wilson, wife of Randy Wilson.

Randy Wilson: dad to Brian Wilson, husband to Stephanie Wilson, con man

Brian Wilson: son of Randy Wilson, Corey's roommate, total fuck-up, dark, mean to animals and women

Heath Talbert: Corey's best friend in school, son of Stephanie Wilson

Jeremy Holder: school friend, roommate

Melinda Boles: Brian Wilson girlfriend, down at Corey's house with roommates at the time of Corey's death, called people and told them not to come to, whatever party they had planned, they had a dead body in the house.

Jana Clark: Jeremy Holder's girlfriend, now wife, she received a phone call that Brian had shot Corey some time that morning early, right after Corey was shot, Jeremy called her.

Brian Reeves: boyfriend of Jana's friend, was with at his house in Lufkin, when call came into Jana, he is the reason I know about the phone call, he says he was told not to go to Corey's house with the girls because Brian was going crazy.

John Havard: became friends with Corey in high school, had reason to lie about Corey and I fighting that night he was listening to the whole conversation and why he told that Corey and I were fighting is still a mystery. He was back on the scene sometime that morning.

Shanoha Havard: John Havard sister, passed Corey's house and must have stopped, she told someone at the memorial hospital, where she worked, one of the 911 calls came from a hospital phone, or one on the road side assistance. She was hysterical when she arrived at work, she talked to a man that relayed this to one of my friends, two months later he killed his wife, and nearly got away with it too. Wow just remembered that, anyway the girl was upset, and when i questioned her, she just agreed with all I said, I ask her to go to district att. She said she went, he Clyde Harrington district attorney for Angelina county, had to step down, crooked official, she is on the run sheet for 911, when I questioned or brought this to the sheriff office attention, I was told she was the dispatcher. More crooks.

This is the phone call from hospital by s.havard the phone was from an emergency phone on the wall of the hospital they are like the emergency phone in call box on highway. Called an verification from phone company.

My mother got the paperwork for Corey's affairs and discovered the checks that were written out of his account, signed by Randy Wilson, so we requested from the bank Corey's account information and the total summary from the time he opened the account. Randy Wilson had stopped writing checks, and someone started withdrawing money out of atm's all over town. Some when Corey was out to sea. The night of his death he withdrew money we requested tape, they have the day before the withdrawal, and the day after, imagine that someone withdrew that money, over 100 dollars, he only had little more than 20 when found.

At this time, I was receiving a preliminary autopsy, from Dr. Randal Bruce, pathologist, another piece of shit no good mother fucker, that did not do his job and was paid for doing it. I worked with his wife's cousin, he told me not to ever be alone with this puke because he would stick me, and that he was a devil worshiper, my mother ask if he would testify to that in a court of law, lol he said he would.

The autopsy was a joke, I found out later it is nothing, I did call the other path in town and get a second opinion, Dr. Gongolas, Corey was more than likely murdered, and for me not to let them close this case, he stated he would not write a letter confirming this but would talk to the judge and ask me to ask him to call him, and I did in court, and at the inquest, he also stated he would not have anything to do with any of them, now I know who they are, Angelina County Crooks in office. So, I called and his nurse when through the autopsy line by line with me, of course, we now know it was a bunch of made-up shit...?

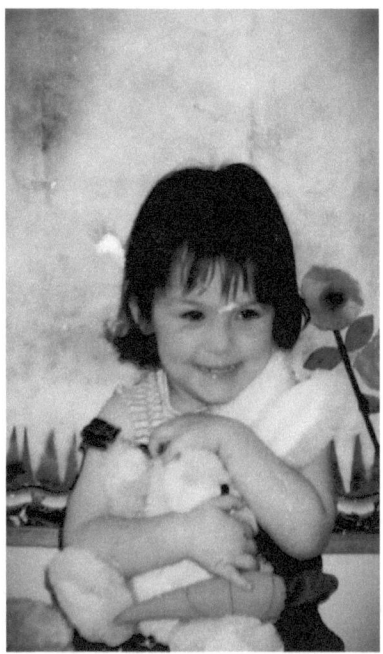

Bailey
Grandbaby that was murdered

My grand baby has also been murdered, Vincent Smith, a key player in Corey's death, well behind the scenes kind of deal with Vinnie, but he was at both Corey's and Bailey's death scene the night before their deaths.

Vincent Smith and wife, Tiffany Smith

My house has also been bombed.

I did not know what to do, knew that things were not adding up, and the questions I was asking were getting answers off the top of these so-called professional men. I have been lied to so much I can tell by the tone of their voice, it is sickening.

STATE FIRE MARSHAL'S OFFICE
INVESTIGATION REPORT
TEXAS DEPARTMENT OF INSURANCE
SENSITIVE

Case #	06-192-12		Priority	3		Investigator	Kyle Morris				Status	Closed
Day of Fire	Wednesday		Date of Fire	12/28/05		Time of Fire	3:30pm		Cause of Fire			Incendiary
Date of Request	12/29/05			Date Case Assigned		12/29/05			Date of Investigation			12/29/05
City of Fire	Huntington					County of Fire		Angelina				
Location of Fire	1379 Walker Road											
Type of Fire Investigation		Residential				Injuries	No	#		Deaths	No	#

OWNER

Full Name	William Earl Lucky						Phone #	936-635-3755
Address	997 Thigpen Road, Pollock, Texas							
Race	White	Other		Sex	Male	Age	46	Date of Birth
Social Security #						Driver's License #		
Insurance	No	Insurance Company Name						
Policy #								
Amount of Policy:	Structure$				Effective Dates		To	
					Contents $			
Adjusters Name					Adjusters Phone #			
Agents Name					Agents Phone #			
Agents Address								

OCCUPANT

Full Name	Roland Rutgrner						Phone #	936-465-1142
Address	1379 Walker Road, Huntington, Texas							
Race	White	Other		Sex	Male	Age	40	Date of Birth
Social Security #	- -					Driver's License #		
Insurance	No	Insurance Company Name						
Policy #								
Amount of Policy:	Structure$				Effective Dates		To	
					Contents $			
Adjusters Name					Adjusters Phone #			
Agents Name					Agents Phone #			
Agents Address								

☒ DISCOVERED ☒ REPORTED FIRE

Full Name	Jennifer Havard					Phone #	936-876-3585
Address	1420 Walker Rd., Huntington, Texas						
Race		Other		Sex		Age	Date of Birth
Social Security #	- -					Driver's License #	

REQUESTOR

Full Name	Jerry LaSalle					Phone #	936-676-6893
Address	Chief Huntington VFD						
Race	White	Other		Sex	Male	Age	Date of Birth
Social Security #	- -					Driver's License #	

MOTOR VEHICLE

Type of Vehicle		Year		Make		Model	
Vehicle Use		Color		V.I.N. #		L.P.#	

OTHER INFORMATION

Other Investigating Agencies	Angelin County SO		
Responding Fire Departments	Huntington VFD		
Weather Conditions		Wind Direction	To			Velocity	

ADMINISTRATIVE SECTION

Arson Lab Utilized		No	Smoke Detectors Present	Unknown		K-9 Utilized		No
Approved By						Date		

RM 2-13-06

Form REP1, Rev 8/2/04

State Fire Marshal's Office Investigation Report
(page 1)

STATE FIRE MARSHAL'S OFFICE
INVESTIGATION REPORT
TEXAS DEPARTMENT OF INSURANCE
SENSITIVE

Case # 06-192-12   Investigator :   Kyle Morris   2004 FEB -2 2:45 Date of Report: 1/30/05

Continuation: Initial Case Report Narrative

REQUEST AND ASSIGNMENT

On December 29, 2005 Fire Chief Jerry LaSalle with the Huntington Volunteer Fire Department contacted this agency and requested the State Fire Marshal's Office assistance with this investigation. I, Deputy State Fire Marshal Kyle Morris, was subsequently contacted by Supervisor Jay Evans and assigned to this case.

SYNOPSIS

On December 28, 2005 at approximately 3:30PM, a structure located at 1379 Walker Rd, Huntington, Texas was heavily damaged by fire. The structure was owned by William Earl Lucky and was unoccupied at the time of the fire, although the last renter still had items in the house. The Huntington Volunteer Fire Department responded to the scene. On December 29, 2005 I conducted a fire scene examination of the fire damaged property. The origin of this fire was determined to be in the area of bedroom #1 and the ignition source was determined to be **incendiary.**

WITNESS INTERVIEWS

The Angelina County Sheriff's Department is obtaining witness statements.

RIGHT OF ENTRY

On December 29, 2005 while speaking with the owner of the damaged property, William Lucky, I informed him that I needed him to sign a consent to search form so I could examine the fire scene. I then explained the State Fire Marshal's standard consent to search form to him and provided William Lucky with a copy of the form. After examining the form, William Lucky signed it and returned the form to me. (See Attached Form).

PROPERTY DESCRIPTION

The property involved in this fire is a one story single family dwelling. This structure was situated on a pier and beam foundation, faced north, measured 60 feet wide and 47 feet long. This structure contained approximately 2820 square feet of living space and contained personal belongings. The interior walls and ceiling coverings consisted of sheetrock. This structure consisted of four bedrooms, one kitchen, one livening room, one dining room, one bathroom and one storage room. The floor coverings consisted of hard wood throughout the structure except for tile in the kitchen and bathrooms. The bedroom floor coverings were carpet. The exterior finish consisted of brick veneer

Page 2

Form REP2, rev 5/26/04

State Fire Marshal's Office Investigation Report

(page 2)

STATE FIRE MARSHAL'S OFFICE
INVESTIGATION REPORT
TEXAS DEPARTMENT OF INSURANCE
SENSITIVE

Case #	06-192-12	Investigator :	Kyle Morris	Date of Report:	1/30/05

Continuation: Initial Case Report Narrative

siding. This structure was equipped with electrical service which was not activated at the time of the fire. The electrical service entered the structure overhead at the west side of the residence.

FATALITY OR INJURY

There were no reported injuries or deaths as a result of this incident.

FIRE SCENE EXAMINATION

EXTERIOR

The exterior examination was initiated with a full 360-degree inspection of the structure. During the exterior examination of the structure, I observed the ceiling, rafter and the roof were completely burned away except for small sections located on the Northeast and Southeast corners of the structure. I also noticed all of the windows were missing; the reason is unknown. This could have been a result of fire suppression activities. I also noted the brick veneer exterior walls were still standing. As I proceeded to the south side of the structure I noted the attached room on the south side had received a lesser amount of fire damage than the rest of the structure.

INTERIOR

The interior examination began at the north exterior door of the structure, which led to the living room area. I observed heavy fire damage had consumed the interior stud walls in the west end of the structure. I also noticed the flooring, ceiling and roof had been consumed on the west end of the structure. As I proceeded in an easterly direction I observed the fire damage became less severe. I also noted the fire pattern was higher on the east end of the structure than on the west end. After inspecting the structure completely I return to the south west section. This area received the most severe fire damage and it also contained the lowest burn pattern in the structure. I removed and examined the fire debris in this area which was determined to be bedroom #1. I did not locate an ignition source which could have ignited this fire. Based on the burn patterns this area was determined to be the area of origin. I examined the electrical wiring and components in this structure and did not observe any evidence of an electrical failure. I also examined the water heater and did not observe any evidence of a failure.

Page 3

Form REP2, rev 5/26/04

State Fire Marshal's Office Investigation Report
(page 3)

STATE FIRE MARSHAL'S OFFICE
INVESTIGATION REPORT
TEXAS DEPARTMENT OF INSURANCE
SENSITIVE

Case # 06-192-12   Investigator :   Kyle Morris   Date of Report: 1/30/05

Continuation: Initial Case Report Narrative

CANINE EXAMINATION

A canine search was not conducted because a canine unit was not available.

EVIDENCE

Photographs were the only evidence removed from the scene by the State Fire Marshal's Office.

ORIGIN AND CAUSE SUMMARY

Based on the evidence described herein it is my professional opinion this fire originated in the south west side of bedroom #1. The exact cause of this fire was determined to be **incendiary**.

CASE STATUS

All leads have been exhausted at this time. The Angelina County Sheriff's Office is conducting follow-up investigation. I recommend this case be **closed** at this time.

Page 4

Form REP2, rev 5/26/04

State Fire Marshal's Office Investigation Report
(page 4)

HUNTINGTON STATE BANK
DATA CHANGE SHEET

Date: 12-14

Changed By: _____

Time: _____

Approved By: _____

Account Name: CORey Wood

Account Number: 10 2230470

Address Change: _____
_____
_____
_____

Field Code	Field Desc	From	To

Reason for Change: Need STAtements from 9-25-1996 to 12-96 ConTACT Person Soy wood. Give to Virginia · HunTington BRanch

Pineywoods Printing Form #070798

Account: 102250470
Check: 681
Amount: 00000138.75
Date cleared: 12/14/98

COREY WOOD 09-96   681
DL 13225597
PH 409-422-3408   88-2366/1131
RT 4 BOX 7020
HUNTINGTON, TX 75949   DATE 12-14-98

PAY TO THE
ORDER OF _____ $ 138 25/xx

One Hundred Thirty-Eight & 75/xx   DOLLARS

HUNTINGTON STATE BANK   ADVANTAGE ACCOUNT

PAID   Corey A Wood by
                        Randy Booth

FOR _____

⑈113123667⑈0681 102250470⑈ 00013875⑈

ENDORSE HERE

DO NOT SIGN / WRITE / STAMP BELOW THIS LINE
FOR FINANCIAL INSTITUTE USE ONLY

Account: 1022504 7
Check: 634
Amount: 00000250.00
Date cleared: 09/04/98

COREY WOOD 09-98   634
DL 13225597
PH 409-422-3408   88-2386/1131
RT 4 BOX 7020
HUNTINGTON, TX 75949   DATE 8-27-98

PAY TO THE
ORDER OF   Michael Thompson $ 250.00

Two Hundred Fifty Dollars   DOLLARS

HUNTINGTON STATE BANK   ADVANTAGE ACCOUNT

FOR Lawnmower Repair   Corey Wood by
                                              Randi

⑈113123667⑈ 0634 1022504 70⑈   00000 25000

PAY TO THE ORDER OF
LUFKIN NATIONAL
FOR DEPOSIT ONLY
ROSS MOTORSPORTS

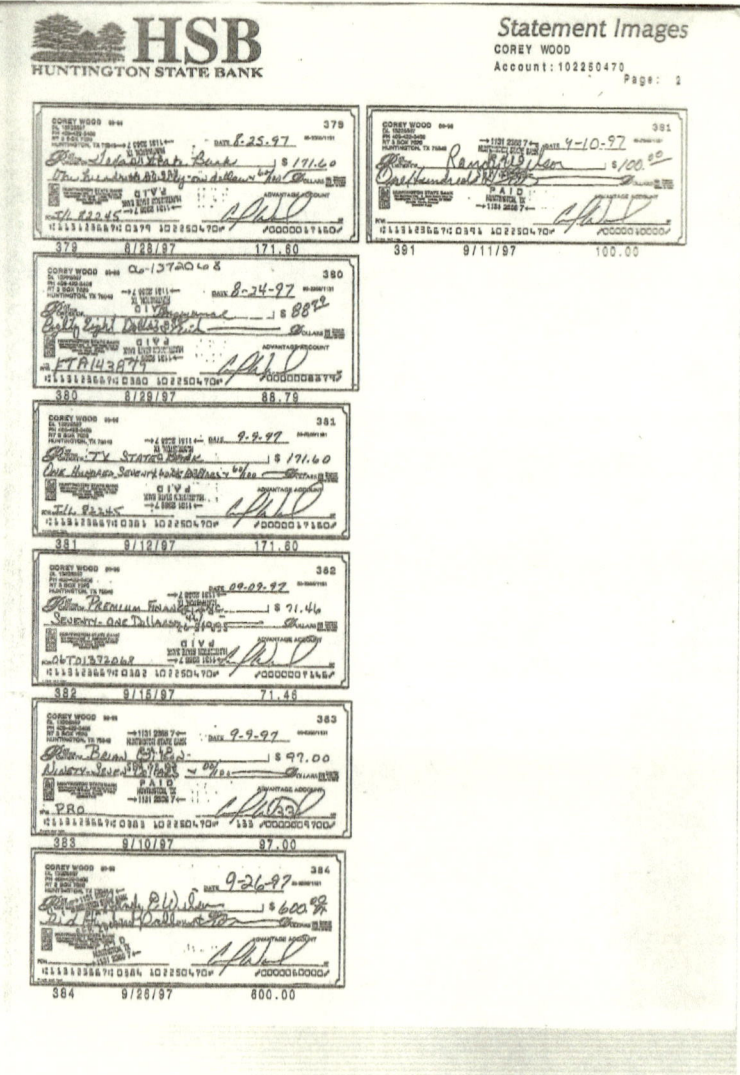

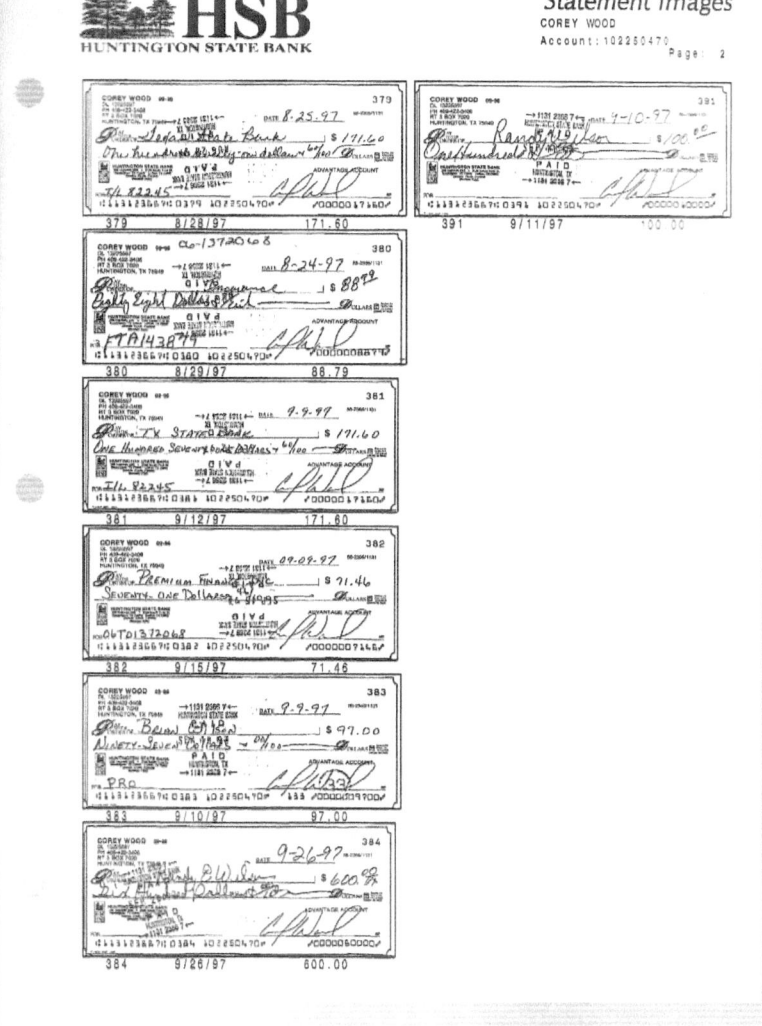

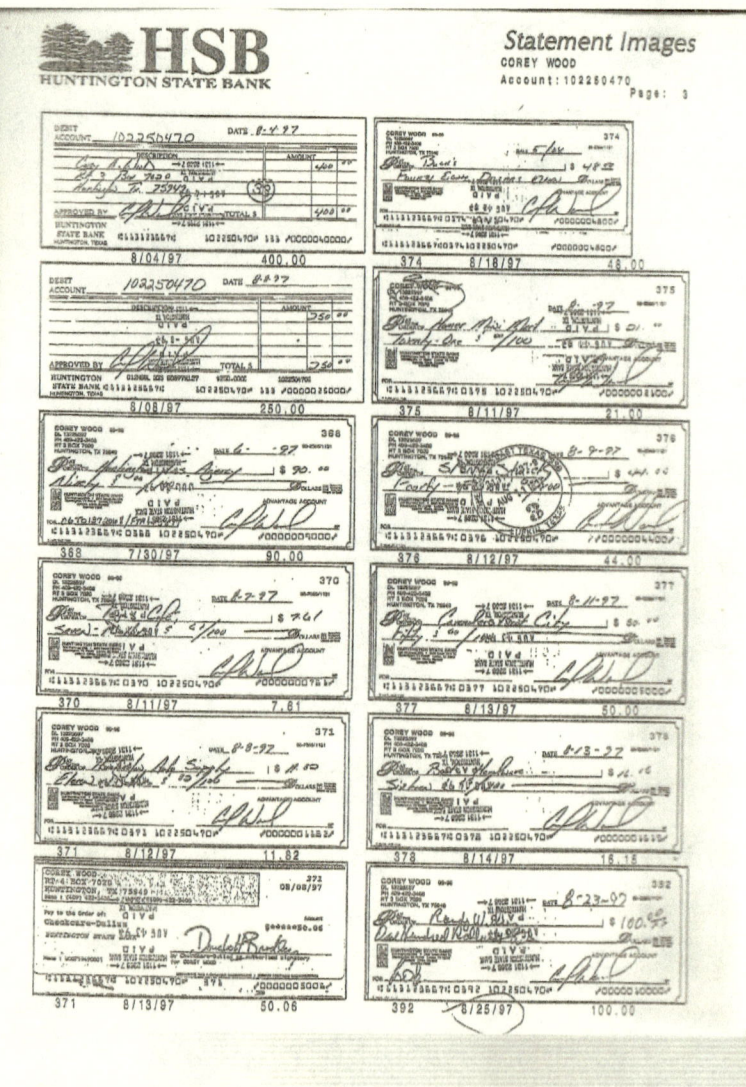

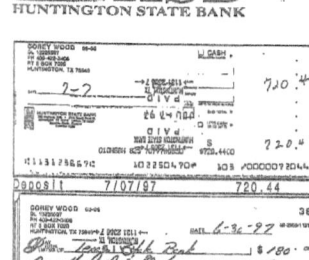

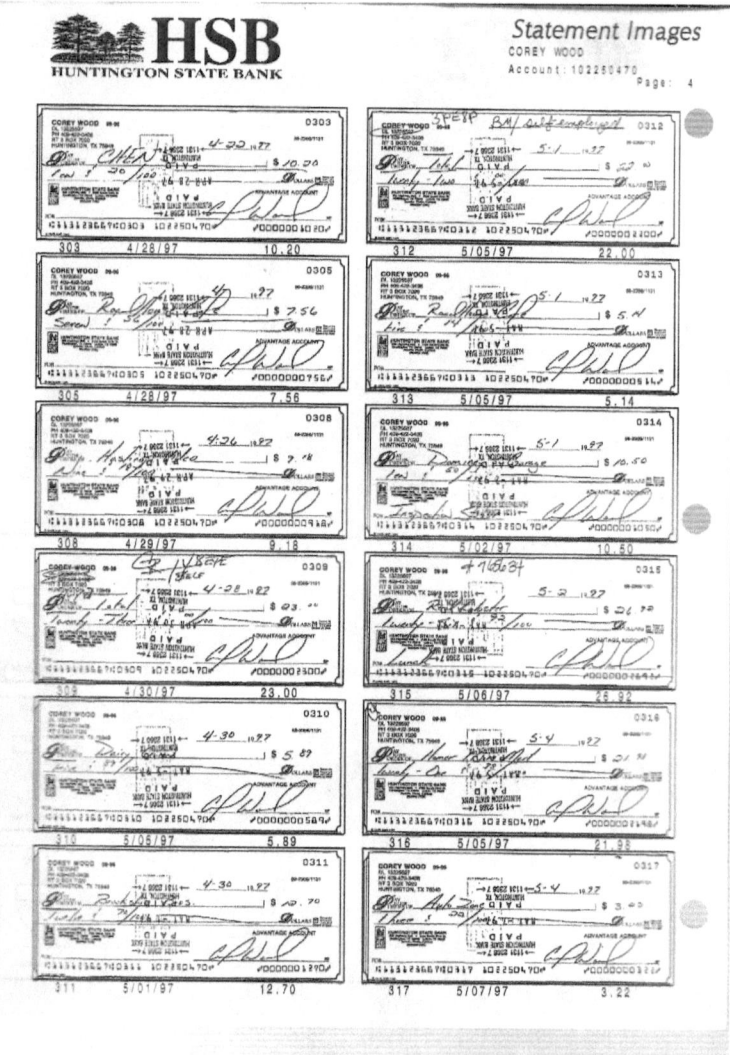

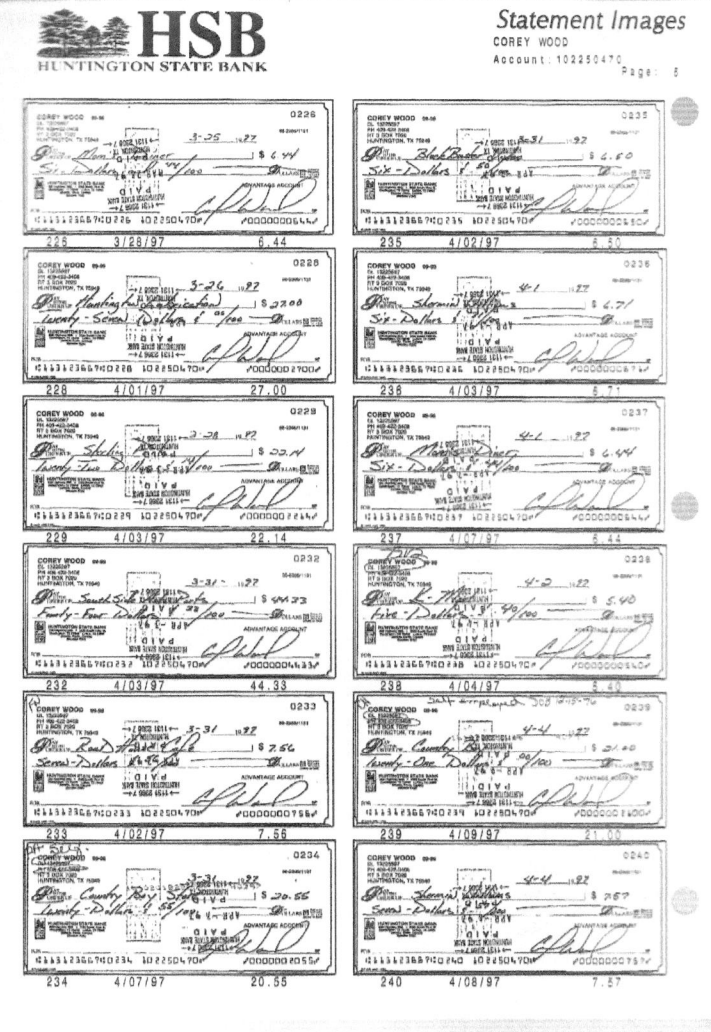

HSB
HUNTINGTON STATE BANK

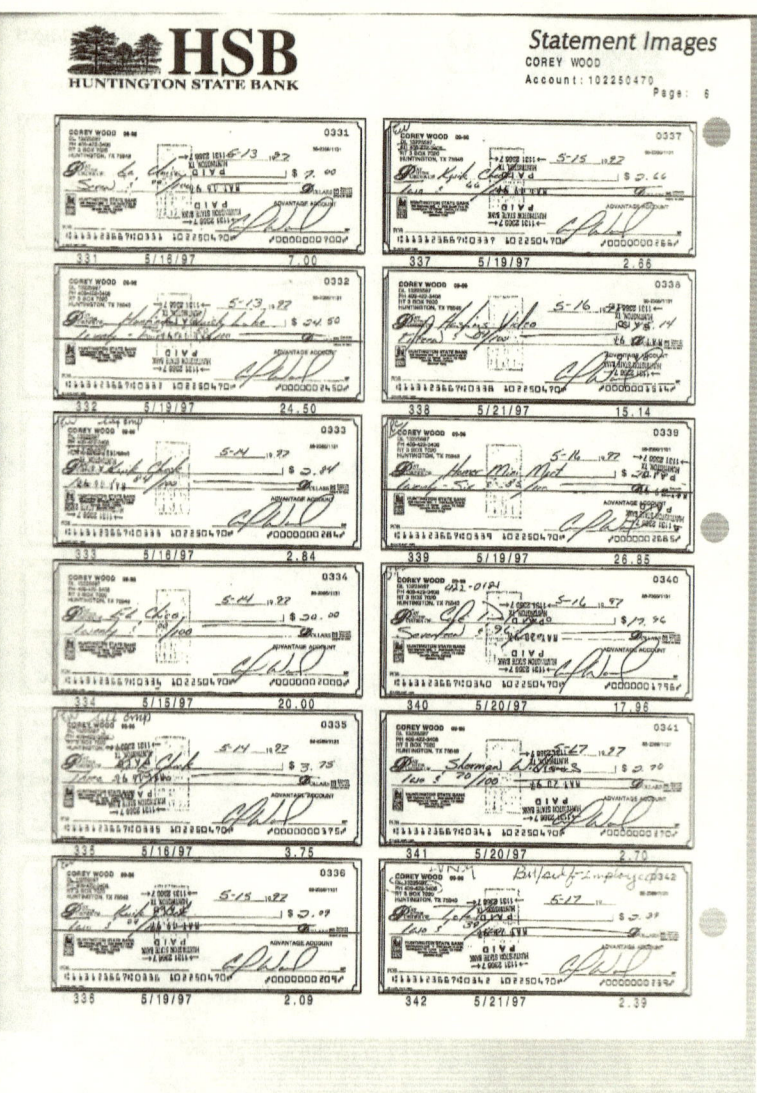

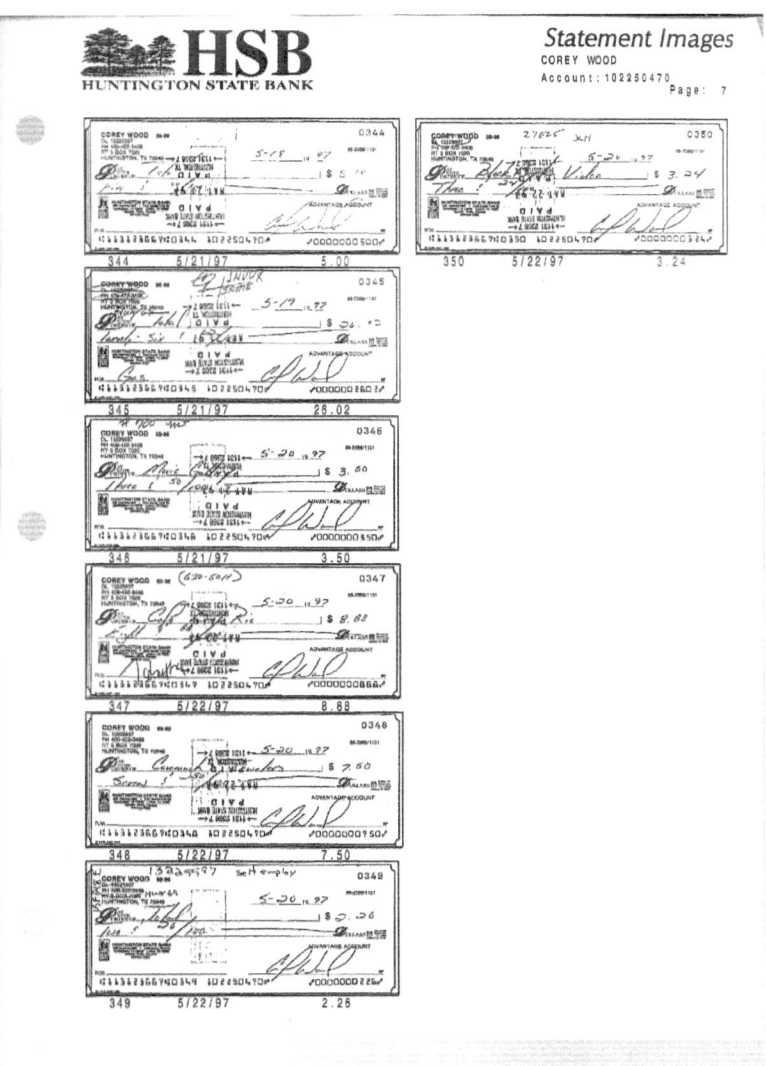

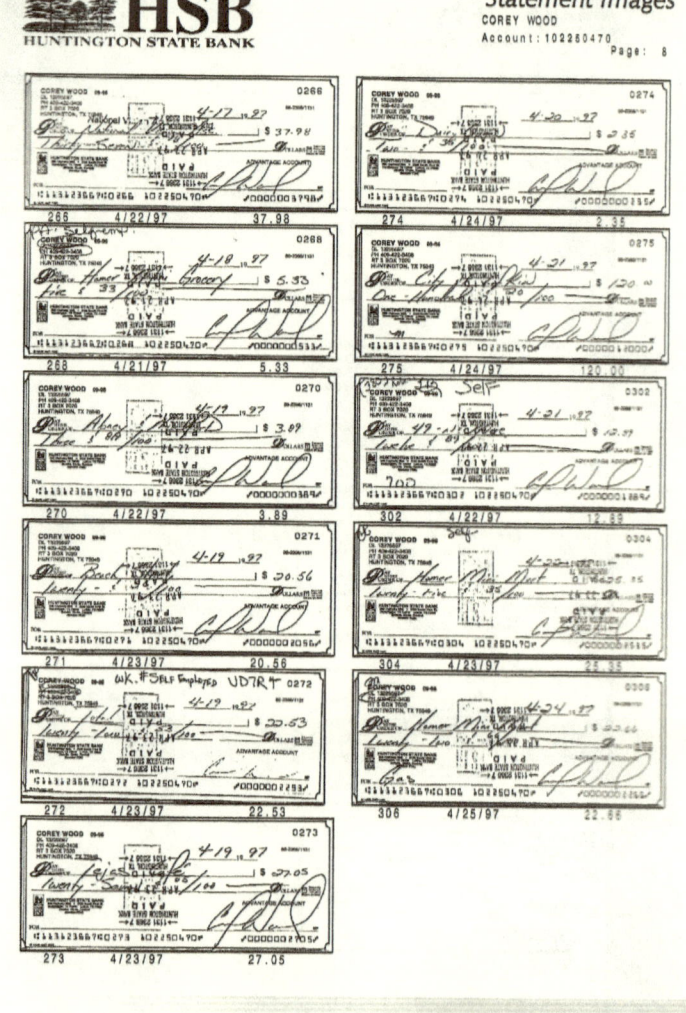

THE EMPTY GRAVE

HUNTINGTON STATE BANK
MEMBER FDIC

HUNTINGTON	LUFKIN	ETOILE	ZAVALLA	CENTRAL
P.O. BOX 1090 • 208 HIGHWAY 69 SOUTH	2120 SOUTH FIRST ST.	HIGHWAY 103 EAST	250 MAIN ST.	3582 NORTH US HWY 69
HUNTINGTON, TEXAS 75949	LUFKIN, TEXAS 75901	ETOILE, TEXAS 75944	ZAVALLA, TEXAS 75980	LUFKIN, TEXAS 75904
(409) 639-5560	(409) 639-5565	(409) 639-5566	(409) 897-9023	(409) 639-5556

ABA 113123667

```
        COREY WOOD                    STATEMENT PERIOD
        RT 3 BOX 7020                 LAST      ENDING
    2   HUNTINGTON TX 75949           3/26/98   4/27/98

                                      PAGE   1

                                      SS# 451 61 3497
```

ACCOUNT NUMBER	PREVIOUS BALANCE	--- CREDITS --- COUNT AMOUNT	--- DEBITS --- COUNT AMOUNT	TOTAL FEE	PRESENT BALANCE
DDA 102250470	843.31	2 2376.12	9 992.15	7.00	2227.28

CHECK NUMBER	DATE	AMOUNT	CHECK NUMBER	DATE	AMOUNT	DATE	BALANCE
CHECKING		102250470					

DAYS IN THIS CYCLE   32

```
********* CHECKS **********
        4/13        63.00 MDB                          3/31        543.31
142 CHARLIE HARDSN       GOLDEN MEADOW LA
        4/23        23.00 MDB                          4/07       1765.15
142 CHARLIE HARDSN       GOLDEN MEADOW LA
        4/27        23.00 MDB                          4/13       1702.15
142 CHARLIE HARDSN       GOLDEN MEADOW LA
        4/27         7.00 SC                           4/14       1202.15
MAINTENANCE FEE
        4/27         1.15 DM                           4/22       2356.43
TRAN FEE
        4/27        52.00 MDB                          4/23       2333.43
HIGHWAY 1                GRAND ISLE   LA
        4/27        23.00 MDB                          4/27       2227.28
142 CHARLIE HARDSN       GOLDEN MEADOW LA
   1009*  3/31     300.00 CCK    1010   4/14    500.00 CCK

********* DEPOSITS **********
        4/07      1221.84 DD
TIDEWATER MARINE PAYROLL
        4/22      1154.28 DD
TIDEWATER MARINE PAYROLL
```

265

HUNTINGTON STATE BANK
MEMBER FDIC

HUNTINGTON	LUFKIN	ETOILE	ZAVALLA	CENTRAL
P.O. BOX 1090 • 208 HIGHWAY 69 SOUTH	2120 SOUTH FIRST ST.	HIGHWAY 103 EAST	250 MAIN ST.	3582 NORTH US HWY 89
HUNTINGTON, TEXAS 75949	LUFKIN, TEXAS 75901	ETOILE, TEXAS 75944	ZAVALLA, TEXAS 75980	LUFKIN, TEXAS 75904
(409) 639-5566	(409) 639-5566	(409) 639-5566	(409) 897-9023	(409) 639-5566

ABA 113123667

```
                                                    STATEMENT PERIOD
        COREY WOOD                                  LAST      ENDING
        RT 3 BOX 7020                               3/26/98   4/27/98
   2    HUNTINGTON TX 75949
                                                    PAGE    1

                                                    SS# 451 61 3497
```

ACCOUNT NUMBER	PREVIOUS BALANCE	--- CREDITS --- COUNT AMOUNT	--- DEBITS --- COUNT AMOUNT	TOTAL FEE	PRESENT BALANCE
DDA 102250470	843.31	2 2376.12	9 992.15	7.00	2227.28

```
CHECK   DATE    AMOUNT   TRANSACTIONS      AMOUNT DATE          BALANCE
NUMBER                   CHECK    DATE
                         NUMBER
CHECKING        102250470
                              DAYS IN THIS CYCLE        32

********* CHECKS **********
          4/13    63.00 MDB                       3/31      543.31
142 CHARLIE HARDSN    GOLDEN MEADOWLA
          4/23    23.00 MDB                       4/07     1765.15
142 CHARLIE HARDSN    GOLDEN MEADOWLA
          4/27    23.00 MDB                       4/13     1702.15
142 CHARLIE HARDSN    GOLDEN MEADOWLA
          4/27     7.00 SC                        4/14     1202.15
MAINTENANCE FEE
          4/27     1.15 DM                        4/22     2356.43
TRAN FEE
          4/27    52.00 MDB                       4/23     2333.43
HIGHWAY 1             GRAND ISLE   LA
          4/27    23.00 MDB                       4/27     2227.28
142 CHARLIE HARDSN    GOLDEN MEADOWLA
     1009* 3/31  300.00 CCK    1010  4/14  500.00 CCK

********* DEPOSITS **********
          4/07  1221.84 DD
TIDEWATER MARINE PAYROLL
          4/22  1154.28 DD
TIDEWATER MARINE PAYROLL
```

HUNTINGTON STATE BANK
Member FDIC

ABA 113123667

COREY WOOD
RT 4 BOX 7020
HUNTINGTON TX 75949

STATEMENT PERIOD
LAST   ENDING
4/27/98   5/26/98

PAGE   2

SS# 451 61 3497

```
********************************TRANSACTIONS********************************
CHECK      DATE     AMOUNT      CHECK      DATE     AMOUNT   DATE          BALANCE
NUMBER                         NUMBER
*************************************************************************
CHECKING            102250470
           5/26      102.00 MDB
400 N TIMBERLAN              LUFKIN      TX
    150*   5/20     2000.00 CK       151  5/19    234.25 CK
   1006*   4/28      500.42 CK

        ******** DEPOSITS *********
           5/07     1074.97 DD
TIDEWATER MARINE PAYROLL
           5/15      749.09 DP
           5/22      917.78 DD
TIDEWATER MARINE PAYROLL
```

HUNTINGTON STATE BANK
MEMBER FDIC

HUNTINGTON	LUFKIN	ETOILE	ZAVALLA	CENTRAL
P.O. BOX 1090 • 208 HIGHWAY 69 SOUTH	2120 SOUTH FIRST ST.	HIGHWAY 103 EAST	250 MAIN ST.	3592 NORTH US HWY 69
HUNTINGTON, TEXAS 75949	LUFKIN, TEXAS 75901	ETOILE, TEXAS 75944	ZAVALLA, TEXAS 75890	LUFKIN, TEXAS 75904
(409) 639-5566	(409) 639-5586	(409) 639-5586	(409) 897-9023	(409) 639-5566

ABA 113123667

```
        COREY WOOD                    STATEMENT PERIOD
        RT 4 BOX 7020                 LAST        ENDING
   11   HUNTINGTON TX 75949           4/27/98     5/26/98

                                      PAGE    1

                                      SS# 451 61 3497
```

ACCOUNT NUMBER	PREVIOUS BALANCE	--- CREDITS --- COUNT	AMOUNT	COUNT	--- DEBITS --- AMOUNT	TOTAL FEE	PRESENT BALANCE
DDA 102250470	2227.28	3	2741.84	27	4188.22	7.00	780.90

CHECK NUMBER	DATE	AMOUNT	TRANSACTIONS CHECK NUMBER	DATE	AMOUNT	DATE	BALANCE
CHECKING		102250470					

DAYS IN THIS CYCLE   29

```
********** CHECKS **********

                4/28     250.00 CK              5/06     250.00 CK   4/28    1476.86
                5/13     101.50 MDB                                  5/06    1226.86
MANHATTEN                         HARVEY   LA
                5/13       1.15 DM                                   5/07    2301.83
TRAN FEE
                5/18      50.00 CK                                   5/13    2199.18
                5/18       1.15 DM                                   5/15    2948.27
TRAN FEE
                5/18      51.50 MDB                                  5/18    2775.22
RT 1 BOX 4705                     LUFKIN   TX
                5/18      50.00 MDB                                  5/19    2269.42
208 HWW 69, HUNTINGTON TX HUNTINGTON  TX
                5/18      20.40 MDB                                  5/20     167.27
400 N TIMBERLAN                   LUFKIN   TX
                5/19     100.00 CK                                   5/22    1033.55
                5/19       1.15 DM                                   5/26     780.90
TRAN FEE
                5/19      20.40 MDB
400 N TIMBERLAN                   LUFKIN   TX
                5/19     100.00 CCK              5/19      50.00 CCK
                5/20      50.00 CCK
                5/20      51.00 MDB
ANGELINA SVGS                     LUFKIN   TX
                5/20       1.15 DM
TRAN FEE
                5/22      51.50 MDB
RT 1 BOX 4705                     LUFKIN   TX
                5/26       7.00 SC
MAINTENANCE FEE
                5/26      41.35 MDB
JOC STOP #20                      LUFKIN   TX
                5/26     100.00 MDB
208 HWW 69, HUNTINGTON TX HUNTINGTON  TX
                5/26       1.15 DM
TRAN FEE
                5/26       1.15 DM
TRAN FEE
```

PLEASE SEE NEXT PAGE

HUNTINGTON STATE BANK
MEMBER FDIC

HUNTINGTON	LUFKIN	ETOILE	ZAVALLA	CENTRAL
P.O. BOX 1090 • 208 HIGHWAY 69 SOUTH	2120 SOUTH FIRST ST.	HIGHWAY 103 EAST	250 MAIN ST.	3592 NORTH US HWY 69
HUNTINGTON, TEXAS 75949	LUFKIN, TEXAS 75901	ETOILE, TEXAS 75944	ZAVALLA, TEXAS 75980	LUFKIN, TEXAS 75904
(409) 639-5566	(409) 639-5566	(409) 833-5566	(409) 897-9021	(409) 639-5566

ABA 113123667

```
          COREY WOOD                        STATEMENT PERIOD
          RT 4 BOX 7020                        LAST      ENDING
     5    HUNTINGTON TX 75949                 5/26/98    6/25/98

                                             PAGE    1

                                             SS# 451 61 3497
```

ACCOUNT NUMBER	PREVIOUS BALANCE	--- CREDITS --- COUNT	AMOUNT	--- DEBITS --- COUNT	AMOUNT	TOTAL FEE	PRESENT BALANCE
DDA 102250470	780.90	2	1551.52	12	740.63	7.00	1591.79

CHECK NUMBER	DATE	AMOUNT	TRANSACTIONS CHECK NUMBER	DATE	AMOUNT	DATE	BALANCE
CHECKING		102250470					

DAYS IN THIS CYCLE   30

```
********** CHECKS **********

              5/29        17.50 OD                          5/27       430.90
NSF CHARGES
              5/29       100.00 CK                          5/28       249.77
              6/01        33.00 MDB                         5/29       132.27
142 CHARLIE HARDSN         GOLDEN MEADOW.A
              6/08        13.00 MDB                         6/01        99.27
142 CHARLIE HARDSN         GOLDEN MEADOW.A
              6/08        13.00 MDB                         6/05       496.51
142 CHARLIE HARDSN         GOLDEN MEADOW.A
              6/22        13.00 MDB                         6/08       470.51
142 CHARLIE HARDSN         GOLDEN MEADOW.A
              6/22        13.00 MDB                         6/22      1598.79
142 CHARLIE HARDSN         GOLDEN MEADOW.A
              6/25         7.00 SC                          6/25      1591.79
MAINTENANCE FEE
     622*     5/27       250.00 CK      651*    5/27       100.00 CK
     652      5/28       129.89 CK      653     5/28        51.24 CK


******** DEPOSITS **********

              6/05       397.24 DD
TIDEWATER MARINE PAYROLL
              6/22      1154.28 DD
TIDEWATER MARINE PAYROLL
```

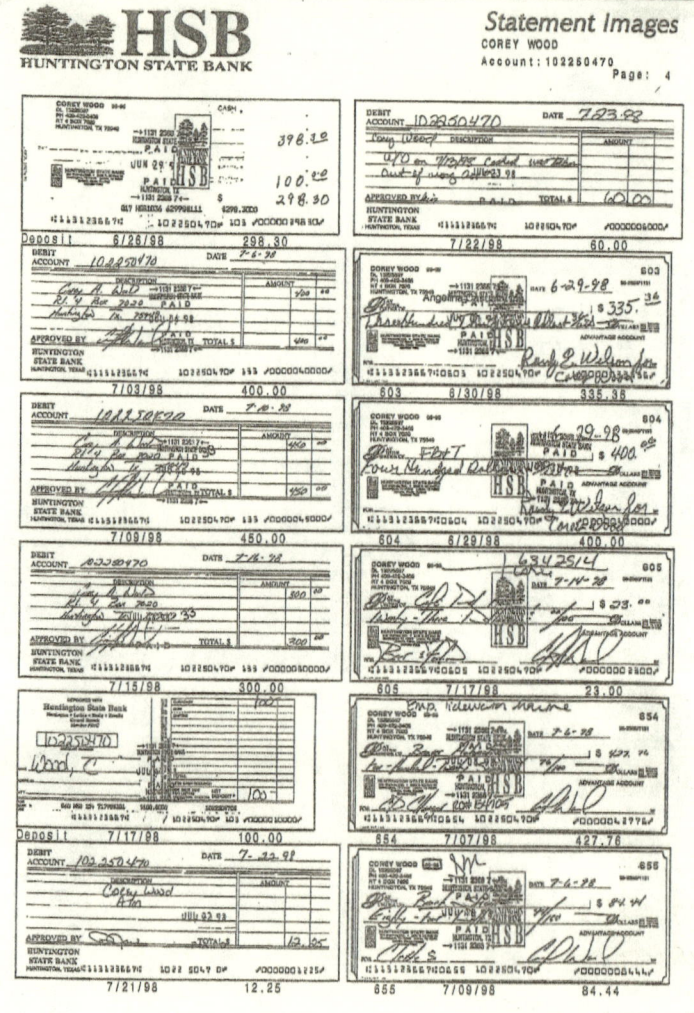

HUNTINGTON STATE BANK
Member FDIC

ABA 113123667

COREY WOOD
RT 4 BOX 7020
HUNTINGTON TX 75949

STATEMENT PERIOD
LAST   ENDING
6/25/98   7/27/98

PAGE   3

SS# 451 61 3497

```
****************************************TRANSACTIONS***********************************
CHECK       DATE      AMOUNT      CHECK      DATE      AMOUNT   DATE              BALANCE
NUMBER                            NUMBER
*************************************************************************************
CHECKING              102250470

           ********* DEPOSITS **********
           6/29        298.30 DP
           7/07       1154.28 DD
TIDEWATER MARINE PAYROLL
           7/17        100.00 DP
           7/22        135.74 DD
TIDEWATER MARINE PAYROLL
```

HSB
HUNTINGTON STATE BANK
Member FDIC

ABA 113123667

COREY WOOD
RT 4 BOX 7020
HUNTINGTON TX 75949

STATEMENT PERIOD
LAST   ENDING
6/25/98   7/27/98

PAGE   2

SS# 451 61 3497

CHECK NUMBER	DATE	AMOUNT	TRANSACTIONS CHECK NUMBER	DATE	AMOUNT	DATE	BALANCE
CHECKING		102250470					
208 HWY 69, HUNTINGTON TX HUNTINGTON				TX			
	7/16	300.00 CCK					
	7/16	41.00 MDB					
111 CHAMPIONS			LUFKIN	TX			
	7/16	51.50 MDB					
RT 1 BOX 4705			LUFKIN	TX			
	7/16	1.15 DM					
TRAN FEE							
	7/16	1.15 DM					
TRAN FEE							
	7/16	100.00 MDB					
208 HWY 69, HUNTINGTON TX HUNTINGTON				TX			
	7/16	51.00 MDB					
111 CHAMPIONS			LUFKIN	TX			
	7/17	41.50 MDB					
*LUFKIN MALL			LUFKIN	TX			
	7/17	1.15 DM					
TRAN FEE							
	7/17	.25 DM					
TRAN FEE							
	7/20	31.50 MDB					
*LUFKIN WEST			LUFKIN	TX			
	7/20	1.15 DM					
TRAN FEE							
	7/20	.25 DM					
TRAN FEE							
	7/21	.25 DM					
TRAN FEE							
	7/21	.25 DM					
TRAN FEE							
	7/21	.25 DM					
TRAN FEE							
	7/21	.25 DM					
TRAN FEE							
	7/21	1.15 DM					
TRAN FEE							
	7/22	12.25 PAY					
LF53 K&B MARRE			MARRERO	LA			
	7/23	60.00 CK					
	7/27	7.00 SC					
MAINTENANCE FEE							
603*	7/01	335.36 CK	604	6/30	400.00 CK		
605	7/17	23.00 PAY					
NSF ITEM							
654*	7/08	427.76 CK	655	7/10	84.44 CK		

PLEASE SEE NEXT PAGE

HUNTINGTON STATE BANK
MEMBER FDIC

HUNTINGTON	LUFKIN	ETOILE	ZAVALLA	CENTRAL
P.O. BOX 1090 • 208 HIGHWAY 69 SOUTH	2120 SOUTH FIRST ST	HIGHWAY 103 EAST	250 MAIN ST	3500 NORTH US HWY 69
HUNTINGTON, TEXAS 75949	LUFKIN, TEXAS 75901	ETOILE, TEXAS 75944	ZAVALLA, TEXAS 75980	LUFKIN, TEXAS 75904
(409) 639-5560	(409) 639-5568	(409) 639-5568	(409) 897-0023	(409) 639-5568

ABA 113123667

```
      COREY WOOD                        STATEMENT PERIOD
      RT 4 BOX 7020                     LAST      ENDING
  12  HUNTINGTON TX 75949               6/25/98   7/27/98

                                        PAGE      1

                                        SS# 451 61 3497
```

ACCOUNT NUMBER	PREVIOUS BALANCE	--- CREDITS --- COUNT	AMOUNT	--- DEBITS --- COUNT	AMOUNT	TOTAL FEE	PRESENT BALANCE
DDA 102250470	1591.79	4	1688.32	46	3212.31	7.00	67.80

CHECK NUMBER	DATE	AMOUNT	TRANSACTIONS CHECK NUMBER	DATE	AMOUNT	DATE	BALANCE
CHECKING		102250470					

DAYS IN THIS CYCLE   32

********** CHECKS **********

```
              7/03     51.00 MDB                                      6/29    1890.09
7102 SIEGEN LANE            BATON ROUGE  LA
              7/03      1.15 DM                                       6/30    1490.09
TRAN FEE
              7/06    400.00 CCK                                      7/01    1154.73
              7/09     51.00 MDB                                      7/03    1102.58
ANGELINA SVGS               LUFKIN        TX
              7/09      1.15 DM                                       7/06     702.58
TRAN FEE
              7/09     51.00 MDB                                      7/07    1856.86
400 N TIMBERLAN            LUFKIN        TX
              7/09      1.15 DM                                       7/08    1429.10
TRAN FEE
              7/10     21.50 MDB                                      7/09    1324.80
RT 1 BOX 4705             LUFKIN        TX
              7/10    450.00 CCK                                      7/10     768.86
              7/13     41.00 MDB                                      7/13     661.56
ANGELINA SVGS             LUFKIN        TX
              7/13     31.50 MDB                                      7/14     619.41
RT 1 BOX 4705             LUFKIN        TX
              7/13     21.00 MDB                                      7/15     608.06
ANGELINA SVGS             LUFKIN        TX
              7/13     11.50 MDB                                      7/16      12.26
RT 1 BOX 4705             LUFKIN        TX
              7/13      1.15 DM                                       7/17      46.36
TRAN FEE
              7/13      1.15 DM                                       7/20      13.46
TRAN FEE
              7/14      1.15 DM                                       7/21      11.31
TRAN FEE
              7/14     41.00 MDB                                      7/22     134.80
111 CHAMPIONS             LUFKIN        TX
              7/15      1.15 DM                                       7/23      74.80
TRAN FEE
              7/15     10.20 MDB                                      7/27      67.80
3023 ANGELINA M           LUFKIN        TX
              7/16     50.00 MDB
```

PLEASE SEE NEXT PAGE

HUNTINGTON STATE BANK
MEMBER FDIC

HUNTINGTON	LUFKIN	ETOILE	ZAVALLA	CENTRAL
P.O. BOX 1090 • 208 HIGHWAY 69 SOUTH	2120 SOUTH FIRST ST.	HIGHWAY 103 EAST	250 MAIN ST.	3592 NORTH US HWY 59
HUNTINGTON, TEXAS 75949	LUFKIN, TEXAS 75901	ETOILE, TEXAS 75944	ZAVALLA, TEXAS 75980	LUFKIN, TEXAS 75904
(409) 639-5506	(409) 639-5506	(409) 639-5506	(409) 897-9023	(409) 639-5506

ABA 113123667

```
        COREY WOOD                    STATEMENT PERIOD
        RT 4 BOX 7020                 LAST      ENDING
   5    HUNTINGTON TX 75949           7/27/98   8/26/98

                                          PAGE    1

                                      SS# 451 61 3497
```

ACCOUNT NUMBER	PREVIOUS BALANCE	CREDITS COUNT	AMOUNT	DEBITS COUNT	AMOUNT	TOTAL FEE	PRESENT BALANCE
DDA 102250470	67.80	3	2056.78	6	777.18	7.00	1347.40

CHECKING   102250470

DAYS IN THIS CYCLE   30

```
********** CHECKS **********

        8/05    17.50 OD                       8/03    277.80
NSF CHARGES
        8/26     7.00 SC                       8/05     39.70-
MAINTENANCE FEE
626*    8/03    40.00 CCK                      8/07    746.68
627     8/05   300.00 PAY                      8/19    584.00
NSF ITEM
628     8/19   162.68 CK    629  8/20  250.00 CCK 8/20  334.00
                                              8/21   1364.40
                                              8/26   1347.40

********** DEPOSITS **********

        8/03   250.00 DP
        8/07   786.38 DD
TIDEWATER MARINE PAYROLL
        8/21  1020.40 DD
TIDEWATER MARINE PAYROLL
```

HSB
HUNTINGTON STATE BANK
Member FDIC

ABA 113123667

COREY WOOD
RT 4 BOX 7020
HUNTINGTON TX 75949

STATEMENT PERIOD
LAST   ENDING
8/26/98   9/27/98

PAGE   2

SS# 451 61 3497

```
****************************************************************************
                              TRANSACTIONS
CHECK       DATE     AMOUNT     CHECK    DATE    AMOUNT   DATE       BALANCE
NUMBER                         NUMBER
****************************************************************************
CHECKING           102250470
TOWNE SQUARE                LUFKIN      TX
            9/14      1.15 DM
TRAN FEE
            9/14       .25 DM
TRAN FEE
            9/15     32.00 MDB
17454 SIDNEY ROAD           GROSSETETE   LA
            9/15      1.15 DM
TRAN FEE
            9/15    300.00 CCK
            9/27      7.00 SC
MAINTENANCE FEE
   402*     9/15     70.00 CCK    607*   9/14    11.67 CK
   630*     8/31    300.00 CK     631    8/31   200.24 CCK
   634*     9/08    250.00 CK     635    8/31   100.00 CK
   636      9/09    200.00 CK     637    9/17   100.00 CK
   638      9/22    100.00 PAY
NSF ITEM
   639      9/18    100.00 CK

         ******** DEPOSITS **********
            9/08   1100.89 DD
TIDEWATER MARINE PAYROLL
            9/22    123.05 DD
TIDEWATER MARINE PAYROLL
```

HUNTINGTON STATE BANK
MEMBER FDIC

HUNTINGTON	LUFKIN	ETOILE	ZAVALLA	CENTRAL
P.O. BOX 1090 • 208 HIGHWAY 69 SOUTH	2120 SOUTH FIRST ST.	HIGHWAY 103 EAST	250 MAIN ST.	3592 NORTH US HWY 89
HUNTINGTON, TEXAS 75949	LUFKIN, TEXAS 75901	ETOILE, TEXAS 75944	ZAVALLA, TEXAS 75980	LUFKIN, TEXAS 75904
(409) 639-5566	(409) 639-9566	(409) 639-5566	(409) 897-9123	(409) 639-5566

ABA 113123667

```
              COREY WOOD                         STATEMENT PERIOD
              RT 4 BOX 7020                        LAST      ENDING
       14     HUNTINGTON TX 75949                 8/26/98    9/27/98

                                                   PAGE     1

                                                 SS# 451 61 3497
```

ACCOUNT NUMBER	PREVIOUS BALANCE	--- CREDITS --- COUNT	AMOUNT	--- DEBITS --- COUNT	AMOUNT	TOTAL FEE	PRESENT BALANCE
DDA 102250470	1347.40	2	1223.94	37	2543.21	7.00	28.13

CHECK NUMBER	DATE	AMOUNT	TRANSACTIONS CHECK NUMBER	DATE	AMOUNT	DATE	BALANCE
CHECKING		102250470					

DAYS IN THIS CYCLE 32

```
********** CHECKS **********
             9/02      1.15 DM                                8/31    747.16
TRAN FEE
             9/02    152.00 MDB                               9/02    594.01
1522 ST. BERNARD A         NEW ORLEANS  LA
             9/03    100.00 CCK                               9/03    494.01
             9/08     21.50 MDB                               9/08   1002.95
AL-SALMAN                  LUFKIN       TX
             9/08    100.00 CCK              9/08   60.00 CCK  9/09    802.95
             9/08      1.15 DM                                9/10    770.80
TRAN FEE
             9/08      1.15 DM                                9/11    679.30
TRAN FEE
             9/08      1.15 DM                                9/14    615.23
TRAN FEE
             9/08       .25 DM                                9/15    212.08
TRAN FEE
             9/08       .25 DM                                9/17    112.08
TRAN FEE
             9/08     51.50 MDB                               9/18     12.08
*LUFKIN MALL               LUFKIN       TX
             9/08     51.50 MDB                               9/22     35.13
*LUFKIN WEST               LUFKIN       TX
             9/08     32.00 MDB                               9/27     28.13
3009 A NW STALLING         NACOGDOCHES  TX
             9/08     31.50 MDB             NACOGDOCHES  TX
             9/10     20.00 MDB
ROUTE 4, BOX 9520          NACOGDOCHES  TX
             9/10     11.00 MDB
208 HWY 69, HUNTINGTON TX  HUNTINGTON   TX
HOLIDAY CH                 LUFKIN       TX
             9/10      1.15 DM
TRAN FEE
             9/11     50.00 MDB
208 HWY 69, HUNTINGTON TX  HUNTINGTON   TX
             9/11     41.50 MDB
RT 1 BOX 4705              LUFKIN       TX
             9/14     51.00 MDB
                    PLEASE SEE NEXT PAGE
```

276

HUNTINGTON STATE BANK

MEMBER FDIC

HUNTINGTON	LUFKIN	ETOILE	ZAVALLA	CENTRAL
P.O. BOX 1090 • 208 HIGHWAY 69 SOUTH	2120 SOUTH FIRST ST	HIGHWAY 103 EAST	250 MAIN ST	3502 NORTH US HWY 59
HUNTINGTON, TEXAS 75949	LUFKIN, TEXAS 75901	ETOILE, TEXAS 75944	ZAVALLA, TEXAS 75980	LUFKIN, TEXAS 75904
(409) 639-5566	(409) 639-5566	(409) 639-5566	(409) 897-9023	(409) 639-5566

ABA 113123667

```
        COREY WOOD                      STATEMENT PERIOD
        RT 4 BOX 7020                     LAST     ENDING
     8  HUNTINGTON TX 75949             9/27/98   10/27/98

                                          PAGE    1

                                        SS# 451 61 3497
```

ACCOUNT NUMBER	PREVIOUS BALANCE	--- CREDITS --- COUNT	AMOUNT	--- DEBITS --- COUNT	AMOUNT	TOTAL FEE	PRESENT BALANCE
DDA 102250470	28.13	2	2175.75	16	2042.15	7.00	161.73

CHECK NUMBER	DATE	AMOUNT	TRANSACTIONS CHECK NUMBER	DATE	AMOUNT	DATE	BALANCE
CHECKING		102250470					

DAYS IN THIS CYCLE   30

```
        ********** CHECKS **********

           10/01      1.15 DM                          10/01        4.98
TRAN FEE
           10/01       .25 DM                          10/02       32.52-
TRAN FEE
           10/01       .25 DM                          10/07      260.66
TRAN FEE
           10/01     21.50 MDB                          10/19       10.66
LAKE FOREST          DAPHNE       AL
           10/02     20.00 PAY                          10/20       10.16
NSF ITEM
           10/02     17.50 OD                           10/22      768.73
NSF CHARGES
           10/20       .25 DM                           10/23      468.73
TRAN FEE
           10/20       .25 DM                           10/26      168.73
TRAN FEE
           10/22    400.00 CCK          10/23   300.00 CCK10/27    161.73
           10/26    200.00 CCK
           10/27      7.00 SC
MAINTENANCE FEE
      644* 10/07    400.00 PAY
NSF ITEM
      646* 10/07    324.00 PAY
NSF ITEM
      647  10/19    250.00 CCK      648  10/26   100.00 CK


        ******** DEPOSITS **********

           10/07    1017.18 DD
TIDEWATER MARINE PAYROLL
           10/22    1158.57 DD
TIDEWATER MARINE PAYROLL
```

HUNTINGTON STATE BANK
MEMBER FDIC

HUNTINGTON	LUFKIN	ETOILE	ZAVALLA	CENTRAL
P.O. BOX 1090 • 208 HIGHWAY 69 SOUTH	2120 SOUTH FIRST ST.	HIGHWAY 103 EAST	210 MAIN ST.	3502 NORTH US HWY 69
HUNTINGTON, TEXAS 75949	LUFKIN, TEXAS 75901	ETOILE, TEXAS 75944	ZAVALLA, TEXAS 75980	LUFKIN, TEXAS 75904
(409) 939-5588	(409) 639-9586	(409) 639-5566	(409) 897-9923	(409) 639-5566

ABA 113123667

```
          COREY WOOD
          RT 4 BOX 7020                   STATEMENT PERIOD
      5   HUNTINGTON TX 75949               LAST      ENDING
                                          10/27/98   11/24/98

                                              PAGE    1

                                          SS# 451 61 3497
```

ACCOUNT NUMBER	PREVIOUS BALANCE	---CREDITS--- COUNT	AMOUNT	---DEBITS--- COUNT	AMOUNT	TOTAL FEE	PRESENT BALANCE
DDA 102250470	161.73	2	1617.40	16	1170.70	7.00	608.43

```
CHECK    DATE     AMOUNT   TRANSACTIONS         AMOUNT DATE          BALANCE
NUMBER                     CHECK    DATE
                           NUMBER
CHECKING          102250470

                                 DAYS IN THIS CYCLE          28

           ********** CHECKS **********
        10/28        1.15 DM                      10/28        68.68
TRAN FEE
        10/28       21.50 MDB                      11/06       790.41
RT 1 BOX 4705            LUFKIN      TX
        10/28       20.40 MDB                      11/09       440.41
ANGELINA VILLAGE        LUFKIN      TX
        10/28       50.00 MDB                      11/10        40.41
208 HWY 69, HUNTINGTON TX  HUNTINGTON  TX
        11/12         .25 DM                       11/12        16.76
TRAN FEE
        11/12         .25 DM                       11/13       250.74-
TRAN FEE
        11/12       22.00 MDB                      11/17       280.24-
4979 E MAIN             GALLIANO    LA
        11/12        1.15 DM                       11/20       615.43
TRAN FEE
        11/13       17.50 OD                       11/24       608.43
NSF CHARGES
        11/17       12.00 PAY
2200 WESTBANK EXPRESSWA   HARVEY      LA
        11/17       17.50 OD
NSF CHARGES
        11/24        7.00 SC
MAINTENANCE FEE
     643* 11/09      50.00 CK
     650* 11/13     250.00 PAY
NSF ITEM
     676* 11/10     400.00 CK       677  11/09     300.00 CK

           ********** DEPOSITS **********
        11/06      721.73 DD
TIDEWATER MARINE PAYROLL
        11/20      895.67 DD
TIDEWATER MARINE PAYROLL
```

278

Account: 102250470
Check: 1001
Amount: 00000180.18
Date cleared: 01/27/98

COREY WOOD
RT 3 BOX 7020
HUNTINGTON, TEXAS 75949

1001

Date 1-28-98 19

Pay to the order of Lufkin State Bank $ 180.18

One hundred eighty & 18/100 Dollars

HSB
HUNTINGTON STATE BANK
HUNTINGTON • LUFKIN • ETOILE • ZAVALLA • CENTRAL

88-2366/1131

PAID
HUNTINGTON STATE BANK
HUNTINGTON, TX
1131 2366 7

For I/L 82245

⑆113123667⑆1001 102250470⑈ ⑈0000018018⑈

01/28/98 -9-085-
113000049
32956196

ENDORSE HERE
DO NOT WRITE, STAMP OR SIGN BELOW THIS LINE
FEDERAL RESERVE

76855079

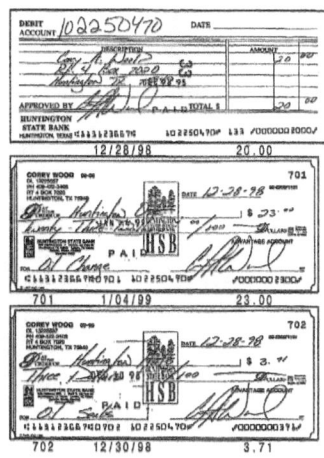

HUNTINGTON STATE BANK
MEMBER FDIC

HUNTINGTON	LUFKIN	ETOILE	ZAVALLA	CENTRAL
P.O. BOX 1090 • 208 HIGHWAY 69 SOUTH	2120 SOUTH FIRST ST.	HIGHWAY 103 EAST	250 MAIN ST.	100 CHIMNEY ROCK
HUNTINGTON, TEXAS 75949	LUFKIN, TEXAS 75901	ETOILE, TEXAS 75944	ZAVALLA, TEXAS 75980	LUFKIN, TEXAS 75904
(409) 422-3600 • (409) 639-2205	(409) 639-5980	(409) 854-2265	(409) 897-9023	(409) 632-4699

ABA 113123667

```
              COREY WOOD
              RT 4 BOX 7020                        STATEMENT PERIOD
       3      HUNTINGTON TX 75949                  LAST      ENDING
                                                   12/27/98   1/25/99

                                                   PAGE    1

                                                   SS# 451 61 3497
```

ACCOUNT NUMBER	PREVIOUS BALANCE	··· CREDITS ··· COUNT	AMOUNT	··· DEBITS ··· COUNT	AMOUNT	TOTAL FEE	PRESENT BALANCE
DDA 102250470	543.33	2	1285.51	16	466.36	7.00	1362.48

CHECK NUMBER	DATE	AMOUNT	TRANSACTIONS CHECK NUMBER	DATE	AMOUNT	DATE	BALANCE
CHECKING		102250470					

DAYS IN THIS CYCLE   29

```
********* CHECKS **********
              12/28        1.15 DM                        12/28      390.68
TRAN FEE
              12/28       21.50 MDB                        12/29      350.68
*LUFKIN MALL              LUFKIN        TX
              12/28       40.00 MDB                        12/30      256.97
208 HWY 69, HUNTINGTON TX HUNTINGTON    TX
              12/28       30.00 MDB                        12/31      106.97
208 HWY 69, HUNTINGTON TX HUNTINGTON    TX
              12/28       20.00 MDB                        1/04        83.97
208 HWY 69, HUNTINGTON TX HUNTINGTON    TX
              12/28       20.00 MDB                        1/08       231.94
208 HWY 69, HUNTINGTON TX HUNTINGTON    TX
              12/28       20.00 CCK                        1/22      1369.48
              12/29       30.00 MDB                        1/26      1362.48
208 HWY 69, HUNTINGTON TX HUNTINGTON    TX
              12/29       10.00 MDR
208 HWY 69, HUNTINGTON TX HUNTINGTON    TX
              12/30       40.00 MDB
100 CHIMNEY ROCK,LUFKINTX  LUFKIN        TX
              12/30       30.00 MDB
208 HWY 69, HUNTINGTON TX HUNTINGTON    TX
              12/30       20.00 MDB
208 HWY 69, HUNTINGTON TX HUNTINGTON    TX
              12/31      150.00 MDB
208 HWY 69, HUNTINGTON TX HUNTINGTON    TX
              1/25        7.00 SC
MAINTENANCE FEE
     701*  1/04       23.00 CK       702  12/30      3.71 CK

********* DEPOSITS **********
              1/08      147.97 DD
TIDEWATER MARINE PAYROLL
              1/22     1137.54 DD
TIDEWATER MARINE PAYROLL
```

HUNTINGTON STATE BANK
MEMBER FDIC

HUNTINGTON	LUFKIN	ETOILE	ZAVALLA	CENTRAL
P.O. BOX 1090 • 208 HIGHWAY 69 SOUTH	2120 SOUTH FIRST ST.	HIGHWAY 103 EAST	250 MAIN ST.	3592 NORTH US HWY 69
HUNTINGTON, TEXAS 75949	LUFKIN, TEXAS 75901	ETOILE, TEXAS 75944	ZAVALLA, TEXAS 75980	LUFKIN, TEXAS 75904
(409) 639-5566	(409) 639-5566	(409) 639-5566	(409) 897-9023	(409) 639-5566

ABA 113123667

```
          COREY WOOD                        STATEMENT PERIOD
          RT 4 BOX 7020                       LAST      ENDING
    3     HUNTINGTON TX 75949               12/27/98   1/25/99

                                              PAGE    1

                                            SS# 451 61 3497
```

ACCOUNT NUMBER	PREVIOUS BALANCE	--- CREDITS --- COUNT	AMOUNT	--- DEBITS --- COUNT	AMOUNT	TOTAL FEE	PRESENT BALANCE
DDA 102250470	543.33	2	1285.51	16	466.36	7.00	1362.48

TRANSACTIONS

CHECK NUMBER	DATE	AMOUNT	CHECK NUMBER	DATE	AMOUNT	DATE	BALANCE
CHECKING		102250470					

DAYS IN THIS CYCLE   29

```
********** CHECKS **********

           12/28      1.15 DM                          12/28    390.68
TRAN FEE
           12/28     21.50 MDB                          12/29    350.68
*LUFKIN MALL              LUFKIN     TX
           12/28     40.00 MDB                          12/30    256.97
208 HWY 69, HUNTINGTON TX  HUNTINGTON  TX
           12/28     30.00 MDB                          12/31    106.97
208 HWY 69, HUNTINGTON TX  HUNTINGTON  TX
           12/28     20.00 MDB                          1/04      83.97
208 HWY 69, HUNTINGTON TX  HUNTINGTON  TX
           12/28     20.00 MDB                          1/08     231.94
208 HWY 69, HUNTINGTON TX  HUNTINGTON  TX
           12/28     20.00 CCK                          1/22    1369.48
           12/29     30.00 MDB                          1/25    1362.48
208 HWY 69, HUNTINGTON TX  HUNTINGTON  TX
           12/29     10.00 MDB
208 HWY 69, HUNTINGTON TX  HUNTINGTON  TX
           12/30     40.00 MDB
100 CHIMNEY ROCK, LUFKIN TX  LUFKIN     TX
           12/30     30.00 MDB
208 HWY 69, HUNTINGTON TX  HUNTINGTON  TX
           12/30     20.00 MDB
208 HWY 69, HUNTINGTON TX  HUNTINGTON  TX
           12/31    150.00 MDB
208 HWY 69, HUNTINGTON TX  HUNTINGTON  TX
           1/25      7.00 SC
MAINTENANCE FEE
   701*  1/04     23.00 CK      702  12/30     3.71 CK


********* DEPOSITS *********

           1/08    147.97 DD
TIDEWATER MARINE PAYROLL
           1/22   1137.54 DD
TIDEWATER MARINE PAYROLL
```

HUNTINGTON STATE BANK
MEMBER FDIC

HUNTINGTON	LUFKIN	ETOILE	ZAVALLA	CENTRAL
P.O. BOX 1090 • 208 HIGHWAY 69 SOUTH	3130 SOUTH FIRST ST.	HIGHWAY 103 EAST	250 MAIN ST.	100 CHIMNEY ROCK
HUNTINGTON, TEXAS 75949	LUFKIN, TEXAS 75901	ETOILE, TEXAS 75944	ZAVALLA, TEXAS 75980	LUFKIN, TEXAS 75904
(409) 421-3000 • (409) 636-2206	(409) 639-9565	(409) 554-2265	(409) 897-9023	(409) 632-4599

ABA 113123667

```
                                  STATEMENT PERIOD
    COREY WOOD                     LAST      ENDING
    RT 4 BOX 7020                  1/25/99   2/22/99
6   HUNTINGTON TX 75949
                                       PAGE    1

                                  SS# 451 61 3497
```

ACCOUNT NUMBER	PREVIOUS BALANCE	··· CREDITS ··· COUNT	AMOUNT	··· DEBITS ··· COUNT	AMOUNT	TOTAL FEE	PRESENT BALANCE
DDA 102250470	1362.48	1	1268.29	29	2422.03	7.00	208.74

CHECK NUMBER	DATE	AMOUNT	TRANSACTIONS CHECK NUMBER	DATE	AMOUNT	DATE	BALANCE
CHECKING		102250470					

DAYS IN THIS CYCLE   28

********** CHECKS **********

```
           1/28      1.15 DM                          1/26      962.48
TRAN FEE
           1/28    101.00 MDB                          1/27      799.80
M C BANK                    MORGAN CITY  LA
           1/29     50.00 CCK          1/29   400.00 CK  1/28      697.65
           2/01     21.00 MDB                          1/29      247.65
111 CHAMPIONS               LUFKIN     TX
           2/01     21.50 MDB                          2/01      203.75
RT 1 BOX 4705               LUFKIN     TX
           2/01      1.15 DM                           2/03      163.75
TRAN FEE
           2/01       .25 DM                           2/04       59.45
TRAN FEE
           2/03     40.00 MDB                          2/05     1297.74
208 HWY 69, HUNTINGTON TX  HUNTINGTON TX
           2/04     51.00 MDB                          2/08      584.29
TOWNE SQUARE               LUFKIN     TX
           2/04     51.00 MDB                          2/09      564.29
TOWNE SQUARE               LUFKIN     TX
           2/04      1.15 DM                           2/10      364.29
TRAN FEE
           2/04      1.15 DM                           2/18      215.74
TRAN FEE
           2/05     30.00 MDB                          2/22      208.74
208 HWY 69, HUNTINGTON TX  HUNTINGTON TX
           2/08     21.50 MDB
RT 1 BOX 4705              LUFKIN     TX
           2/08    600.00 CK
           2/08      1.15 DM
TRAN FEE
           2/08     50.00 MDB
100 CHIMNEY ROCK,LUFKINTX  LUFKIN     TX
           2/08     40.80 MDB
ANGELINA VILLAGE           LUFKIN     TX
           2/09     20.00 MDB
208 HWY 69, HUNTINGTON TX  HUNTINGTON TX
           2/10    200.00 CK
```

PLEASE SEE NEXT PAGE

285

HUNTINGTON STATE BANK
Member FDIC

ABA 113123667

COREY WOOD
RT 4 BOX 7020
HUNTINGTON TX 75949

STATEMENT PERIOD
LAST   ENDING
1/25/99   2/22/99

PAGE   2

SS# 451 61 3497

```
••••••••••••••••••••••••••••••••••TRANSACTIONS••••••••••••••••••••••••••••••••••••••••
CHECK      DATE      AMOUNT      CHECK      DATE      AMOUNT   DATE          BALANCE
NUMBER                          NUMBER
••••••••••••••••••••••••••••••••••••••••••••••••••••••••••••••••••••••••••••••••••••••••
CHECKING             102250470
             2/18       43.00 MDB
BELLE PASS                     GOLDEN MEADO LA
             2/18      103.00 MDB
BELLE PASS                     GOLDEN MEADO LA
             2/18        1.15 DM
TRAN FEE
             2/18        1.15 DM
TRAN FEE
             2/18         .25 DM
TRAN FEE
             2/22        7.00 SC
MAINTENANCE FEE
    727*    1/26      400.00 CK      729*   1/27     162.68 CK

         •••••••• DEPOSITS ••••••••••
             2/05     1268.29 DD
TIDEWATER MARINE PAYROLL
```

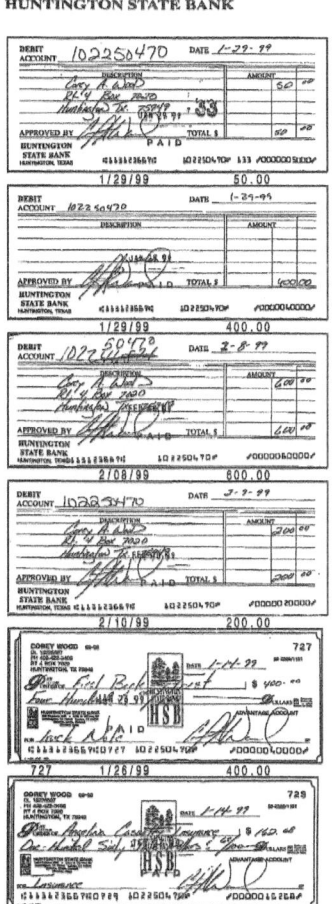

287

HUNTINGTON STATE BANK
MEMBER FDIC

HUNTINGTON	LUFKIN	ETOILE	ZAVALLA	CENTRAL
P.O. BOX 1090 • 208 HIGHWAY 69 SOUTH	2120 SOUTH FIRST ST.	HIGHWAY 103 EAST	250 MAIN ST.	3592 NORTH US HWY 98
HUNTINGTON, TEXAS 75949	LUFKIN, TEXAS 76901	ETOILE, TEXAS 75944	ZAVALLA, TEXAS 75980	LUFKIN, TEXAS 75904
(409) 639-5566	(409) 838-5566	(409) 639-5566	(409) 897-9023	(409) 639-5566

ABA 113123667

```
        COREY WOOD                          STATEMENT PERIOD
        RT 4 BOX 7020                       LAST      ENDING
    6   HUNTINGTON TX 75949                 1/25/99   2/22/99

                                            PAGE    1
                                            SS# 451 61 3497
```

ACCOUNT NUMBER	PREVIOUS BALANCE	--- CREDITS --- COUNT	AMOUNT	--- DEBITS --- COUNT	AMOUNT	TOTAL FEE	PRESENT BALANCE
DDA 102250470	1362.48	1	1268.29	29	2422.03	7.00	208.74

CHECK NUMBER	DATE	AMOUNT	TRANSACTIONS CHECK NUMBER	DATE	AMOUNT	DATE	BALANCE
CHECKING		102250470					

DAYS IN THIS CYCLE   28

```
********** CHECKS **********

              1/28      1.15 DM                                      1/26      962.48
TRAN FEE
              1/28    101.00 MDB                                     1/27      799.80
M C BANK              MORGAN CITY LA
              1/29     50.00 CCK             1/29    400.00 CK       1/28      697.65
              2/01     21.00 MDB                                     1/29      247.65
111 CHAMPIONS              LUFKIN     TX
              2/01     21.50 MDB                                     2/01      203.76
RT 1 BOX 4705             LUFKIN     TX
              2/01      1.15 DM                                      2/03      163.76
TRAN FEE
              2/01       .25 DM                                      2/04       59.45
TRAN FEE
              2/03     40.00 MDB                                     2/05     1297.74
208 HWY 69, HUNTINGTON TX  HUNTINGTON   TX
              2/04     51.00 MDB                                     2/08      584.29
TOWNE SQUARE              LUFKIN     TX
              2/04     51.00 MDB                                     2/09      584.29
TOWNE SQUARE              LUFKIN     TX
              2/04      1.15 DM                                      2/10      364.29
TRAN FEE
              2/04      1.15 DM                                      2/18      215.74
TRAN FEE
              2/05     30.00 MDB                                     2/22      208.74
208 HWY 69, HUNTINGTON TX  HUNTINGTON   TX
              2/08     21.50 MDB
RT 1 BOX 4705             LUFKIN     TX
              2/08    600.00 CK
              2/08      1.15 DM
TRAN FEE
              2/08     50.00 MDB
100 CHIMNEY ROCK,LUFKINTX  LUFKIN     TX
              2/08     40.80 MDB
ANGELINA VILLAGE          LUFKIN     TX
              2/09     20.00 MDB
208 HWY 69, HUNTINGTON TX  HUNTINGTON   TX
              2/10    200.00 CK

                    PLEASE SEE NEXT PAGE
```

HSB
HUNTINGTON STATE BANK
Member FDIC

ABA 113123667

COREY WOOD
RT 4 BOX 7020
HUNTINGTON TX 75949

STATEMENT PERIOD
LAST   ENDING
1/25/99   2/22/99

PAGE   2

SS# 451 61 3497

TRANSACTIONS

CHECK NUMBER	DATE	AMOUNT	CHECK NUMBER	DATE	AMOUNT	DATE	BALANCE
CHECKING		102250470					
	2/18	43.00 MDB					
BELLE PASS			GOLDEN MEADO LA				
	2/18	103.00 MDB					
BELLE PASS			GOLDEN MEADO LA				
	2/18	1.15 DM					
TRAN FEE							
	2/18	1.15 DM					
TRAN FEE							
	2/18	.25 DM					
TRAN FEE							
	2/22	7.00 SC					
MAINTENANCE FEE							
727*	1/26	400.00 CK	729*	1/27	162.68 CK		

********* DEPOSITS **********

	2/05	1268.29 DD
TIDEWATER MARINE PAYROLL		

DEBIT ACCOUNT 102250470   DATE 1-29-99

DESCRIPTION	AMOUNT
Corey A. Wood	50 00
Rt 4 Box 7020	
Huntington, Tx. 75949	
APPROVED BY	**TOTAL $** 50 00

HUNTINGTON STATE BANK
HUNTINGTON, TEXAS   PAID

1/29/99   50.00

DEBIT ACCOUNT 102250470   DATE 1-29-99

DESCRIPTION	AMOUNT
APPROVED BY	**TOTAL $** 400 00

HUNTINGTON STATE BANK
HUNTINGTON, TEXAS   PAID

1/29/99   400.00

DEBIT ACCOUNT 102250470   DATE 2-8-99

DESCRIPTION	AMOUNT
Corey A. Wood	600 00
Rt 4 Box 7020	
Huntington, Texas	
APPROVED BY	**TOTAL $** 600 00

HUNTINGTON STATE BANK
HUNTINGTON, TEXAS   PAID

2/08/99   600.00

DEBIT ACCOUNT 102250470   DATE 2-9-99

DESCRIPTION	AMOUNT
Corey A. Wood	200 00
Rt 4 Box 7020	
Huntington, Texas	
APPROVED BY	**TOTAL $** 200 00

HUNTINGTON STATE BANK
HUNTINGTON, TEXAS   PAID

2/10/99   200.00

COREY WOOD   727
DATE 1-14-99
$ 400.00
Four Hundred 00   DOLLARS
PAID
727   1/26/99   400.00

COREY WOOD   729
DATE 1-14-99
$ 162.68
One Hundred Sixty   DOLLARS
PAID
729   1/27/99   162.68

HUNTINGTON STATE BANK
MEMBER FDIC

HUNTINGTON	LUFKIN	ETOILE	ZAVALLA	CENTRAL
P.O. BOX 1090 • 208 HIGHWAY 69 SOUTH	2120 SOUTH FIRST ST.	HIGHWAY 103 EAST	250 MAIN ST.	3592 NORTH US HWY 69
HUNTINGTON, TEXAS 75949	LUFKIN, TEXAS 75901	ETOILE, TEXAS 75944	ZAVALLA, TEXAS 75980	LUFKIN, TEXAS 75904
(409) 639-5566	(409) 639-5566	(409) 639-5566	(409) 897-9023	(409) 829-6666

ABA 113123667

COREY WOOD
RT 4 BOX 7020
6   HUNTINGTON TX 75949

STATEMENT PERIOD
LAST   ENDING
2/22/99   3/17/99

PAGE   1

SS# 451 61 3497

ACCOUNT NUMBER	PREVIOUS BALANCE	--- CREDITS --- COUNT	AMOUNT	--- DEBITS --- COUNT	AMOUNT	TOTAL FEE	PRESENT BALANCE
DDA 102250470	208.74	3	2766.62	29	1520.75	7.00	1454.61

TRANSACTIONS

CHECK NUMBER	DATE	AMOUNT	CHECK NUMBER	DATE	AMOUNT	DATE	BALANCE
CHECKING	102250470						

DAYS IN THIS CYCLE   23

********** CHECKS ***********

TRAN FEE	2/24	.25 DM		2/23	672.02
TRAN FEE	3/01	.25 DM		2/24	671.77
TRAN FEE	3/08	1.15 DM		3/01	671.52
TRAN FEE	3/08	.25 DM		3/05	2974.86
TRAN FEE	3/08	101.00 MDB		3/08	2472.06
600 W. GULFWAY		PORT BOLIVAR TX			
	3/10	62.00 MDB		3/10	2242.26
808 LAKESHORE DR		LAKE CHARLES LA			
	3/10	1.15 DM		3/11	2192.26
TRAN FEE	3/10	1.15 DM		3/12	2045.76
TRAN FEE	3/10	1.15 DM		3/15	1811.61
TRAN FEE	3/10	.25 DM		3/16	1641.61
TRAN FEE	3/10	.25 DM		3/17	1454.61
TRAN FEE	3/10	.25 DM			
TRAN FEE	3/10	102.00 MDB			
808 LAKESHORE DR		LAKE CHARLES LA			
	3/10	62.00 MDB			
808 LAKESHORE DR		LAKE CHARLES LA			
	3/11	50.00 CCK			
	3/12	21.50 MDB			
RT 1 BOX 4705		LUFKIN TX			
	3/12	100.00 MDB			
208 HWY 69, HUNTINGTON TX		HUNTINGTON TX			
	3/15	100.00 CCK			
	3/15	31.50 MDB			
*LUFKIN MALL		LUFKIN TX			
	3/15	1.15 DM			

PLEASE SEE NEXT PAGE

291

HUNTINGTON STATE BANK
Member FDIC

ABA 113123667

COREY WOOD
RT 4 BOX 7020
HUNTINGTON TX 75949

STATEMENT PERIOD
LAST   ENDING
2/22/99   3/17/99

PAGE   2

SS# 451 61 3497

```
********************************TRANSACTIONS**************************************
CHECK     DATE    AMOUNT      CHECK      DATE   AMOUNT  DATE          BALANCE
NUMBER                        NUMBER
********************************************************************************
CHECKING           102250470
TRAN FEE
          3/15       51.50 MDB
RT 1 BOX 4705                  LUFKIN     TX
          3/15       50.00 MDB
208 HWY 69, HUNTINGTON TX  HUNTINGTON    TX
          3/16       50.00 MDB
208 HWY 69, HUNTINGTON TX  HUNTINGTON    TX
          3/17        7.00 SC
MAINTENANCE FEE
          3/17       20.00 MDB
208 HWY 69, HUNTINGTON TX  HUNTINGTON    TX
610*      3/08      400.00 CK  612*      3/12    25.00 CK
614*      3/16      120.00 CK  615       3/17   160.00 CK


         ******** DEPOSITS *********
          2/23      463.28 DD
TIDEWATER MARINE PAYROLL
          3/05     1362.98 DD
US TREASURY 220  TAX REFUND
          3/05      940.36 DD
TIDEWATER MARINE PAYROLL
```

3/11/99   50.00

3/15/99   100.00

610   3/08/99   400.00

612   3/12/99   25.00

614   3/16/99   120.00

615   3/17/99   160.00

HSB
HUNTINGTON STATE BANK
Member FDIC

ABA 113123667

COREY WOOD
RT 4 BOX 7020
HUNTINGTON TX 75949

STATEMENT PERIOD
LAST   ENDING
3/17/99   4/26/99

PAGE   2

SS# 451 61 3497

TRANSACTIONS

CHECK NUMBER	DATE	AMOUNT	CHECK NUMBER	DATE	AMOUNT	DATE	BALANCE
CHECKING		102250470					
RT 1 BOX 4705			LUFKIN	TX			
	4/05	30.00 CCK				4/20	287.79
	4/06	50.00 MDB				4/21	246.39
208 HWY 69, HUNTINGTON TX			HUNTINGTON	TX			
	4/07	.25 DM				4/23	445.39
TRAN FEE							
	4/07	51.00 MDB				4/26	288.39
ANGELINA VILLAGE			LUFKIN	TX			
	4/07	1.15 DM					
TRAN FEE							
	4/08	30.00 MDB					
208 HWY 69, HUNTINGTON TX			HUNTINGTON	TX			
	4/09	1.15 DM					
TRAN FEE							
	4/09	.25 DM					
TRAN FEE							
	4/09	41.00 MDB					
1873 WEST FRANK			LUFKIN	TX			
	4/12	20.00 MDB					
208 HWY 69, HUNTINGTON TX			HUNTINGTON	TX			
	4/12	11.00 MDB					
100 N. PECAN			NACOGDOCHES	TX			
	4/12	20.00 MDB					
208 HWY 69, HUNTINGTON TX			HUNTINGTON	TX			
	4/12	100.00 CCK					
	4/12	1.15 DM					
TRAN FEE							
	4/12	21.50 MDB					
ROUTE 4, BOX 8520			NACOGDOCHES	TX			
	4/15	11.50 MDB					
ROUTE 4, BOX 8520			NACOGDOCHES	TX			
	4/15	11.00 MDB					
111 CHAMPIONS			LUFKIN	TX			
	4/15	10.00 MDB					
208 HWY 69, HUNTINGTON TX			HUNTINGTON	TX			
	4/15	1.15 DM					
TRAN FEE							
	4/16	20.00 MDB					
208 HWY 69, HUNTINGTON TX			HUNTINGTON	TX			
	4/16	10.00 MDB					
208 HWY 69, HUNTINGTON TX			HUNTINGTON	TX			
	4/19	100.00 MDB					
208 HWY 69, HUNTINGTON TX			HUNTINGTON	TX			
	4/21	41.00 MDB					
107 QUITMAN STREET			EMORY,	TX			

PLEASE SEE NEXT PAGE

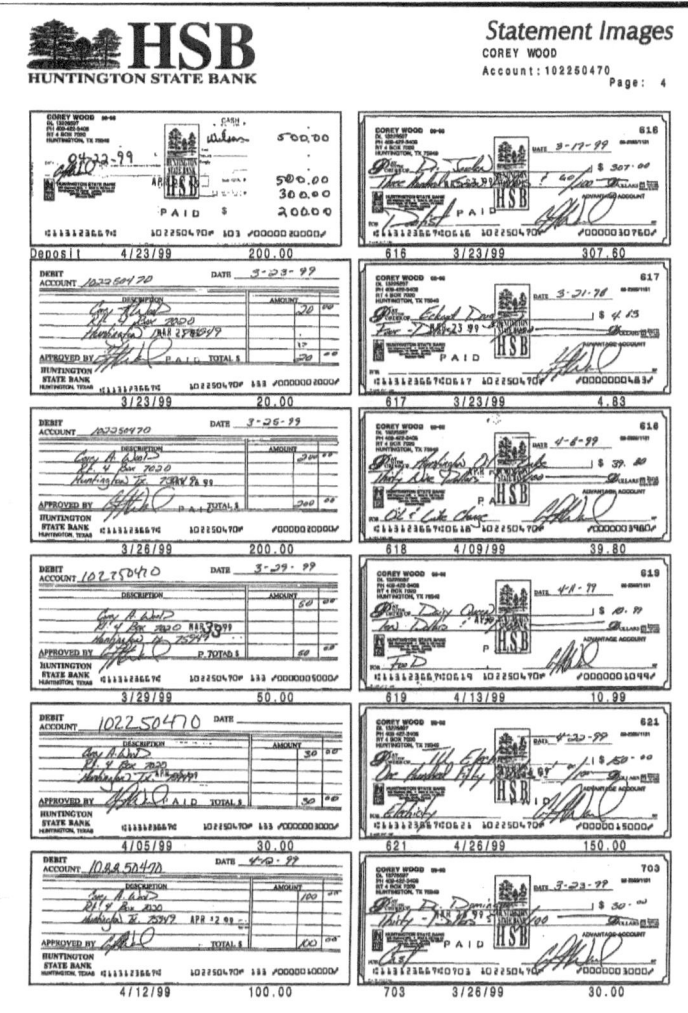

HUNTINGTON STATE BANK
Member FDIC

ABA 113123667

COREY WOOD
RT 4 BOX 7020
HUNTINGTON TX 75949

STATEMENT PERIOD
LAST   ENDING
3/17/99   4/26/99

PAGE   3

SS# 451 61 3497

CHECK NUMBER	DATE	AMOUNT	TRANSACTIONS CHECK NUMBER	DATE	AMOUNT	DATE	BALANCE
CHECKING		102250470					
	4/21	.25 DM					
TRAN FEE							
	4/21	1.15 DM					
TRAN FEE							
	4/26	7.00 SC					
MAINTENANCE FEE							
616*	3/23	307.60 CK	617	3/23	4.83 CK		
618	4/09	39.80 CK	619	4/13	10.99 CK		
621*	4/26	150.00 CK	703*	3/26	30.00 CK		
706*	4/19	22.02 CK	707	4/19	4.15 CK		
709*	4/20	3.13 CK					

********** DEPOSITS **********

	3/22	700.80 DD					
TIDEWATER MARINE PAYROLL							
	4/23	200.00 DP					

HUNTINGTON STATE BANK
MEMBER FDIC

HUNTINGTON	LUFKIN	ETOILE	ZAVALLA	CENTRAL
P.O. BOX 1090 • 208 HIGHWAY 69 SOUTH	2120 SOUTH FIRST ST.	HIGHWAY 103 EAST	250 MAIN ST	3592 NORTH US HWY 69
HUNTINGTON, TEXAS 75949	LUFKIN, TEXAS 75901	ETOILE, TEXAS 75944	ZAVALLA, TEXAS 75980	LUFKIN, TEXAS 75904
(409) 639-5566	(409) 639-5566	(409) 639-5566	(409) 897-9023	(409) 639-5566

ABA 113123667

```
              COREY WOOD
              RT 4 BOX 7020                    STATEMENT PERIOD
     15       HUNTINGTON TX 75949              LAST      ENDING
                                              3/17/99    4/26/99

                                                 PAGE    1

                                              SS# 451 61 3497
```

ACCOUNT NUMBER	PREVIOUS BALANCE	--- CREDITS --- COUNT AMOUNT	--- DEBITS --- COUNT AMOUNT	TOTAL FEE	PRESENT BALANCE
DDA 102250470	1454.61	2 900.80	56 2087.02	7.00	288.39

```
CHECK    DATE     AMOUNT      TRANSACTIONS
NUMBER                       CHECK      DATE    AMOUNT   DATE            BALANCE
                             NUMBER
CHECKING          102250470

                                     DAYS IN THIS CYCLE          40

          ********** CHECKS **********
              3/18        1.15 DM                             3/18       1363.06
TRAN FEE
              3/18       50.00 MDB                            3/19       1320.91
208 HWY 69, HUNTINGTON TX  HUNTINGTON    TX
              3/18       20.40 MDB                            3/22       1898.71
ANGELINA VILLAGE            LUFKIN        TX
              3/18       20.00 MDB                            3/23       1546.28
208 HWY 69, HUNTINGTON TX  HUNTINGTON    TX
              3/19        1.15 DM                             3/25       1523.63
TRAN FEE
              3/19       41.00 MDB                            3/26       1293.63
107 QUITMAN STREET         EMORY,        TX
              3/22       51.50 MDB                            3/29       1243.63
ROUTE 4, BOX 8520          NACOGDOCHES   TX
              3/22       51.50 MDB                            3/30       1033.63
RT 1 BOX 4705              LUFKIN        TX
              3/22       20.00 MDB                            3/31       1013.63
208 HWY 69, HUNTINGTON TX  HUNTINGTON    TX
              3/23       20.00 MDB                            4/02        961.48
208 HWY 69, HUNTINGTON TX  HUNTINGTON    TX
              3/23       20.00 CCK                            4/05        879.98
              3/26       21.50 MDB                            4/06        829.98
*LUFKIN MALL               LUFKIN        TX
              3/26        1.15 DM                             4/07        777.58
TRAN FEE
              3/26      200.00 CK          3/29     50.00 CCK 4/08        747.58
              3/30      200.00 MDB                            4/09        665.38
100 CHIMNEY ROCK,LUFKINTX  LUFKIN        TX
              3/30       10.00 MDB                            4/12        491.73
100 CHIMNEY ROCK,LUFKINTX  LUFKIN        TX
              3/31       20.00 MDB                            4/13        480.74
208 HWY 69, HUNTINGTON TX  HUNTINGTON    TX
              4/02        1.15 DM                             4/15        447.09
TRAN FEE
              4/02       51.00 MDB                            4/16        417.09
2510 W FRANK               LUFKIN        TX
              4/05       51.50 MDB                            4/19        290.92
                              PLEASE SEE NEXT PAGE
```

HSB
HUNTINGTON STATE BANK
Member FDIC

ABA 113123667

COREY WOOD
RT 4 BOX 7020
HUNTINGTON TX 75949

STATEMENT PERIOD
LAST   ENDING
3/17/99   4/26/99

PAGE   2

SS# 451 61 3497

CHECK NUMBER	DATE	AMOUNT	TRANSACTIONS CHECK NUMBER	DATE	AMOUNT	DATE	BALANCE
CHECKING		102250470					
RT 1 BOX 4706			LUFKIN	TX			
	4/05	30.00 CCK				4/20	287.79
	4/06	50.00 MDB				4/21	245.39
208 HWY 69, HUNTINGTON TX			HUNTINGTON	TX			
	4/07	.25 DM				4/23	445.39
TRAN FEE							
	4/07	51.00 MDB				4/26	288.39
ANGELINA VILLAGE			LUFKIN	TX			
	4/07	1.15 DM					
TRAN FEE							
	4/08	30.00 MDB					
208 HWY 69, HUNTINGTON TX			HUNTINGTON	TX			
	4/09	1.15 DM					
TRAN FEE							
	4/09	.25 DM					
TRAN FEE							
	4/09	41.00 MDB					
1873 WEST FRANK			LUFKIN	TX			
	4/12	20.00 MDB					
208 HWY 69, HUNTINGTON TX			HUNTINGTON	TX			
	4/12	11.00 MDB					
100 N. PECAN			NACOGDOCHES	TX			
	4/12	20.00 MDB					
208 HWY 69, HUNTINGTON TX			HUNTINGTON	TX			
	4/12	100.00 CCK					
	4/12	1.15 DM					
TRAN FEE							
	4/12	21.50 MDB					
ROUTE 4, BOX 8520			NACOGDOCHES	TX			
	4/15	11.50 MDB					
ROUTE 4, BOX 8520			NACOGDOCHES	TX			
	4/15	11.00 MDB					
111 CHAMPIONS			LUFKIN	TX			
	4/15	10.00 MDB					
208 HWY 69, HUNTINGTON TX			HUNTINGTON	TX			
	4/15	1.15 DM					
TRAN FEE							
	4/16	20.00 MDB					
208 HWY 69, HUNTINGTON TX			HUNTINGTON	TX			
	4/16	10.00 MDB					
208 HWY 69, HUNTINGTON TX			HUNTINGTON	TX			
	4/19	100.00 MDB					
208 HWY 69, HUNTINGTON TX			HUNTINGTON	TX			
	4/21	41.00 MDB					
107 QUITMAN STREET			EMORY,	TX			

PLEASE SEE NEXT PAGE

HSB
HUNTINGTON STATE BANK
Member FDIC

ABA 113123667

COREY WOOD
RT 4 BOX 7020
HUNTINGTON TX 75949

STATEMENT PERIOD
LAST   ENDING
3/17/99   4/26/99

PAGE   3

SS# 451 61 3497

```
••••••••••••••••••••••••••••••••••TRANSACTIONS•••••••••••••••••••••••••••••••••••••••
CHECK      DATE     AMOUNT       CHECK       DATE     AMOUNT  DATE            BALANCE
NUMBER                          NUMBER
••••••••••••••••••••••••••••••••••••••••••••••••••••••••••••••••••••••••••••••••••••••
CHECKING            102250470
           4/21          .25 DM
TRAN FEE
           4/21         1.15 DM
TRAN FEE
           4/26         7.00 SC
MAINTENANCE FEE
616*       3/23       307.60 CK    617      3/23        4.83 CK
618        4/09        39.80 CK    619      4/13       10.99 CK
621*       4/26       150.00 CK    703*     3/26       30.00 CK
706*       4/19        22.02 CK    707      4/19        4.15 CK
709*       4/20         3.13 CK

•••••••••• DEPOSITS •••••••••
           3/22       700.80 DD
TIDEWATER MARINE PAYROLL
           4/23       200.00 DP
```

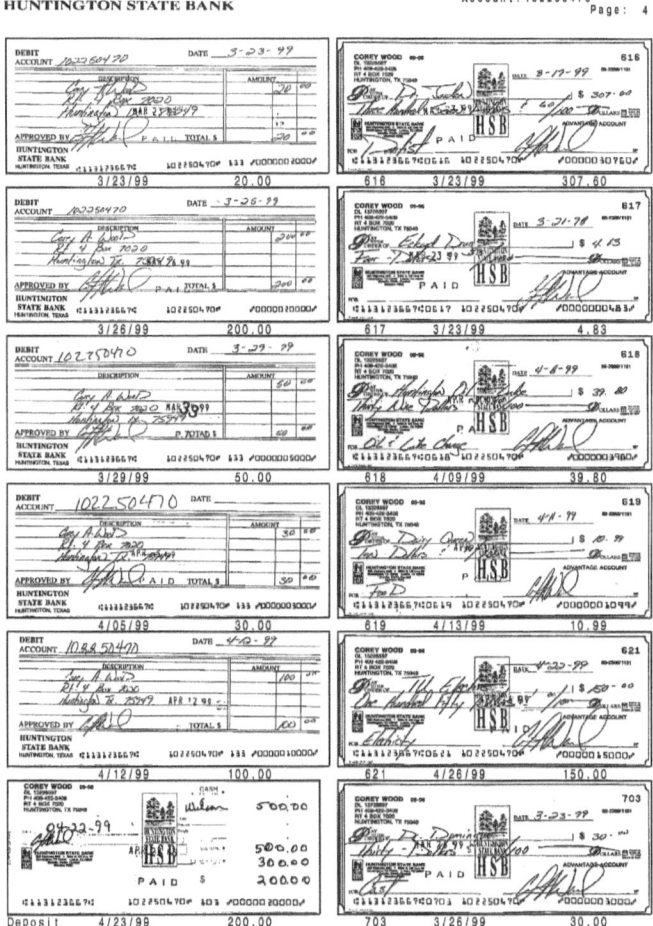

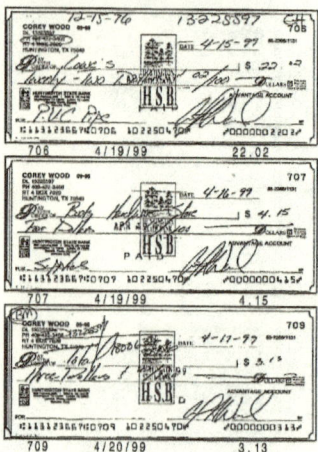

HUNTINGTON STATE BANK
MEMBER FDIC

HUNTINGTON	LUFKIN	ETOILE	ZAVALLA	CENTRAL
P.O. BOX 1090 • 202 HIGHWAY 69 SOUTH	2120 SOUTH FIRST ST.	HIGHWAY 103 EAST	290 MAIN ST.	3510 NORTH LOZ HWY 94
HUNTINGTON, TEXAS 75949	LUFKIN, TEXAS 75901	ETOILE, TEXAS 75944	ZAVALLA, TEXAS 75980	LUFKIN, TEXAS 75904
(409) 639-5506	(409) 639-5506	(409) 639-5660	(409) 897-5003	(409) 639-5040

ABA 113123667

```
                                           STATEMENT PERIOD
       COREY WOOD                          LAST        ENDING
       RT 4 BOX 7020                       4/26/99     5/24/99
   8   HUNTINGTON TX 75949
                                           PAGE    1

                                           SS# 451 61 3497
```

ACCOUNT NUMBER	PREVIOUS BALANCE	--- CREDITS --- COUNT AMOUNT	--- DEBITS --- COUNT AMOUNT	TOTAL FEE	PRESENT BALANCE
DDA 102250470	288.39	2 1131.15	21 879.67	7.00	539.87

```
                              TRANSACTIONS
CHECK    DATE     AMOUNT   CHECK   DATE   AMOUNT DATE          BALANCE
NUMBER                     NUMBER
CHECKING          102250470
                              DAYS IN THIS CYCLE        28

         ********** CHECKS **********
         4/28     20.00 CK          4/29    20.00 CCK 4/28    223.38
         4/30     21.50 MDB                            4/29    203.38
DANDY DOUB          LUFKIN    TX
         4/30      1.15 DM                             4/30     20.48
TRAN FEE
         4/30       .25 DM                             5/03      8.52
TRAN FEE
         4/30     20.00 MDB
208 HWY 69, HUNTINGTON TX  HUNTINGTON  TX             5/04    130.48-
         4/30    100.00 MDB
208 HWY 69, HUNTINGTON TX  HUNTINGTON  TX             5/10    147.98-
         4/30     40.00 MDB
208 HWY 69, HUNTINGTON TX  HUNTINGTON  TX             5/18    152.02
         5/03      1.15 DM
TRAN FEE                                              5/21    983.17
         5/04     17.50 OD
NSF CHARGES                                           5/24    539.87
         5/04     20.00 PAY
208 HWY 69, HUNTINGTON TX  HUNTINGTON  TX
         5/04    101.50 PAY
DANDY DOUB          LUFKIN    TX
         5/10     17.50 OD
NSF CHARGES
         5/24     22.00 MDB
10183 HWY. 90 E     MORGAN CITY  LA
         5/24      7.00 SC
MAINTENANCE FEE
         5/24      1.15 DM
TRAN FEE
         5/24      1.15 DM
TRAN FEE
         5/24     12.00 MDB
PO BOX 814 17178 HWY 90  ALLENMARK   LA
     578* 5/24    400.00 CK      620* 4/28    45.01 CK
     624* 5/03     10.81 CK
                 PLEASE SEE NEXT PAGE
```

303

HSB
HUNTINGTON STATE BANK
Member FDIC

ABA 113123667

COREY WOOD
RT 4 BOX 7020
HUNTINGTON TX 75949

STATEMENT PERIOD
LAST   ENDING
4/26/99   5/24/99

PAGE   2

SS# 451 61 3497

```
****************************** TRANSACTIONS *******************************
CHECK    DATE    AMOUNT     CHECK      DATE    AMOUNT  DATE          BALANCE
NUMBER                      NUMBER
**************************************************************************
CHECKING          102250470

********* DEPOSITS *********

         5/18    300.00 DP
         5/21    831.15 DD
TIDEWATER MARINE PAYROLL
```

Statement Images
COREY WOOD
Account: 102250470
Page: 3

4/28/99   20.00

4/28/99   45.01

4/29/99   20.00

5/03/99   10.81

5/04/99   20.00

5/04/99   101.50

Deposit   5/18/99   300.00

578   5/24/99   400.00

305

HUNTINGTON STATE BANK
MEMBER FDIC

HUNTINGTON	LUFKIN	ETOILE	ZAVALLA	CENTRAL
P.O. BOX 1080 • 206 HIGHWAY 69 SOUTH	2120 SOUTH FIRST ST.	HIGHWAY 103 EAST	250 MAIN ST.	100 CHIMNEY ROCK
HUNTINGTON, TEXAS 75949	LUFKIN, TEXAS 75901	ETOILE, TEXAS 75944	ZAVALLA, TEXAS 75980	LUFKIN, TEXAS 75904
(409) 422-3000 • (409) 639-2208	(409) 639-5586	(409) 854-2265	(409) 897-9023	(409) 632-4589

ABA 113123667

```
        COREY WOOD
        RT 4 BOX 7020            STATEMENT PERIOD
     8  HUNTINGTON TX 75949      LAST      ENDING
                                 4/26/99   5/24/99

                                 PAGE    1

                                 SS# 451 61 3497
```

ACCOUNT NUMBER	PREVIOUS BALANCE	CREDITS COUNT	AMOUNT	DEBITS COUNT	AMOUNT	TOTAL FEE	PRESENT BALANCE
DDA 102250470	288.39	2	1131.15	21	879.67	7.00	539.87

```
CHECK    DATE    AMOUNT      TRANSACTIONS         DATE  AMOUNT  DATE      BALANCE
NUMBER                       CHECK
                             NUMBER

CHECKING          102250470
                                    DAYS IN THIS CYCLE          28

           ********** CHECKS **********
           4/28    20.00 CK        4/29    20.00 CCK 4/28     223.38
           4/30    21.50 MDB                        4/29     203.38
DANDY DOUB              LUFKIN   TX
           4/30     1.15 DM                          4/30      20.48
TRAN FEE
           4/30      .25 DM                          5/03       8.52
TRAN FEE
           4/30    20.00 MDB                         5/04     130.48-
208 HWY 69, HUNTINGTON TX HUNTINGTON  TX
           4/30   100.00 MDB                         5/10     147.98-
208 HWY 69, HUNTINGTON TX HUNTINGTON  TX
           4/30    40.00 MDB                         5/18     152.02
208 HWY 69, HUNTINGTON TX HUNTINGTON  TX
           5/03     1.15 DM                          5/21     983.17
TRAN FEE
           5/04    17.50 OD                          5/24     539.87
NSF CHARGES
           5/04    20.00 PAY
208 HWY 69, HUNTINGTON TX HUNTINGTON  TX
           5/04   101.50 PAY
DANDY DOUB              LUFKIN   TX
           5/10    17.50 OD
NSF CHARGES
           5/24    22.00 MDB
10183 HWY. 90 E        MORGAN CITY LA
           5/24     7.00 SC
MAINTENANCE FEE
           5/24     1.15 DM
TRAN FEE
           5/24     1.15 DM
TRAN FEE
           5/24    12.00 MDB
PO BOX 814 17178 HWY 90  ALLENMARK   LA
      578*  5/24   400.00 CK       620*  4/28    45.01 CK
      624*  5/03    10.81 CK
                    PLEASE SEE NEXT PAGE
```

HUNTINGTON STATE BANK
Member FDIC

ABA 113123667

COREY WOOD
RT 4 BOX 7020
HUNTINGTON TX 75949

STATEMENT PERIOD
LAST   ENDING
4/26/99   5/24/99

PAGE   2

SS# 451 61 3497

```
••••••••••••••••••••••••••••••••••••••••••••••••••••••••••••••••••••••••••••••••••
                                 TRANSACTIONS
CHECK      DATE     AMOUNT     CHECK      DATE     AMOUNT   DATE          BALANCE
NUMBER                        NUMBER
••••••••••••••••••••••••••••••••••••••••••••••••••••••••••••••••••••••••••••••••••
CHECKING          102250470  ·

           •••••••• DEPOSITS •••••••••
           5/18      300.00 DP
           5/21      831.15 DD
TIDEWATER MARINE PAYROLL
```

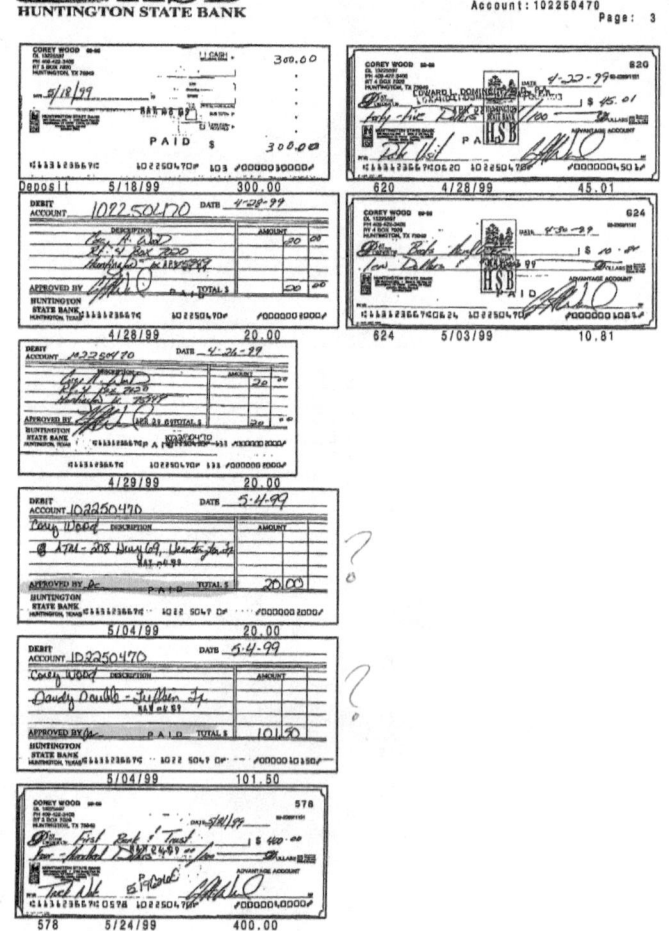

HUNTINGTON STATE BANK
MEMBER FDIC

HUNTINGTON	LUFKIN	ETOILE	ZAVALLA	CENTRAL
P.O. BOX 1090 • 208 HIGHWAY 69 SOUTH	2120 SOUTH FIRST ST.	HIGHWAY 103 EAST	252 MAIN ST.	3592 NORTH US HWY 59
HUNTINGTON, TEXAS 75949	LUFKIN, TEXAS 75901	ETOILE, TEXAS 75944	ZAVALLA, TEXAS 75980	LUFKIN, TEXAS 75904
(409) 639-5566	(409) 638-5566	(409) 639-5566	(409) 897-9023	(409) 639-5566

ABA 113123667

```
        COREY WOOD                    STATEMENT PERIOD
        RT 4 BOX 7020                 LAST        ENDING
     8  HUNTINGTON TX 75949           5/24/99     6/24/99

                                      PAGE      1

                                      SS# 451 61 3497
```

ACCOUNT NUMBER	PREVIOUS BALANCE	··· CREDITS ··· COUNT AMOUNT	··· DEBITS ··· COUNT AMOUNT	TOTAL FEE	PRESENT BALANCE
DDA 102250470	539.87	2 2206.30	25 1581.78	7.00	1164.39

TRANSACTIONS

CHECK NUMBER	DATE	AMOUNT	CHECK NUMBER	DATE	AMOUNT	DATE	BALANCE
CHECKING		102250470					

DAYS IN THIS CYCLE   31

********** CHECKS **********

				DATE	BALANCE
TRAN FEE	5/28	1.15 DM		5/28	466.72
10183 HWY. 90 E	5/28	52.00 MDB MORGAN CITY LA		6/01	142.02
	5/28	20.00 CK		6/02	41.69
TRAN FEE	6/01	1.15 DM		6/03	88.38-
TRAN FEE	6/01	1.15 DM		6/04	184.45-
208 HWY 69	6/01	200.00 MDB HUNTINGTON TX		6/07	218.33-
TOWNE SQUARE	6/01	20.40 MDB LUFKIN TX		6/08	776.38
NEW ORLEANS AIRPOR	6/01	102.00 MDB T KENNER LA		6/14	702.36
TRAN FEE	6/02	1.15 DM		6/16	677.36
TRAN FEE	6/02	1.15 DM		6/17	359.80
TRAN FEE	6/02	1.15 DM		6/22	1571.39
GLORIETA COLON	6/02	51.46 MDB CAJERO 4120 MEX		6/24	1164.39
SUC REFORMA	6/02	40.27 MDB MEXICO MEX			
GLORIETA COLON	6/02	5.15 MDB CAJERO 4120 MEX			
NSF CHARGES	6/03	17.50 OD			
NSF CHARGES	6/04	17.50 OD			
NSF CHARGES	6/07	17.50 OD			
MAINTENANCE FEE	6/24	7.00 SC			
409*	6/17	317.56 CK	412* 6/14	74.02 CK	
414*	6/07	16.38 PAY			

PLEASE SEE NEXT PAGE

309

HUNTINGTON STATE BANK
MEMBER FDIC

HUNTINGTON	LUFKIN	ETOILE	ZAVALLA	CENTRAL
P.O. BOX 1000 • 208 HIGHWAY 69 SOUTH	2120 SOUTH FIRST ST.	HIGHWAY 103 EAST	250 MAIN ST.	3592 NORTH US HWY 69
HUNTINGTON, TEXAS 75949	LUFKIN, TEXAS 75901	ETOILE, TEXAS 75944	ZAVALLA, TEXAS 75980	LUFKIN, TEXAS 75904
(409) 639-5566	(409) 639-5566	(409) 639-5566	(409) 897-9023	(409) 639-5566

ABA 113123667

```
                    COREY WOOD                          STATEMENT PERIOD
                    RT 4 BOX 7020                       LAST      ENDING
         8          HUNTINGTON TX 75949                 5/24/99   6/24/99

                                                        PAGE   1

                                                        SS# 451 61 3497
```

ACCOUNT NUMBER	PREVIOUS BALANCE	··· CREDITS ··· COUNT AMOUNT	··· DEBITS ··· COUNT AMOUNT	TOTAL FEE	PRESENT BALANCE
DDA 102250470	539.87	2 2206.30	25 1581.78	7.00	1164.39

```
CHECK    DATE     AMOUNT      TRANSACTIONS
NUMBER                        CHECK     DATE     AMOUNT   DATE          BALANCE
                              NUMBER

CHECKING          102250470

                                        DAYS IN THIS CYCLE        31


                ********** CHECKS **********
                5/28        1.15 DM                          5/28      466.72
    TRAN FEE
                5/28       52.00 MDB                          6/01      142.02
    10183 HWY. 90 E         MORGAN CITY  LA
                5/28       20.00 CK                           6/02       41.69
                6/01        1.15 DM                           6/03       88.38-
    TRAN FEE
                6/01        1.15 DM                           6/04      184.45-
    TRAN FEE
                6/01      200.00 MDB                          6/07      218.33-
    208 HWY 69             HUNTINGTON     TX
                6/01       20.40 MDB                          6/08      776.38
    TOWNE SQUARE          LUFKIN          TX
                6/01      102.00 MDB                          6/14      702.36
    NEW ORLEANS AIRPOR T KENNER          LA
                6/02        1.15 DM                           6/16      677.36
    TRAN FEE
                6/02        1.15 DM                           6/17      359.80
    TRAN FEE
                6/02        1.15 DM                           6/22     1571.39
    TRAN FEE
                6/02       51.46 MDB                          6/24     1164.39
    GLORIETA COLON        CAJERO 4120 MEX
                6/02       40.27 MDB
    SUC REFORMA           MEXICO         MEX
                6/02        5.15 MDB
    GLORIETA COLON        CAJERO 4120 MEX
                6/03       17.50 OD
    NSF CHARGES
                6/04       17.50 OD
    NSF CHARGES
                6/07       17.50 OD
    NSF CHARGES
                6/24        7.00 SC
    MAINTENANCE FEE
    409*   6/17      317.56 CK      412*  6/14    74.02 CK
    414*   6/07       16.38 PAY
                              PLEASE SEE NEXT PAGE
```

HSB
HUNTINGTON STATE BANK
Member FDIC

ABA 113123667

COREY WOOD
RT 4 BOX 7020
HUNTINGTON TX 75949

STATEMENT PERIOD
LAST   ENDING
5/24/99   6/24/99

PAGE   2

SS# 451 61 3497

```
********************************TRANSACTIONS*******************************************
CHECK      DATE     AMOUNT     CHECK      DATE     AMOUNT   DATE            BALANCE
NUMBER                         NUMBER
*********************************************************************************
CHECKING            102250470
NSF ITEM
    416*   6/24     400.00 CK
    577*   6/03     112.57 PAY
NSF ITEM
    585*   6/04      78.57 PAY
NSF ITEM
    623*   6/16      25.00 CK

         ********* DEPOSITS **********

           6/08     994.71 DD
TIDEWATER MARINE PAYROLL
           6/22    1211.59 DD
TIDEWATER MARINE PAYROLL
```

HUNTINGTON STATE BANK
MEMBER FDIC

HUNTINGTON	LUFKIN	ETOILE	ZAVALLA	CENTRAL
P.O. BOX 1090 • 208 HIGHWAY 69 SOUTH	2120 SOUTH FIRST ST.	HIGHWAY 103 EAST	250 MAIN ST.	100 CHIMNEY ROCK
HUNTINGTON, TEXAS 75949	LUFKIN, TEXAS 75901	ETOILE, TEXAS 75944	ZAVALLA, TEXAS 75980	LUFKIN, TEXAS 75904
(409) 422-3000 • (409) 636-2206	(409) 639-5566	(409) 854-2205	(409) 897-9023	(409) 632-4589

ABA 113123667

```
              COREY WOOD                    STATEMENT PERIOD
              RT 4 BOX 7020                 LAST      ENDING
        15    HUNTINGTON TX 75949           3/17/99   4/26/99

                                            PAGE   1

                                            SS# 451 61 3497
```

ACCOUNT NUMBER	PREVIOUS BALANCE	CREDITS COUNT	AMOUNT	DEBITS COUNT	AMOUNT	TOTAL FEE	PRESENT BALANCE
DDA 102250470	1454.61	2	900.80	56	2067.02	7.00	288.39

```
CHECK   DATE   AMOUNT   TRANSACTIONS
NUMBER                  CHECK   DATE   AMOUNT  DATE       BALANCE
                        NUMBER

CHECKING       102250470          DAYS IN THIS CYCLE      40

********** CHECKS **********
        3/18    1.15 DM                            3/18   1363.06
TRAN FEE
        3/18   50.00 MDB                           3/19   1320.91
208 HWY 69, HUNTINGTON TX  HUNTINGTON  TX
        3/18   20.40 MDB                           3/22   1898.71
ANGELINA VILLAGE            LUFKIN      TX
        3/18   20.00 MDB                           3/23   1546.28
208 HWY 69, HUNTINGTON TX  HUNTINGTON  TX
        3/19    1.15 DM                            3/25   1523.63
TRAN FEE
        3/19   41.00 MDB                           3/26   1293.63
107 QUITMAN STREET         EMORY,      TX
        3/22   51.50 MDB                           3/29   1243.63
ROUTE 4, BOX 8520          NACOGDOCHES TX
        3/22   51.50 MDB                           3/30   1033.63
RT 1 BOX 4705              LUFKIN      TX
        3/22   20.00 MDB                           3/31   1013.63
208 HWY 69, HUNTINGTON TX  HUNTINGTON  TX
        3/23   20.00 MDB                           4/02    961.48
208 HWY 69, HUNTINGTON TX  HUNTINGTON  TX
        3/25   21.50 MDB                           4/05    879.98
*LUFKIN MALL               LUFKIN      TX          4/06    829.98
        3/25    1.15 DM                            4/07    777.58
TRAN FEE
        3/26  200.00 CK         3/29   50.00 CCK 4/08     747.58
        3/30  200.00 MDB                          4/09    666.38
100 CHIMNEY ROCK,LUFKINTX  LUFKIN      TX
        3/30   10.00 MDB                           4/12    491.73
100 CHIMNEY ROCK,LUFKINTX  LUFKIN      TX
        3/31   20.00 MDB                           4/13    480.74
208 HWY 69, HUNTINGTON TX  HUNTINGTON  TX
        4/02    1.15 DM                            4/15    447.09
TRAN FEE
        4/02   51.00 MDB                           4/16    417.09
2510 W FRANK               LUFKIN      TX
        4/05   51.50 MDB                           4/19    290.92
                       PLEASE SEE NEXT PAGE
```

MEMBER FDIC

HUNTINGTON	LUFKIN	ETOILE	ZAVALLA	CENTRAL
P.O. BOX 1090 • 208 HIGHWAY 69 SOUTH	2100 SOUTH FIRST ST.	HIGHWAY 103 EAST	250 MAIN ST.	2592 NORTH US HWY 69
HUNTINGTON, TEXAS 75949	LUFKIN, TEXAS 75901	ETOILE, TEXAS 75944	ZAVALLA, TEXAS 75980	LUFKIN, TEXAS 75904
(409) 833-5368	(409) 639-5566	(409) 897-5586	(409) 897-9022	(409) 639-5566

ABA 113123667

```
        COREY WOOD                    STATEMENT PERIOD
        RT 4 BOX 7020                 LAST        ENDING
   8    HUNTINGTON TX 75949           5/24/99     6/24/99

                                            PAGE     1

                                      SS# 451 61 3497
```

ACCOUNT NUMBER	PREVIOUS BALANCE	--- CREDITS --- COUNT	AMOUNT	--- DEBITS --- COUNT	AMOUNT	TOTAL FEE	PRESENT BALANCE
DDA 102250470	539.87	2	2206.30	25	1581.78	7.00	1164.39

TRANSACTIONS

CHECK NUMBER	DATE	AMOUNT	CHECK NUMBER	DATE	AMOUNT	DATE	BALANCE
CHECKING		102250470					

DAYS IN THIS CYCLE   31

```
********** CHECKS **********

              5/28      1.15 DM                               5/28      466.72
TRAN FEE      5/28     52.00 MDB                              6/01      142.02
10183 HWY. 90 E        MORGAN CITY  LA
              5/28     20.00 CK                               6/02       41.69
              6/01      1.15 DM                               6/03       88.38-
TRAN FEE
              6/01      1.15 DM                               6/04      184.45-
TRAN FEE
              6/01    200.00 MDB                              6/07      218.33-
208 HWY 69             HUNTINGTON    TX
              6/01     20.40 MDB                              6/08      776.38
TOWNE SQUARE           LUFKIN        TX
              6/01    102.00 MDB                              6/14      702.36
NEW ORLEANS AIRPOR     T KENNER      LA
              6/02      1.15 DM                               6/16      677.36
TRAN FEE
              6/02      1.15 DM                               6/17      359.80
TRAN FEE
              6/02      1.15 DM                               6/22     1571.39
TRAN FEE
              6/02     51.46 MDB                              6/24     1164.39
GLORIETA COLON         CAJERO 4120 MEX
              6/02     40.27 MDB
SUC REFORMA            MEXICO       MEX
              6/02      5.15 MDB
GLORIETA COLON         CAJERO 4120 MEX
              6/03     17.50 OD
NSF CHARGES
              6/04     17.50 OD
NSF CHARGES
              6/07     17.50 OD
NSF CHARGES
              6/24      7.00 SC
MAINTENANCE FEE
        409* 6/17    317.56 CK        412* 6/14      74.02 CK
        414* 6/07     16.38 PAY
                          PLEASE SEE NEXT PAGE
```

313

HUNTINGTON STATE BANK
Member FDIC

ABA 113123667

COREY WOOD
RT 4 BOX 7020
HUNTINGTON TX 75949

STATEMENT PERIOD
LAST   ENDING
5/24/99   6/24/99

PAGE   2

SS# 451 61 3497

•••••••••••••••••••••••••••••••••••••• TRANSACTIONS ••

CHECK NUMBER	DATE	AMOUNT	CHECK NUMBER	DATE	AMOUNT	DATE	BALANCE

CHECKING   102250470
NSF ITEM
    416*   6/24   400.00 CK
    577*   6/03   112.57 PAY
NSF ITEM
    585*   6/04   78.57 PAY
NSF ITEM
    623*   6/16   25.00 CK

•••••••••• DEPOSITS ••••••••••

              6/08   994.71 DD
TIDEWATER MARINE PAYROLL
              6/22   1211.59 DD
TIDEWATER MARINE PAYROLL

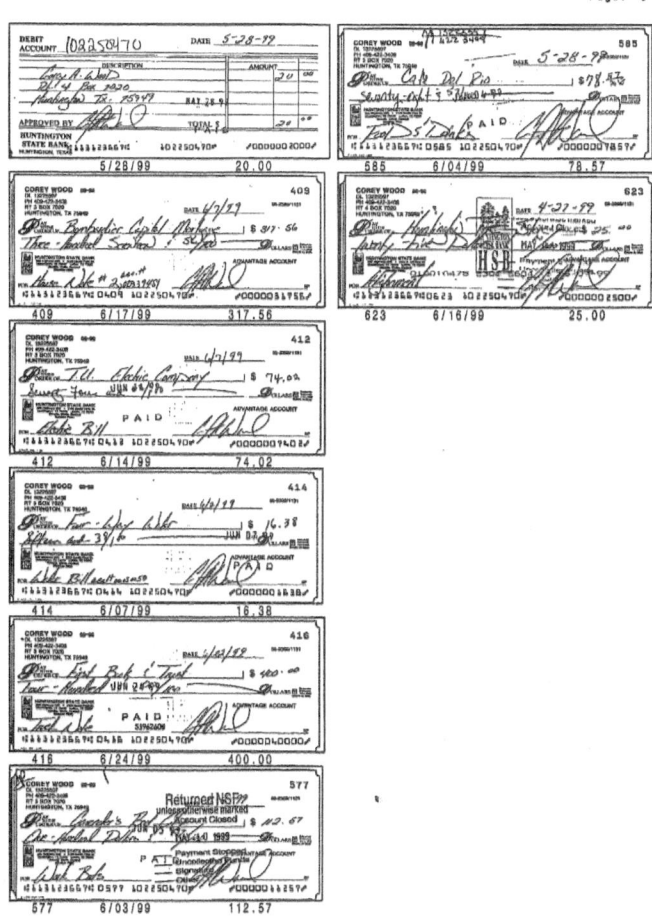

HUNTINGTON STATE BANK

MEMBER FDIC

HUNTINGTON	LUFKIN	ETOILE	ZAVALLA	CENTRAL
P.O. BOX 1090 • 206 HIGHWAY 69 SOUTH	2120 SOUTH FIRST ST.	HIGHWAY 103 EAST	250 MAIN ST.	3592 NORTH US HWY 69
HUNTINGTON, TEXAS 75949	LUFKIN, TEXAS 75901	ETOILE, TEXAS 75944	ZAVALLA, TEXAS 75980	LUFKIN, TEXAS 75904
(409) 639-5566	(409) 639-5566	(409) 639-5566	(409) 897-9023	(409) 639-5566

ABA 113123667

```
                                                          STATEMENT PERIOD
        COREY WOOD                                         LAST      ENDING
        RT 4 BOX 7020                                     6/24/99    7/26/99
   4    HUNTINGTON TX 75949
                                                          PAGE    1

                                                          SS# 451 61 3497
```

ACCOUNT NUMBER	PREVIOUS BALANCE	--- CREDITS --- COUNT	AMOUNT	--- DEBITS --- COUNT	AMOUNT	TOTAL FEE	PRESENT BALANCE
DDA 102250470	1164.39	2	2376.79	5	915.02	7.00	2626.16

CHECK NUMBER	DATE	AMOUNT	TRANSACTIONS CHECK NUMBER	DATE	AMOUNT	DATE	BALANCE

CHECKING   102250470

DAYS IN THIS CYCLE   32

```
********** CHECKS **********
            7/26        7.00 SC                                    7/08     2255.31
MAINTENANCE FEE
    404*    7/26      400.00 CK      410*   7/14   317.56 CK       7/09     2139.12
    413*    7/09      116.19 CK      415*   7/08    74.27 CK       7/14     1821.56
                                                                  7/22     3033.16
                                                                  7/26     2626.16

********* DEPOSITS **********
            7/08     1165.19 DD
TIDEWATER MARINE PAYROLL
            7/22     1211.60 DD
TIDEWATER MARINE PAYROLL
```

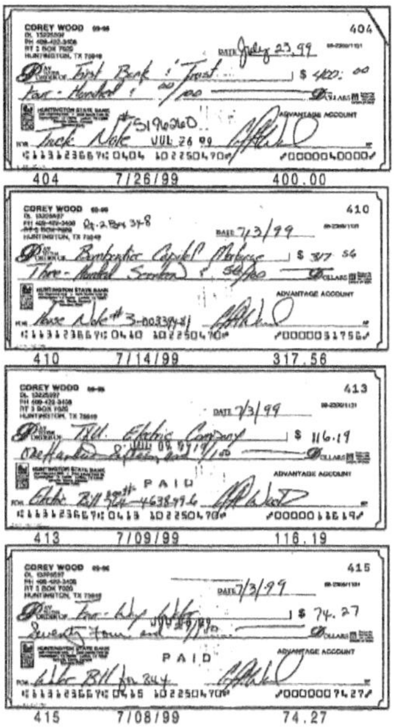

HUNTINGTON STATE BANK
MEMBER FDIC

HUNTINGTON	LUFKIN	ETOILE	ZAVALLA	CENTRAL
P.O. BOX 1090 • 268 HIGHWAY 69 SOUTH	2120 SOUTH FIRST ST.	HIGHWAY 103 EAST	250 MAIN ST.	3582 NORTH US HWY 69
HUNTINGTON, TEXAS 75949	LUFKIN, TEXAS 75901	ETOILE, TEXAS 75944	ZAVALLA, TEXAS 75980	LUFKIN, TEXAS 75904
(409) 839-5566	(409) 639-5566	(409) 639-5566	(409) 897-9023	(409) 639-5566

ABA 113123667

```
        COREY WOOD
        RT 4 BOX 7020                     STATEMENT PERIOD
    4   HUNTINGTON TX 75949               LAST      ENDING
                                          6/24/99   7/26/99

                                             PAGE   1

                                          SS# 451 61 3497
```

ACCOUNT NUMBER	PREVIOUS BALANCE	--- CREDITS --- COUNT	AMOUNT	--- DEBITS --- COUNT	AMOUNT	TOTAL FEE	PRESENT BALANCE
DDA 102250470	1164.39	2	2376.79	5	915.02	7.00	2626.16

TRANSACTIONS

CHECK NUMBER	DATE	AMOUNT	CHECK NUMBER	DATE	AMOUNT	DATE	BALANCE
CHECKING		102250470					

DAYS IN THIS CYCLE   32

```
********** CHECKS **********
        7/26      7.00 SC                               7/08    2255.31
MAINTENANCE FEE
    404*  7/26    400.00 CK   410*  7/14  317.56 CK  7/09    2139.12
    413*  7/09    116.19 CK   415*  7/08   74.27 CK  7/14    1821.56
                                                     7/22    3033.16
                                                     7/26    2626.16

********* DEPOSITS *********
        7/08    1165.19 DD
TIDEWATER MARINE PAYROLL
        7/22    1211.60 DD
TIDEWATER MARINE PAYROLL
```

HUNTINGTON STATE BANK

COREY WOOD
Account: 102250470
Page: 2

404	7/26/99	400.00
410	7/14/99	317.56
413	7/07/99	116.19
415	7/08/99	74.27

HUNTINGTON STATE BANK
MEMBER FDIC

HUNTINGTON	LUFKIN	ETOILE	ZAVALLA	CENTRAL
P.O. BOX 1090 • 206 HIGHWAY 69 SOUTH	2120 SOUTH FIRST ST.	HIGHWAY 103 EAST	250 MAIN ST.	3592 NORTH US HWY 59
HUNTINGTON, TEXAS 75949	LUFKIN, TEXAS 75901	ETOILE, TEXAS 75944	ZAVALLA, TEXAS 75980	LUFKIN, TEXAS 75901
(409) 639-5566	(409) 639-5566	(409) 639-6508	(409) 897-9023	(409) 639-9500

ABA 113123667

```
COREY WOOD                    STATEMENT PERIOD
RT 4 BOX 7020                 LAST      ENDING
5   HUNTINGTON TX 75949       7/26/99   8/24/99
                              PAGE     1
                              SS# 451 61 3497
```

ACCOUNT NUMBER	PREVIOUS BALANCE	... CREDITS ... COUNT AMOUNT	... DEBITS ... COUNT AMOUNT	TOTAL FEE	PRESENT BALANCE
DDA 102250470	2626.16	2 2443.57	6 1342.31	7.00	3727.42

TRANSACTIONS

CHECK NUMBER	DATE	AMOUNT	CHECK NUMBER	DATE	AMOUNT	DATE	BALANCE

CHECKING   102250470

DAYS IN THIS CYCLE   29

********** CHECKS ***********

MAINTENANCE FEE	8/24	7.00 SC				8/05	2544.05
405*	8/12	400.00 CK	411*	8/09	317.56 CK	8/06	3776.03
579*	8/12	400.00 CK	580	8/05	82.11 CK	8/09	3458.47
582*	8/10	135.64 CK				8/10	3322.83
						8/12	2522.83
						8/20	3734.42
						8/24	3727.42

********** DEPOSITS **********

| | 8/06 | 1231.98 DD |
| TIDEWATER MARINE PAYROLL |
| | 8/20 | 1211.59 DD |
| TIDEWATER MARINE PAYROLL |

HUNTINGTON STATE BANK

MEMBER FDIC

HUNTINGTON	LUFKIN	ETOILE	ZAVALLA	CENTRAL
P.O. BOX 1090 • 208 HIGHWAY 69 SOUTH	2120 SOUTH FIRST ST.	HIGHWAY 103 EAST	260 MAIN ST.	3592 NORTH US HWY 69
HUNTINGTON, TEXAS 75949	LUFKIN, TEXAS 75901	ETOILE, TEXAS 75944	ZAVALLA, TEXAS 75980	LUFKIN, TEXAS 75904
(409) 639-0566	(409) 639-8566	(409) 639-5566	(409) 897-9023	(409) 639-8566

ABA 113123667

COREY WOOD
RT 4 BOX 7020
12   HUNTINGTON TX 75949

STATEMENT PERIOD
LAST   ENDING
8/24/99   9/26/99

PAGE   1

SS# 451 61 3497

ACCOUNT NUMBER	PREVIOUS BALANCE	... CREDITS ... COUNT AMOUNT	... DEBITS ... COUNT AMOUNT	TOTAL FEE	PRESENT BALANCE
DDA 102250470	3727.42	2 1979.67	43 4529.21	7.00	1177.88

CHECK NUMBER	DATE	AMOUNT	TRANSACTIONS CHECK NUMBER	DATE	AMOUNT	DATE	BALANCE

CHECKING   102250470

DAYS IN THIS CYCLE   33

********** CHECKS **********

	DATE	AMOUNT		DATE	BALANCE
TRAN FEE	8/26	1.15 DM		8/26	3359.89
TRAN FEE	8/26	1.15 DM		9/02	2959.89
TRAN FEE	8/26	1.15 DM		9/07	3906.09
TRAN FEE	8/26	1.15 DM		9/08	2706.09
TRAN FEE	8/26	1.15 DM		9/09	2239.09
TRAN FEE	8/26	1.15 DM		9/10	1639.09
TRAN FEE	8/26	1.15 DM		9/16	1537.09
TRAN FEE	8/26	1.15 DM		9/17	1337.09
	8/26	108.58 MDB		9/20	837.09
336 OFICINA CEN	8/26	108.58 MDB	VERACRUZ, MEX	9/21	1429.43
BANAMEX			MEX		
BANAMEX	8/26	54.29 MDB	MEX	9/22	1327.03
	8/26	21.72 MDB		9/23	1184.88
336 OFICINA CEN	8/26	21.72 MDB	VERACRUZ, MEX	9/26	1177.88
336 OFICINA CEN	8/26	21.72 MDB	VERACRUZ, MEX		
BANAMEX			MEX		
BANAMEX	8/26	10.86 MDB	MEX		
BANAMEX	8/26	10.86 MDB	MEX		
	9/07	21.67 MDB			
MULTIBANCO COMERMEX			BCO INVERLAT		
TRAN FEE	9/07	1.15 DM			
	9/07	1.15 DM			

PLEASE SEE NEXT PAGE

MEMBER FDIC

HUNTINGTON	LUFKIN	ETOILE	ZAVALLA	CENTRAL
P.O. BOX 1090 • 208 HIGHWAY 69 SOUTH	2120 SOUTH FIRST ST.	HIGHWAY 103 EAST	250 MAIN ST.	3502 NORTH US HWY 69
HUNTINGTON, TEXAS 75949	LUFKIN, TEXAS 75901	ETOILE, TEXAS 75944	ZAVALLA, TEXAS 75980	LUFKIN, TEXAS 75904
(409) 539-5566	(409) 639-5566	(409) 639-6560	(409) 897-9022	(409) 639-1560

ABA 113123667

```
                 COREY WOOD              STATEMENT PERIOD
                 RT 4 BOX 7020           LAST      ENDING
       3         HUNTINGTON TX 75949     9/26/99   10/28/99

                                             PAGE   1

                                         SS# 451 61 3497
```

ACCOUNT NUMBER	PREVIOUS BALANCE	--- CREDITS --- COUNT AMOUNT	--- DEBITS --- COUNT AMOUNT	TOTAL FEE	PRESENT BALANCE
DDA 102250470	1177.88		7 1177.88		*CLOSED ACCT*

CHECK NUMBER	DATE	AMOUNT	CHECK NUMBER	TRANSACTIONS DATE	AMOUNT	DATE	BALANCE

CHECKING   102250470

DAYS IN THIS CYCLE   32

********** CHECKS **********

```
              9/27       60.00  MDB                              9/27      973.99
208 HW 69                       HUNTINGTON   TX
              9/27       60.00  MDB                              9/28      966.76
208 HW 69                       HUNTINGTON   TX
              9/27       20.00  MDB                              10/15       0.00
208 HW 69                       HUNTINGTON   TX
              9/27       13.89  MDB
2215 SOUTH FIRST STUS           LUFKIN       TX    10/15    966.76 CLO
              9/27       50.00  CCK
      590*    9/28        7.23  CK
```

********** DEPOSITS **********

HUNTINGTON STATE BANK
Member FDIC

ABA 113123667

COREY WOOD
RT 4 BOX 7020
HUNTINGTON TX 75949

STATEMENT PERIOD
LAST   ENDING
8/24/99   9/26/99

PAGE   2

SS# 451 61 3497

●●●●●●●●●●●●●●●●●●●●●●●●●●●●●●●●●TRANSACTIONS●●●●●●●●●●●●●●●●●●●●●●●●●●●●●●●●●●●●●

CHECK NUMBER	DATE	AMOUNT	CHECK NUMBER	DATE	AMOUNT	DATE	BALANCE
CHECKING		102250470					
TRAN FEE	9/07	1.15 DM					
TRAN FEE	9/07	162.55 MDB					
CD DEL CARMEN			CD DEL CARMEN				
	9/07	107.88 MDB					
BANAMEX			MEX				
	9/08	800.00 CCK		9/08	400.00 CK		
	9/10	500.00 CCK					
	9/10	100.00 MDB					
208 HWY 69			HUNTINGTON	TX			
	9/17	200.00 CCK		9/20	500.00 CCK		
	9/21	40.00 MDB					
208 HWY 69			HUNTINGTON	TX			
	9/22	1.15 DM					
TRAN FEE	9/22	.25 DM					
TRAN FEE	9/22	101.00 MDB					
111 CHAMPIONS			LUFKIN	TX			
	9/23	1.15 DM					
TRAN FEE	9/23	40.00 MDB					
208 HWY 69			HUNTINGTON	TX			
	9/23	101.00 MDB					
2510 W FRANK			LUFKIN	TX			
	9/26	7.00 SC					
MAINTENANCE FEE							
403*	9/02	400.00 CK	581*	9/07	36.58 CK		
583*	9/09	149.44 CK	584	9/09	317.56 CK		
586*	9/16	32.00 CK	587	9/16	70.00 CK		
588	9/21	69.00 CK					

********* DEPOSITS *********

	9/07	1278.33 DD
TIDEWATER MARINE PAYROLL		
	9/21	701.34 DD
TIDEWATER MARINE PAYROLL		

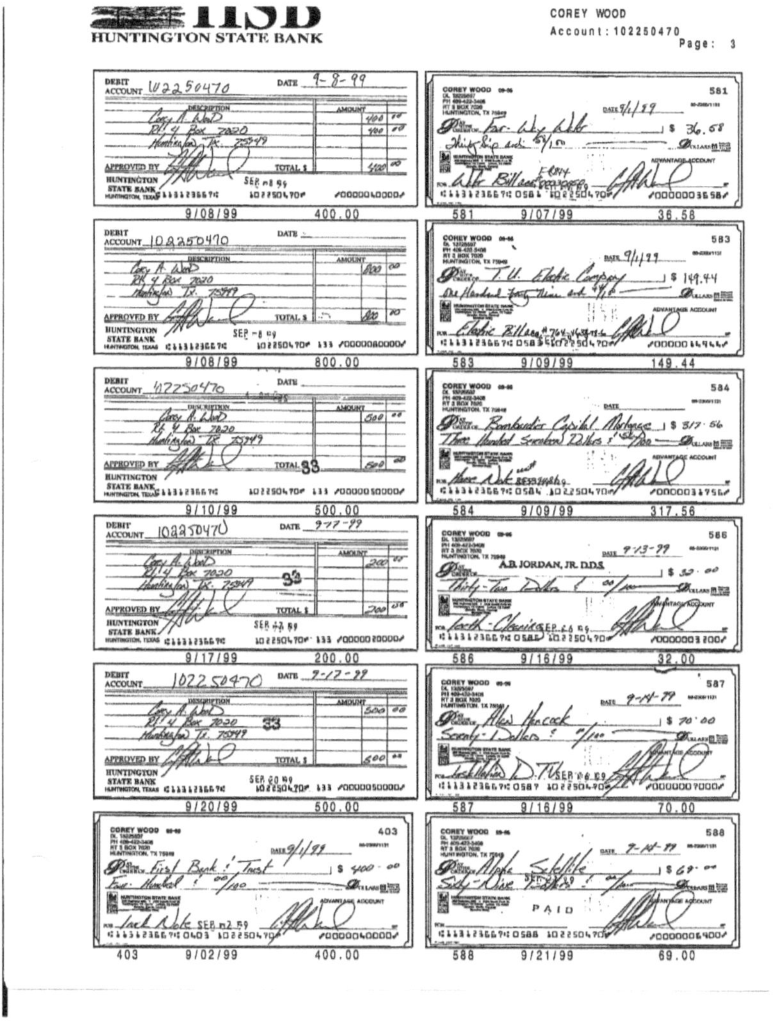
HUNTINGTON STATE BANK
COREY WOOD
Account: 102250470
Page: 3
9/08/99 400.00
581 9/07/99 36.58
9/08/99 800.00
583 9/09/99 149.44
9/10/99 500.00
584 9/09/99 317.56
9/17/99 200.00
586 9/16/99 32.00
9/20/99 500.00
587 9/16/99 70.00
403 9/02/99 400.00
588 9/21/99 69.00

HUNTINGTON STATE BANK

MEMBER FDIC

HUNTINGTON	LUFKIN	ETOILE	ZAVALLA	CENTRAL
P.O. BOX 1090 • 208 HIGHWAY 69 SOUTH HUNTINGTON, TEXAS 75949 (409) 639-5566	2130 SOUTH FIRST ST. LUFKIN, TEXAS 75901 (409) 639-5566	HIGHWAY 103 EAST ETOILE, TEXAS 75944 (409) 639-5566	250 MAIN ST ZAVALLA, TEXAS 75980 (409) 897-9023	3592 NORTH US HWY 69 LUFKIN, TEXAS 75904 (409) 639-5566

ABA 113123667

```
        COREY WOOD                     STATEMENT PERIOD
        RT 4 BOX 7020                  LAST        ENDING
   5    HUNTINGTON TX 75949            7/26/99      8/24/99

                                       PAGE     1

                                       SS# 451 61 3497
```

ACCOUNT NUMBER	PREVIOUS BALANCE	--- CREDITS --- COUNT	AMOUNT	--- DEBITS --- COUNT	AMOUNT	TOTAL FEE	PRESENT BALANCE
DDA 102250470	2626.16	2	2443.57	6	1342.31	7.00	3727.42

CHECK NUMBER	DATE	AMOUNT	TRANSACTIONS CHECK NUMBER	DATE	AMOUNT	DATE	BALANCE
CHECKING		102250470					

DAYS IN THIS CYCLE   29

********** CHECKS **********

	8/24	7.00 SC				8/05	2544.05
MAINTENANCE FEE							
405*	8/12	400.00 CK	411*	8/09	317.56 CK	8/06	3776.03
579*	8/12	400.00 CK	580	8/05	82.11 CK	8/09	3458.47
582*	8/10	135.64 CK				8/10	3322.83
						8/12	2522.83
						8/20	3734.42
						8/24	3727.42

********* DEPOSITS **********

	8/06	1231.98 DD
TIDEWATER MARINE PAYROLL		
	8/20	1211.59 DD
TIDEWATER MARINE PAYROLL		

326

HUNTINGTON	LUFKIN	ETOILE	ZAVALLA	CENTRAL
P.O. BOX 1090 • 208 HIGHWAY 69 SOUTH	2120 SOUTH FIRST ST.	HIGHWAY 103 EAST	250 MAIN ST.	3592 NORTH US HWY 69
HUNTINGTON, TEXAS 75949	LUFKIN, TEXAS 75901	ETOILE, TEXAS 75944	ZAVALLA, TEXAS 75980	LUFKIN, TEXAS 75904
(409) 639-8686	(409) 639-5586	(409) 639-5586	(409) 897-9023	(409) 639-5586

ABA 113123667

```
                  COREY WOOD                          STATEMENT PERIOD
                  RT 4 BOX 7020                        LAST      ENDING
        12        HUNTINGTON TX 75949                  8/24/99   9/26/99

                                                     PAGE    1

                                                     SS# 451 61 3497
```

ACCOUNT NUMBER	PREVIOUS BALANCE	... CREDITS ... COUNT	AMOUNT	... DEBITS ... COUNT	AMOUNT	TOTAL FEE	PRESENT BALANCE
DDA 102250470	3727.42	2	1979.67	43	4529.21	7.00	1177.88

CHECK NUMBER	DATE	AMOUNT	TRANSACTIONS CHECK NUMBER	DATE	AMOUNT	DATE	BALANCE

```
CHECKING          102250470
                                    DAYS IN THIS CYCLE          33


          ********** CHECKS **********
              8/26        1.15 DM                          8/26      3359.89
TRAN FEE      8/26        1.15 DM                          9/02      2959.89
TRAN FEE      8/26        1.15 DM                          9/07      3906.09
TRAN FEE      8/26        1.15 DM                          9/08      2706.09
TRAN FEE      8/26        1.15 DM                          9/09      2239.09
TRAN FEE      8/26        1.15 DM                          9/10      1639.09
TRAN FEE      8/26        1.15 DM                          9/16      1537.09
TRAN FEE      8/26        1.15 DM                          9/17      1337.09
TRAN FEE      8/26      108.68 MDB                         9/20       837.09
336 OFICINA CEN          VERACRUZ, MEX
              8/26      108.58 MDB                         9/21      1429.43
BANAMEX                  MEX
              8/26       54.29 MDB                         9/22      1327.03
BANAMEX                  MEX
              8/26       21.72 MDB                         9/23      1184.88
336 OFICINA CEN          VERACRUZ, MEX
              8/26       21.72 MDB                         9/26      1177.88
336 OFICINA CEN          VERACRUZ, MEX
              8/26       21.72 MDB
BANAMEX                  MEX
              8/26       10.86 MDB
BANAMEX                  MEX
              8/26       10.86 MDB
BANAMEX                  MEX
              9/07       21.67 MDB
MULTIBANCO COMERMEX      BCO INVERLAT
              9/07        1.15 DM
TRAN FEE
              9/07        1.15 DM

                        PLEASE SEE NEXT PAGE
```

9/27/99   50.00

10/15/99   966.76

590   9/28/99   7.23

HUNTINGTON STATE BANK
Member FDIC

ABA 113123667

COREY WOOD
RT 4 BOX 7020
HUNTINGTON TX 75949

STATEMENT PERIOD
LAST   ENDING
8/24/99   9/26/99

PAGE   2

SS# 451 61 3497

```
****************************TRANSACTIONS****************************
CHECK      DATE      AMOUNT     CHECK       DATE     AMOUNT   DATE          BALANCE
NUMBER                         NUMBER
****************************************************************************
CHECKING              102250470
TRAN FEE
           9/07         1.15 DM
TRAN FEE
           9/07       162.55 MDB
CD DEL CARMEN                    CD DEL CARMEN
           9/07       107.88 MDB
BANAMEX                          MEX
           9/08       800.00 CCK            9/08     400.00 CK
           9/10       500.00 CCK
           9/10       100.00 MDB
208 HWY 69                      HUNTINGTON   TX
           9/17       200.00 CCK            9/20     500.00 CCK
           9/21        40.00 MDB
208 HWY 69                      HUNTINGTON   TX
           9/22         1.15 DM
TRAN FEE
           9/22          .25 DM
TRAN FEE
           9/22       101.00 MDB
111 CHAMPIONS                   LUFKIN       TX
           9/23         1.15 DM
TRAN FEE
           9/23        40.00 MDB
208 HWY 69                      HUNTINGTON   TX
           9/23       101.00 MDB
2510 W FRANK                    LUFKIN       TX
           9/26         7.00 SC
MAINTENANCE FEE
           403*  9/02  400.00 CK     581*  9/07     36.58 CK
           583*  9/09  149.44 CK     584   9/09    317.56 CK
           586*  9/16   32.00 CK     587   9/16     70.00 CK
           588   9/21   69.00 CK

           ******** DEPOSITS *********
                 9/07     1278.33 DD
TIDEWATER MARINE PAYROLL
                 9/21      701.34 DD
TIDEWATER MARINE PAYROLL
```

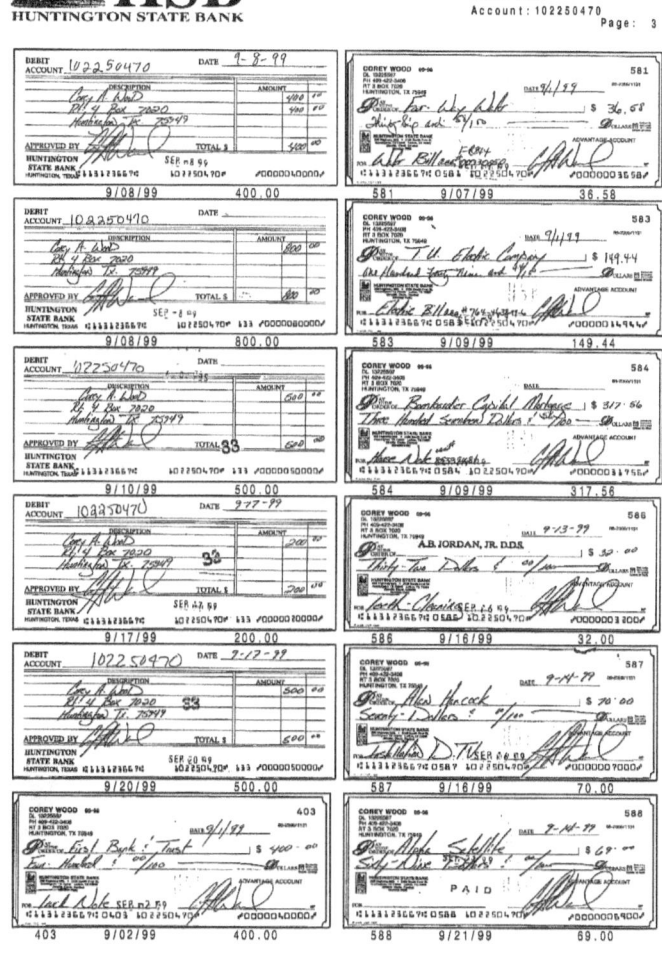

HUNTINGTON STATE BANK

MEMBER FDIC

HUNTINGTON	LUFKIN	ETOILE	ZAVALLA	CENTRAL
P.O. BOX 1090 • 208 HIGHWAY 69 SOUTH	2120 SOUTH FIRST ST.	HIGHWAY 103 EAST	250 MAIN ST.	3592 NORTH US HWY 69
HUNTINGTON, TEXAS 75949	LUFKIN, TEXAS 75901	ETOILE, TEXAS 75944	ZAVALLA, TEXAS 75980	LUFKIN, TEXAS 75904
(409) 639-5566	(409) 639-5566	(409) 639-5566	(409) 897-9023	(409) 639-5591

ABA 113123667

```
                COREY WOOD                        STATEMENT PERIOD
                RT 3 BOX 7020                      LAST      ENDING
        3       HUNTINGTON TX 75949                1/26/98   2/25/98

                                                   PAGE      1

                                                   SS# 451 61 3497
```

ACCOUNT NUMBER	PREVIOUS BALANCE	---CREDITS--- COUNT AMOUNT	---DEBITS--- COUNT AMOUNT	TOTAL FEE	PRESENT BALANCE
DDA 102250470	713.31	2 2342.34	7 1052.83	7.00	2002.82

CHECK NUMBER	DATE	AMOUNT	TRANSACTIONS CHECK NUMBER	DATE	AMOUNT DATE	BALANCE
CHECKING		102250470				

DAYS IN THIS CYCLE   30

********** CHECKS **********

```
        1/29    53.00 MDB                                    1/28      533.13
142 CHARLIE HARDSN         GOLDEN MEADOW LA
        2/10   201.50 MDB                                    1/29      480.13
3723 GULFWAY DR           PORT ARTHUR  TX
        2/10     1.15 DM                                     2/06     1668.19
TRAN FEE
        2/26     7.00 SC                                     2/10     1465.54
MAINTENANCE FEE
   1001*  1/28  180.18 CK        1004*  2/17   280.00 CCK 2/17     1185.54
   1005   2/25  330.00 CK                                    2/20     2339.82
                                                            2/25     2002.82
```

********** DEPOSITS **********

```
        2/06  1188.06 DD
TIDEWATER MARINE PAYROLL
        2/20  1154.28 DD
TIDEWATER MARINE PAYROLL
```

FDIC
Federal Deposit Insurance Corporation
1910 Pacific Avenue, 20th Floor
Dallas, TX 75201

Division of Compliance and Consumer Affairs
(972) 761-8016

October 12, 2000
Ref. No.: CAC2000D-000262-0

Sharon Joy Brunner
Rt. 2, Box 159-D
Huntington, TX 75949

Dear Sharon Joy Brunner:

Subject: Consumer Complaint Against
Huntington State Bank, Huntington, Texas

Mr. Rex Lowery, Chief Executive Officer of the subject bank, has responded to our inquiry of your complaint concerning alleged forged checks on your deceased son's checking account.

We have investigated your complaint by reviewing information provided by both you and the bank. Information obtained from the bank disclosed that Corey Wood (your son) opened a checking account at the bank on September 25, 1996 and it was closed on October 15, 1999. You are correct that according to the signature card on file, Mr. Wood was the only signer on the account. Mr. Lowery agrees that upon inspection of the checks that accompanied your complaint, they do indicate that a Mr. Randy Wilson's signature is on some of the checks usually signed "Corey Wood by Randy Wilson or Randy Wilson for Corey Wood." It appears that these checks cover a period of time from February 16, 1998 through November 5, 1998. Federal regulations do not mandate that the banking industry manually verify each check that passes through a financial institution.

You questioned the legality of several withdrawals from Mr. Wood's account. It appears that the withdrawals in question occurred during 1997 and 1998. Mr. Lowery stated Huntington State Bank makes every effort to assure that their depositors' funds are safeguarded from theft or embezzlement. It is the assumption of the bank that Mr. Wood was receiving the statements since the statements were not returned to the bank. In accordance with federal regulations Mr. Wood had 60 days to respond to any discrepancies in his account. Mr. Lowery further stated that to his knowledge and that of the employees of Huntington State Bank, they never received any complaints from Mr. Wood regarding his account.

The Federal Deposit Insurance Corporation (FDIC) is the primary federal regulator for Huntington State Bank and is responsible for enforcing compliance by that institution with

Regulation E, it was necessary for Mr. Wood to inform the Bank of an error or an unauthorized transaction in a timely manner. Unfortunately, the Bank maintains that Mr. Wood never alleged an error or unauthorized transaction, and there is no evidence to indicate otherwise.

We recognize your frustration in attempting to resolve your concerns with the Bank, but it appears that the Bank acted in accordance with Regulation E. The circumstances surrounding Mr. Wood's death are most regrettable. While this matter does not fall under the jurisdiction of FDIC's regulatory supervision, it may be more appropriately handled by law enforcement officials. Should you wish to pursue this matter, you may want to consult with law enforcement authorities or an attorney about legal remedies that may be available to you.

Your interest in this matter is appreciated. If you have further questions, the Division of Compliance and Consumer Affairs may be reached at (800) 934-3342.

Sincerely,

Donna Gambrell
Deputy Director

Enclosures

FDIC
Federal Deposit Insurance Corporation
1910 Pacific Avenue, 20th Floor
Dallas, TX 75201

Division of Compliance and Consumer Affairs
(972) 761-8016

September 29, 2000
Ref. No.: CAC2000D-000262-0

Sharon Joy Brunner
Rt. 2, Box 159-D
Huntington, TX 75949

Dear Sharon Joy Brunner:

Subject: Consumer Complaint Against
Huntington State Bank, Huntington, Texas

This office has received your recent correspondence regarding your complaint against the subject bank.

Additional time is needed for our office to contact the bank in order to obtain the information necessary to thoroughly review your complaint. It is the practice of the Division of Compliance and Consumer Affairs to inform you of our findings within 60 calendar days.

We will advise you of our findings as soon as possible.

Sincerely,

Doris F. Jones
Consumer Affairs Specialist

HUNTINGTON STATE BANK
Huntington · Lufkin · Etoile · Zavalla · Central
Member FDIC

DEAR CUSTOMER:

YOUR DECEMBER BANK STATEMENT WAS RETURNED TO US BY THE POST
OFFICE STATING THAT IT WAS UNCLAIMED . IT IS BEING HELD IN OUR
HUNTINGTON OFFICE, AND YOU MAY PICK IT UP DURING REGULAR
BUSINESS HOURS. IF THIS IS NOT CONVENIENT FOR YOU, CONTACT ME AT
409-422-3000 TO MAKE OTHER ARRANGEMENTS.

SINCERELY,

SHELLEY MATHEWS
OPERATIONS DEPT.

P.O. Box 1090 · Huntington, Texas 75949
Telephone (409) 422-3000 · Fax (409) 422-3500

Tidewater Marine

October 22, 1999

To Whom It May Concern:

I, Hunter J. Chaisson, was the supervisor for Cory Wood at Tidewater Marine. I am writing this letter to state the future of Cory Wood's planning with Tidewater Marine. On Friday 9/24-99 Cory called me stating that he would be able to go to work the following Monday. I had Cory scheduled to report to the M/V Gulf Ace II for 0800 on Monday 9/27/99. Monday morning at 0900 Cory called me at the office and said he would not make it to the office because he needed to see a doctor for a cold. I rescheduled Cory for Wednesday 9/29/99 again for the M/V Gulf Ace II. Cory asked if 1100 A. M. would be fine instead of 0800 due to some last minute errands he had to run, bills to pay, hair cut, etc. Cory claimed, what he could not finish he would get his Grandmother to finish for him. Cory's was preparing to upgrade for his Mates license with the help of his Captain, Terry Hunter. Captain Hunter acknowledges Cory did not have the complete time in for the license but already started training Cory at the wheel, of the vessel.

In my own opinion, I feel that Cory would never take his own life. Cory was the type of person who was what I call "high on life". Cory was always cheerful and willing to learn and help with any task given to him on the vessel or in the office. For such a young man, Cory was always looking toward the future to better himself professionally and personally. I can say he loves his family dearly. Cory was always talking about how close they were. Again in my opinion I can not see a young man taking his own life with so much to give to those around him. After talking to Cory's mother, Joy, I can tell that Cory was loved just as much by his family. I ask that if there is anything I might be able to answer or elaborate on concerning Cory's investigation that I am contacted to clarify for the sake of Cory's memory.

I am sending this letter to Judge Marshall and the others involved in Cory's case; in hopes that I may be able to help enlighten any other opinion of Cory's life and attitude towards life that anyone else may have of a young man that they do not know. If there is any need for you to contact me for further questioning, I ask that you reach me at my office phone 1 800 634 5806.

Sincerely yours,

Hunter Chaisson

CHAPTER 10

Sunday morning June 19, 2016 have thought of John Havard today this morning. My daughter just had her 20-year reunion and John married one of the girls in her class, he had the audacity to sake her and my son-in-law's hand, and of course Darci wish's now she would have hit him with her beer bottle.

I have just in the past 6 months moved out of the bottom as I call it, I lived across the street from Jeremy Holder's parents, one country block from John Havard, and over yonder that is a ways away, I thought I would never get to use this or would never use yonder, but Vincint Smith, lived a yonder way and that really would be ways, he lived yonder ways. About 3 miles up out of the woods from me, did I mention I lived in the bottom? Vincent Smith: at both death scenes the night before both of my kids were killed, that in itself is a big problem for me not to look at, devil worshiper? I have been told that; he talks in riddles around I have ask him if he is with me on this, he was in Corey and Darci's lives since daycare. He says he is, but i do not believe he is true to his word. I did confront him about both deaths, he conveniently turned his self into sheriff office when the insurance investigator came to investigate Corey's death.

When I ask him about the baby's death and why was he down there, he said he wasn't at Darci's, but she saw him, this is how I knew he was there; we may have argued he may have said nothing, I do remember his wife, saying to him that Rex Lowery set you up, he set you up, I really don't remember how this ended them walking or riding off yes, they were on 4 wheelers, same ole girl thought I wasn't home one day and was being smart and drove through my circle drive.

I thought she was another one of my friends. I ran out the front door, I know like I was trying to catch someone. I was my friend, the bitch ducked, last time Vincint rode by my house, on the way out, oh yeah one way in one way out, I was on the porch shotgun showing, and he looked at his boy riding beside him, he also told Darci he was a hit man. In reality the gun he showed her may have been the gun that shot Corey, sick little bastard no telling what parts he has played in many lives.

CHAPTER 11

August 21, 2016: On this day I am having anxiety attacks because of this book, not writing it, Corey was sat up as a suicide, because he was used as insurance fraud, money has been stolen out of his checking account. A life insurance policy was on him from Randy Wilson, the prick, he manipulated his son into killing Corey, not only his son but stepson and I am sure his wife. Surely all these people were not led by the devil.

I must tell you something blood was rubbed down the side of Corey's house where he was found or placed, the man across the street told me that devil worshipers were in my yard. My grand baby was also murdered 2 and a half years after Corey, this is the counties MO and that is why nobody will or has come forward these men whoever they may be, will kill you family members if you bring them to the attention of anyone in power what a cluster fuck this was...

Well, I am back after a long time, working on getting the salon and my new business off the ground... So, need to finish this book. Long story short so tired of getting angry lol understatement of the century went into the oldest mason building last Sunday and Jesus' face is on the front noticed it yesterday. Youngest son just came in and going for a ride on the beach, I am out of here, have to write a bio on myself before anyone even sees this, lol that should be something, may even tell the truth lol

January 2019: moved now living in a place I can pay for, having a blast, can hear the ocean, sitting outside, praising for all Jesus has given me, because I obeyed. There were times I fought not to confront, law enforcement, judges, murderers, not really murderers, I look for Corey's and must say hope i see them

What is now going on in Corey's case is the sheriff of Angelina Co. Texas has agreed to let anyone we would like to come in and investigate so cold justice has been contacted twice.

www.ingramcontent.com/pod-product-compliance
Lightning Source LLC
Chambersburg PA
CBHW021702120626
46545CB00004B/1363